FOUNDATIONS OF ACCOUNTING

Edited by
RICHARD P. BRIEF
New York University

A GARLAND SERIES

Law and Accounting

Nineteenth Century American Legal Cases

Edited with an introduction by
JEAN MARGO REID

GARLAND PUBLISHING, INC.

NEW YORK & LONDON 1988

For a list of Garland's publications in accounting,
see the final pages of this volume.

Library of Congress Cataloging-in-Publication Data

Law and accounting.

(Foundations of accounting)
Bibliography: p.
1. Accounting—Law and legislation—United States—Cases.
I. Reid, Jean Margo. II. Series
KF1357.A7L38 1988 346.73'063 88-24382
ISBN0-8240-6130-6 (alk. paper) 347.30663

Design by Renata Gomes

The volumes in this series are printed on
acid-free, 250-year-life paper.

Printed in the United States of America

Contents

Introduction

This book contains fifty-three nineteenth-century American legal cases in which courts discussed accounting issues. The cases are in chronological order and have been edited to exclude material not relevant to accounting issues. The names of a few of these cases will be familiar. The meaning of *Wood v. Drummer* (1824), in which Justice Story said that a corporation's capital is a trust fund for the benefit of its creditors, was hotly debated for the remainder of the century. Whatever conclusion was reached regarding whether a "trust" was created, this case was the foundation for the idea that capital could not be returned to shareholders and it was this restriction which made it necessary to distinguish between income and capital. This case preceded the famous 1849 British case, *Burnes v. Pennell*,[1] which is often cited as the source of the rule that dividends cannot be paid except from profits. Another well known American case is *Eyster v. Centennial Board of Finance* (1876), in which the Supreme Court of the United States said that depreciation was not a deductible expense since "The public, when referring to the profits of the business of a merchant, rarely ever take into account the depreciation of the buildings in which the business is carried on."

But most of the cases in this book are not well-known. In fact, it is often assumed that few American legal cases on accounting matters were decided in the nineteenth century. For example, Littleton[2] discusses only English legal cases in his classic text on the evolution of accounting in the nineteenth century. Early American accounting texts like Dickinson and Hatfield[3] also tend to stress British influence on United States accounting thought, although occasional mention is made of an American case. And legal writers like Reiter also emphasize British antecedents with comments like "it is in the English statutes and cases that the background is found for American rules governing the valuation of balance sheet items."[4]

American accounting thought is usually assumed to have originated in this century and the general belief is that the earlier literature dealt "with the particulars of accounting practice rather than with the conceptual underpinnings."[5] The first references to accounting concepts and principles in the United States are the *Journal of Accountancy*, first published in 1905, and works by Sprague, Cole, Hatfield, and Montgomery.[6]

However, a search of numerous nineteenth and early twentieth century treatises on corporate law[7] and other books and articles about accounting and about dividend law[8] produced citations to 120 legal cases decided in federal and state courts from 1824 to 1899 in which courts discussed a variety of accounting issues. Fifty-three of these cases are included here. Many of them preceded the earliest British legal cases that discussed accounting issues. Some concerned dividend law. Others considered how to compute taxable income or remuneration under employee and leasehold profit sharing agreements. In still others public utility rate setting depended on income determination. And statutory reporting requirements of banks and other kinds of corporations were at issue in a few cases.

These cases are of interest for several reasons. First, they show that government regulation of accounting predated the modern regulatory era. As is commonly known, legislation restricted the payment of dividends to profits, or earned surplus, or forbade dividends when capital was impaired. But other accounting regulation also existed and it contained reporting requirements and sometimes mandated methods of profit computation. For example, banks chartered by the state of Maine, like that in *Wood v. Drummer* (1824), were required to produce semi-annual financial statements and the state retained the right to inspect their affairs.[9] New York banking law contained quarterly reporting requirements which specified that, among other information, the amount of loans due from directors be reported to the superintendent of the banking department. The superintendent also required that the largest single borrower and extent of its indebtedness be identified. As the court noted in *People v. Vail* (1879), this information was necessary to obtain a "true picture" of the condition of the bank. New York also regulated, at least in part, how profits were to be computed. For example, as discussed in *Dykman v. Keeney* (1897), banks were required to deduct from profits all losses including debts "which shall have remained due without prosecution and upon which no interest shall have been paid for more than one year." Similar legislation governed national banks and the banks of other states as well.

Some states required that manufacturing corporations publish annual reports. For example, a New York statute, the interpretation of which was at issue in *Whitney Arms Company v. Barlow* (1876), provided that if annual reports were not filed, the directors were personally liable for all debts thereafter contracted. Rhode Island also required, as discussed in *Wing & Evans v. Slater* (1896), that manufacturing companies file an annual certificate which stated their paid in capital, assessed value of real estate, value of personal assets, and outstanding debts and liabilities. These reporting statutes thus mandated that particular accounting information be provided to potential creditors and investors.

Other legislation under which some railroads were incorporated and financed contained other accounting regulation designed to protect the railroad from insolvency while retiring the debt owing to the government. Thus federal legislation, discussed in *Union Pacific Railroad Company v. United States* (1878), specified that the railroad was to devote five percent of its net earnings to retire its bonded debt owing to the government and that interest on the road's first mortgage bonds and current expenses were deductable expenses. Congress later enacted the Thurman Act, discussed in *United States v Central Pacific Railroad Company* (1891), which provided that deductions should include "the necessary expenses actually paid within the year in operating the same and keeping the same in a state of repair." Other regulation on public utility rate setting and taxation of income also involved the courts in decisions regarding the meaning of income and profits.

Second, these cases illustrate that sometimes, but not often, private contracts specified a particular accounting treatment and that accounting, therefore, served to define private rights. For example, in *Barry v. Missouri, Kansas & Texas Railway Co.* (1886) the income bondholder's contract provided that the entire income, "after the payment of the expenses of operating and keeping the said railway and property in repair, and of the interest on the incumbrances prior hereto . . . is pledged to the payment of these bonds." However, court interpretation frequently appeared to frustrate the parties' expectations, particularly in the case of shareholders' contracts specifying the fund out of which directors were supposed to pay dividends. And in most cases courts were left to determine the meaning of the word profits without guidance of either legislation or private contract.

Third, these cases illustrate that American courts discussed accrual accounting problems as early as 1837 and that a cash concept of profits was not the norm. In that year, in *De Peyster v. The American Fire Insurance Company*, a New York court first decided that "unearned premiums on which the risks assumed by the company are still running . . . are not *surplus profits* . . . without leaving a sufficient surplus on hand to meet the probable losses which may accrue." A wide variety of other problems of income and expense recognition and asset valuation arose in these cases. In *Davis v. Flagstaff Silver Company of Utah* (Utah, 1877) the court decided that payments received for ores to be delivered in the future were not income. In some cases income was connected with cash receipts, as in *United States v. Schillinger* (S.D.N.Y., 1876), a tax case, where a federal circuit court decided that "Income must be taken to mean money, and not the expectation of receiving it." Similarly, in *Jennery v. Olmstead* (New York, 1885), which involved an employee profit sharing agreement, the court refused to permit a company to recognize income due to appreciation in market value of government bonds, since "the bond unsold is only called worth so many dollars . . . whereas the bond when sold has actually brought so many dollars." A dissenting judge argued otherwise and he asked "Are not [the employee's] services shown to be valuable when an investment which he made has increased in value?" In other cases such as *Van Dyke v. McQuade* (New York, 1881) courts permitted companies to accrue income when earned, since "In any just transaction [profits] must be earned before they are due, and when due they are earned, although not received."

Other cases involved expense recognition. In several, like *Gratz v. Redd* (Kentucky, 1843), the issue was whether "interest" on capital during the period of construction was an expenditure or an asset. In another early case, *Grant v. Hartford and New Haven Railroad Company* (1876), the United States Supreme Court stated a general rule to distinguish expenses from assets. The latter included expenditures for permanent improvements which had "an additional value to what they had before, with an increased capacity for producing future profits," although the court admitted to difficulty in applying the rule in practice. In *Hubbard v. Weare* (Iowa, 1890) and *Davenport v. Lines* (Conn. 1899), the court had to determine whether expenditures for advertising and research and development were expenditures or assets. In *Davenport* the court decided advertising expenditures were expenses, since "the court has failed to find that as an asset it had any value."

Non cash expenditures also came in for their share of scrutiny. In an early New York case, *Sagory v. Dubois* (1846), the court determined that corporations must take account of doubtful debts in the calculation of profits available for dividends. A similar decision was reached in an 1874 federal circuit court case, *Main v. Mills*. These cases contrast with British cases of this period, which in general required that only known bad debts had to enter into the profit calculation.[10]

This book contains edited versions of other well-known depreciation cases of this era, *Tutt v. Land* (Georgia, 1873) and *United States v. Kansas Pacific Railway Company* (Supreme Court of the United States, 1878), and some less well known cases on this topic, including *Little Miami & Columbus & Xenia Railroad Company v. United States* (United States Supreme Court, 1883) and *Whittaker v. Amwell National Bank* (New Jersey, 1894). In addition, there are three Pennsylvania cases, *Ford v. Locust Mountain Coal Co.* (1868), *Commonwealth v. The Ocean Oil Company* (1868), and *Commonwealth v. The Penn Gas Coal Company* (1869), which considered the deductability of depletion in wasting asset companies. These cases may be the source of the wasting asset doctrine, which is often attributed to an 1886 work by Morawetz[11] or the famous British case, *Lee v. Neuchatel Asphalte Company* (1889).[12] In one of these, *Commonwealth v. The Penn Gas Coal Company* (1869), which was a tax case, the court explained that "All capitals of mining companies . . . are nominal . . . and fixed by their promoters at such large figures, that, by applying the principle contended for by the appellees, the whole annual income would have to be retained to supply the loss of capital, which would disappoint the stockholders of their dividends, and the state of her taxes." Later cases like *People v. Roberts* (New York, 1898) agreed with this view.

Nineteenth-century American courts also were called upon to determine whether contingent liabilities should be recognized as expenses in *Carpenter v. The New York & New Haven Railroad Company* (New York, 1857), *Whitney Arms Company v. Barlow* (New York, 1876), *Witherow v. Slayback* (New York, 1895), and *Wing & Evans v. Slater* (Rhode Island, 1896).

As in the British court decisions during this formative period in the history of accounting thought and practice,[13] the early American cases often contain inconsistent views on particular issues. But the important point is that many of the courts seem to be aware of basic accounting issues which, even today, continue to be debated. This book makes these legal cases more accessible to those interested in these early developments.

NOTES

1. 2 H. L. Cas. 497.

2. A. C. Littleton, *Accounting Evolution to 1900* (1933), reprinted by the University of Alabama Press, University, Alabama, 1981.

3. A. L. Dickinson, *Accounting Practice and Procedure* (1913), reprinted by Scholars Book Co., Houston, 1975; H. R. Hatfield, *Modern Accounting* (New York & London: D. Appleton and Company, 1909).

4. P. Reiter, *Profits, Dividends and the Law* (1926), reprinted by Arno Press, New York, 1976.

5. American Accounting Association, Committee on Concepts and Standards for External Reports, *Statement on Accounting Theory and Theory Acceptance* (American Accounting Association, 1977).

6. C. E. Sprague, *Philosophy of Accounts* (New York: 1907); W. M. Cole, *Accounts: Their Construction and Interpretation* (Boston: Houghton and Mifflin Company, 1908); Hatfield, *op. cit.* note 3; and R. H. Montgomery, *Auditing Theory and Practice* (1912),

reprinted by Arno Press, New York, 1976.

7. These include J. Grant, *A Practical Treatise on the Law of Corporations* (Philadelphia: T. & J. W. Johnson, 1854); J. K. Angell and S. Ames, *Treatise on the Law of Private Corporations Aggregate,* Fifth Edition (Boston: Little, Brown and Company, 1855); P. Potter, *Treatise on the Law of Corporations* (New York: Banks & Brothers, 1881); V. Morawetz, *A Treatise on the Law of Private Corporations,* First and Second Editions (Boston: Little, Brown and Company, 1882, 1886); H. O. Taylor, *A Treatise on the Law of Private Corporations Having Capital Stock* (1884); C. T. Boone, *Manual of the Law Applicable to Corporations* (San Francisco: Bancroft-Whitney, 1887); W. L. Clark and W. L. Marshall, *Marshall on Private Corporations* (Saint Paul: Keefe-Davidson, 1902); and W. W. Cook *A Treatise on the Law of Corporations,* Fifth Edition, Vol. 2 (Chicago: Calaghan & Company, 1903).

8. These include P. Reiter, *op. cit.* note 4; Annotation, "Right or duty of corporation to pay dividends; and liability for wrongful payment," *American Law Reports Annotated,* Vol. 55 (Rochester: Lawyers Cooperative Publishing Company, 1928), pp. 8—147; J. L. Weiner, "Theory of Anglo-American Dividend Law: American Statutes and Cases," *Columbia Law Review* (April, 1929), pp. 461—482; J. L. Weiner and J. C. Bonbright, "Theory of Anglo-American Dividend Law: Surplus and Profits," *Columbia Law Review* (March and November, 1930), pp. 330—358 and pp. 954—985; L. L. Briggs, "Asset Valuation in Dividend Decisions," *The Accounting Review* (September, 1934), pp. 184—191; D. Kehl, "The Origin and Early Development of American Dividend Law," *Harvard Law Review* (November, 1939), pp. 36—67 and *Corporate Dividends* (1941), reprinted by Arno Press, New York, 1976; A. A. Berle, Jr. and F. S. Fisher, Jr., "Elements of the Law of Business Accounting," *Columbia Law Review* (April, 1932), pp. 573—622; and G. S. Hills, "The Law of Accounting: I" and "The Law of Accounting: II," *Columbia Law Review* (January and November, 1954), pp. 1—53 and 1049—1106.

9. This regulation is detailed in *Vose V. Grant,* 55 Mass. 505 (1819), which involved the same bank as the later *Wood v. Drummer* case.

10. British legal cases on accounting that were decided before 1889 are identified and discussed in J. M. Reid, "Judicial Intervention in Accounting Behavior: A Reevaluation of the Nineteenth Century Experience," *Journal of Accounting and Public Policy* (Spring, 1987), pp. 9—34, and "Judicial Views on Accounting in Britain Before 1889," *Accounting and Business Research* (Summer, 1987), pp. 247—258.

11. Morawetz, *Op. cit.* Note 7.

12. L.R. 41 Ch. D. 1.

13. Edited versions of thirty British legal cases decided in the nineteenth century before *Lee v. Neuchatel Asphalte Company,* L.R. 41 Ch. D. 1 (1889) can be found in J. M. Reid, ed., *Law and Accounting: Pre-1889 British Legal Cases* (New York and London: Garland Publishing, Inc., 1986).

WOOD v. DRUMMER

30 Fed. Cas. 435, Fed. Case No. 17,944 (1824)
United States Circuit Court
District of Maine

STORY, Circuit Justice. The Hallowell and Augusta Bank was incorporated in March, 1804, by the legislature of Massachusetts, with a capital stock of $200,000, divided into shares of $100 each, for a term which expired on the first Monday of October, 1812, with the usual rights and privileges belonging to the banks in the same state. In June, 1812, the legislature passed an act (Act of 1812, c. 57) continuing all the banks, whose charters would expire on the first Monday of October, 1812, as corporate bodies until the first Monday of October, 1816, "for the sole purpose of enabling said banks gradually to settle and close their concerns, and divide their capital stock." And by a further act, passed in December, 1816 (Act of 1816, c. 110), the term was prolonged for three years from the passing of this last act. In January, 1813, at a meeting of the stockholders of the Hallowell and Augusta Bank, a vote was passed, ordering a dividend to be made among the stockholders of the bank of fifty per cent. of the capital stock thereof; and in October in the same year, a vote was passed for a further dividend of twenty-five per cent. of the capital stock, making in the whole a dividend of seventy-five per cent. of the whole capital stock among the stockholders. The notes of the bank continued to circulate in good credit until after November, 1814; and the plaintiffs were, in October and November, 1814, owners in their several rights of notes of the same bank to a sum in the aggregate amounting to more than $29,000, which were presented for payment to the bank, and payment refused. The plaintiffs received certain notes of the directors as collateral security, but these were never paid. In fact one quarter part of the capital stock of the bank had never been paid in, but was secured by the notes of the stockholders, called "stock notes"; and about $90,000 of debts (beside stock notes) were due from certain directors of the bank, who became insolvent and utterly unable to pay the same. So that nearly three quarters of the stock was lost or unpaid, either from insolvency or some other cause, and left the bank involved, after the division of the stock, in deep insolvency. In June, 1812, another and new bank was incorporated, composed in part of the same persons, with the same corporate name. The new bank, for a considerable time, continued to give credit to, and circulate the notes of the old bank; and the bill asserted the new bank to have become possessed of the funds of the old bank to a very large amount.

Such are the principal facts; and the claim of the plaintiffs is to be reimbursed by the defendants, (who are owners of three hundred and twenty shares) out of the dividends of the capital stock received by them, the amount of the debts so due to the plaintiffs respectively, for the bank notes above stated.

The case is full of difficulties. The bill is 1
drawn in a very loose and inartificial manner. It proceeds principally upon the grounds of a gross over issue of bank notes, and other violations of the charter, and of a fraudulent dividend by the stockholders with a knowledge of their insolvency; grounds, which are denied by the answers, and are not in the slightest degree established in the proofs. It does not directly proceed upon the ground, that the defendants hold a trust fund applicable to the payment of the debts of the corporation; but leaves this to be picked up in fragments by a minute analysis of the bill. I pass, however, over these objections, for the purpose of considering that, which is the principal point argued in the cause, whether the capital stock in the hands of the stockholders is liable to the payment of the debts of the bank.

It appears to me very clear upon general principles, as well as the legislative intention, that the capital stock of banks is to be deemed a pledge or trust fund for the payment of the debts contracted by the bank. The public, as well as the legislature, have always supposed this to be a fund appropriated for such purpose. The individual stockholders are not liable for the debts of the bank in their private capacities. The charter relieves them from personal responsibility, and substitutes the capital stock in its stead. Credit is universally given to this fund by the public, as the only means of repayment. During the existence of the corporation it is the sole property of the corporation, and can be applied only according to its charter, that is, as a fund for payment of its debts, upon the security of which it may discount and circulate notes. Why, otherwise, is any capital stock required by our charters? If the stock may, the next day after it is paid in, be withdrawn by the stockholders without payment of the debts of the corporation, why is its amount so studiously provided for, and its

payment by the stockholders so diligently required? To me this point appears so plain upon principles of law, as well as common sense, that I cannot be brought into any doubt, that the charters of our banks make the capital stock a trust fund for the payment of all the debts of the corporation. The bill-holders and other creditors have the first claims upon it; and the stockholders have no rights, until all the other creditors are satisfied. They have the full benefit of all the profits made by the establishment, and cannot take any portion of the fund, until all the other claims on it are extinguished. Their rights are not to the capital stock, but to the residuum after all demands on it are paid. On a dissolution of the corporation, the bill-holders and the stockholders have each equitable claims, but those
2 of the bill-holders possess, as I conceive, a prior exclusive equity. The same doctrine has been recognized by the supreme court of Massachusetts in Vose v. Grant, 15 Mass. 505, 517, 522, and Spear v. Grant, 16 Mass. 9, 15.

If I am right in this position, the principal difficulty in the cause is overcome. If the capital stock is a trust fund, then it may be followed by the creditors into the hands of any persons, having notice of the trust attaching to it. As to the stockholders themselves, there can be no pretence to say, that, both in law and fact, they are not affected with the most ample notice....

The next consideration is, whether the bill makes out a case, which upon the facts proved or admitted, entitles the plaintiffs to relief. I have already adverted to the loose structure of the bill. It primarily charges the case, as a case of fraud; that is now abandoned. If it can stand at all, it must be simply on the fact, that the defendants have the funds in their possession. That alone could not entitle the parties to relief, without allegations of insolvency on the part of the corporation or of the non-existence of other funds. Now the bill does not allege, that the corporation is insolvent, nor that it is dissolved, nor that there is no other corporate property, out of which the debts can be paid. These are extraordinary omissions; and if there had been a demurrer to the bill, it would be difficult for the court to have strained hard enough to support it. But these defects are in some degree helped by the answers, which admit the insolvency of the corporation, and show, that in fact no sufficient funds for payment of its debts are in existence, independent of the capital stock. Then again the bill (notwithstanding the intimations thrown out by the court on a former hearing of the cause) does not charge, that the capital stock is a trust fund, appropriated by law and the charter to the payment of the debts, and that the surplus only, after such payment, belongs to the stockholders. Such an allegation was most fit to have been made upon the grounds, on which ultimately the plaintiffs concluded to rest their case at the hearing. The court is therefore compelled to thread it out by inference and intendment and exposition of the charter, as made part of the pleadings. . . .

Upon the whole, my opinion is, that the objection of the want of sufficient parties cannot be maintained. We may then proceed to the merits of the defence, as disclosed in the answers. One ground there taken is, that the demands of the plaintiffs respectively are barred by the statute of limitations. But this bar to a decree cannot, upon the facts, be sustained. The rights of the plaintiffs accrued as against the defendants within six years; for until a refusal of payment by the bank of its notes, followed by an inability to discharge them, there was no cause of proceeding in equity against the defendants. There is no positive bar to suits in equity; but whenever any limitation is adopted, it is ordinarily regulated by analogy to the common law. Here, the claim is against a trust fund in the hands of the defendants; and in cases, not of constructive, but of express trusts, so long, at least, as they are not encountered by an adverse possession and denial of right, the statute of limitations does not begin to run. I should have very great difficulty in allowing a bar of the statute of limitations to operate in a case of this nature, unless where the circumstances of negligence on one side, and of positive denial of right on the other were very cogent. Here the capital stock was actually divided, to the amount of $150,000, in January and October, 1813, at a time when it was perfectly well known, or ought to have been known, that a very large number of bank notes, amounting, I believe, to more than $90,000, were due, and outstanding against the bank. If what has fallen from the bar be correct, this large amount remains yet unpaid. How was its payment provided for? Simply by the notes due to the bank, then outstanding, the productiveness of which could not be then ascertained, and the utter insolvency of the debtors has been since fully established. These notes, indeed, to an amount of more than $140,000 (including the stock notes, for the unpaid quarter part of the capital stock,) were due almost entirely from the directors of the bank, from whose official misconduct the stockholders ought certainly to derive no benefit, if they are not to be affected with any private responsibility.

The only other ground, suggested as a defence by the defendants is, that they have been guilty of no fraud, and that the division of the capital stock was an act authorized by law; and there is no equity to relieve the plaintiffs by throwing the loss on the stockholders. The answer to this argument, for such it is, has already been given. The stockholders have no right to any thing but the residuum of the capital stock, after payment of all the debts of the bank. The funds in their hands, therefore, have an equity attached to them, in favour of the creditors, which it is against conscience to resist. . . .

Taking into consideration the manifest defects of the present bill, the long delay in instituting the present suit (which is not accounted for in any averments framed for this purpose,) the possible, nay, probable intermediate insolvencies of some of the stockholders, the injustice which may arise to other creditors of the bank, not before the court, by any other course, I have come to the conclusion, that our duty is best performed by holding the plaintiffs entitled to a decree, that the defendants pay out of the dividends of the capital stock received by them, so much of the debts due to the plaintiffs, as the number of shares held by them in the same capital stock (viz. 320 shares) bears to the whole number of shares in the capital stock (viz. 2,000 shares).

There is much force in the suggestion, that the corporation books have been withdrawn and secreted, so that the plaintiffs were unable originally to ascertain who the other stockholders were. But this difficulty might, in some measure, have been overcome by apt averments in the bill; and the disclosure of the names of several stockholders in the answers puts the plaintiffs in possession of facts, by which, at their choice, they might by an amendment have brought those persons before the court, or have assigned a sufficient 3
reason for the omission.

My judgment accordingly is, that the defendants are to pay the plaintiffs, in the proportion already intimated, and no further. Decree accordingly, with costs.

PEOPLE ex. rel. COMMERCIAL INSURANCE COMPANY OF THE CITY OF NEW YORK v. THE SUPERVISORS OF THE CITY AND COUNTY OF NEW YORK

18 Wend. (N.Y.) 605 (1836)
Supreme Court of the State of New York

This is a motion for a peremptory mandamus against the board of supervisors of the city and county of New-York, to compel them to strike from the tax list for the year 1835, and from the warrant of the collector, the name of the Commercial Insurance Company.

It appears from the return of the board to the alterna-
4 tive mandamus, that the president of the company filed with the clerk of the board an affidavit stating that they were not in the receipt of *any profits* or *income*, nor had they received any for the then last twelve months, and that during that period, as well as at the time of making the affidavit, the property of the company was not equal to the amount of capital stock paid in. This affidavit was presented to the board of supervisors at their annual meeting in 1835, in order that the name of the company might be stricken from the assessment roll, and no tax imposed. The application was denied, and the company assessed $1320....

By the Court, NELSON, J. The statute, 1 *R.S.*416, [section] 9, provides, that if the president or other proper officer of any incorporated company named in the assessment roll, shall show to the satisfaction of the board of supervisors, at their annual meeting, within two days from the commencement thereof, by an affidavit of such officer to be filed with the clerk of the board, that such company is not in the receipt of any *profits* or *income*, the name of such company shall be stricken out of the assessment roll, and no tax shall be imposed upon it. Though the affidavit shews a state of facts *literally* corresponding with the terms of this section, it was conceded on the argument that the company had been in operation the preceding year, and was so at the time of the application to the board; and that the affidavit was made under the advice and belief that by the terms *profits* or *income*, the statute intended *net profit and income*. The president did not mean to swear that the company had not been for the year, and was not at the time, in the receipt of *any income*; in other words, that it was not in operation. The question then presented before the board, upon the affidavit, involved the true construction of this section: whether, by the terms "any profit or income," the legislature intended *net profit and income*, or not.

The first act on this subject was passed 23d April, 1823. *Statutes, Session of* 1823, *p*. 390. The 14th [section], p. 395, provides, that all incorporated companies, *receiving a regular income* from the employment of capital, shall be considered persons, within the meaning of this act, and assessed accordingly. The section then 5
goes on and prescribes the mode levying and collecting the tax upon the real and personal estate of the companies. The next (and section 15) gives to the companies their election to pay ten per cent. upon all "*dividends, profits or income*" made, in lieu of the tax before directed. This act was amended 20th April, 1825. The 7th section provided for the payment of the tax by the proper officer of the company, and for a deduction to the amount from the dividends of the stockholders; it also provided that any turnpike or bridge company, any canal company, or company employed wholly or principally in manufacturing, might elect to pay five per cent. upon all "the *profits* or *income*" made by them; but that no such company, whose "*net income* or *profits*" exceeded five per cent. on the capital stock paid in, &c. should have this privilege. The 15th section of the act of 1823 was repealed, which of course limited the privilege of commutation to the companies above specified. The 1st section of the revised act, 2 *R*.*S*. 414, provides that "all monied or stock corporations deriving *an income* or *profit* from their capital, shall be liable to taxation on their capital." The 11th section gives the privilege to all companies employed wholly or principally in manufacturing, and all marine insurance companies, whose *net annual income* shall not exceed five per cent. on the capital stock paid in, &c. to commute for their taxes by paying five per cent. upon such *net income* made during the year. Section 12th exempts from taxation all turnpike, bridge or canal companies whose *net annual income* shall not exceed five per cent. on the capital stock, &c. Section

13th prescribes the mode of ascertaining whether the net annual income exceeds or falls short of the five per cent. The proper officer shall make an affidavit stating the capital stock paid in and secured to be paid in, together with the *income and profits*, and the *total expeditures during the preceeding year,* &c. And by section 14th, the proper officers of each company electing to commute, must also make an afffidavit stating the amount of such *net income*, &c.

It is apparent from the various provisions above referred to, that the legislature, in using the phrase "any profits or income," did not intend to convey the
6 same idea as that indicated by the words "net income."
Whenever the assessment of the tax is made to depend upon the clear profit arising from the employment of the capital of the corporation, the phrase "net annual income" is used. See 1 *R*. *S*. 416, 417, [section] 11, 12, 14. A very striking illustration of the meaning of the legislature may be found in the 13th section, *p*. 417, which prescribes the mode of ascertaining net annual income. It directs the "*income and profits*" and the total expenditures of the company for the year to be stated in the affidavit, which is to be delivered to the assessors. By these data the assessors can readily ascertain the net income or profits.

In all the discussions of the assessment law, we are not aware that the principle was ever advanced or defended, that taxation of capital should depend upon the question whether it had been profitably employed or not. Certainly no such rule has ever been applied in the assessment of individual property. The injustice of it is apparent. It would be taxing the skill and industry used in the employment of the capital, rather than the capital itself.

The comptroller, in a letter of instructions to the several boards of supervisors, 23d September, 1826, expresses the view above taken of the statutes of 1823, 1825, and there has been no change by the revised statutes upon the point in question. He says, "It is the duty of the assessors to put on the assessment roll not only every company deriving a profit from its business, but every company deriving an income, even if this income is much less than its expenses."

The preliminary objections taken to this proceeding, namely, that the court could not interfere in this summary way, consistent with the exercise of the discretion of the board, under the 1st section above cited, or require them to do an act which seems not to be within their power, would probably have been sufficient to deny the motion; but we have looked into the merits at the request of the counsel, and put the case upon that ground.

DE PEYSTER v. THE AMERICAN FIRE INSURANCE COMPANY

6 Paige (N.Y.) 486 (1837)
Cases in Chancery, New York

THIS was an appeal from a decree of the vice chancellor of the first circuit dismissing the complainant's bill. Previous to the great fire in New York, by which the American Fire Insurance Company lost its whole capital and was rendered insolvent, the complainant loaned to the company, for the purpose of paying a loss which had occurred, $2000, which amount the company agreed to repay to the complainant with interest, on demand. And as the company had a surplus on hand, in addition to its capital, of about
8 $6000 at the time of the fire, the complainant claimed a preference in payment to the full amount of his debt out of this surplus fund. He therefore brought his action against the company, and having obtained judgment for the amount and issued an execution thereon, which was returned unsatisfied, he filed his bill in this cause against the corporation and the receivers appointed under the act of January, 1836, for the purpose of obtaining such preference in payment of the assets of the company in the hands of the receivers. The vice chancellor decided against the claim; from which decree the complainant appealed.

THE CHANCELLOR. There is no legal or equitable foundation for the claim of preference in payment which the complainant is attempting to establish in this case. Although the assets of the company are in the nature of a trust fund for the payment of the debts due to the creditors of the corporation, no one of those creditors is entitled to any preference in payment over another, unless he has obtained a specific appropriation of or prior equitable lien upon some particular part of the fund. In this case it is not pretended that the identical $2000 which the complainant loaned to the company did in fact constitute any part of the assets of the company which remained on hand at the time the insolvency occurred, and which have gone into the hands of the receivers. On the contrary it appears that the money was loaned to pay off a loss which had previously taken place; and was undoubtedly applied for that object. The complainainant, therefore, was a mere creditor at large at the time of the appointment of the receivers, without any specific lien whatever. His claim then appears to be based entirely upon the erroneous supposition that the creditors

who became such by reason of the destruction of their property by the fire have no claim upon the assets of the company beyond the amount of the capital stock; and that as the money loaned went to pay off a previous loss which must otherwise have been paid out of the surplus on hand at the time of the fire, the lender is entitled to a preference in payment out of such surplus. The capital stock, however, is not the primary or natural fund for the payment of losses which may happen by the destruction of property insured by the company. The charters of all these companies con
template the capital stock merely as a collateral security 9
for the payment of extraordinary losses, and only to be resorted to when the primary fund for the payment of the debts of the company shall prove insufficient. The premiums received and the interest of the capital stock, which constitute what is called the surplus fund of the company, is the primary and natural fund out of which losses should be paid; and the residue only of such premiums and interest, after providing for the payment of all such losses and debts, should be divided among the stockholders. The directors are only authorized to declare dividends of the surplus profits. And unearned premiums on which the risks assumed by the company are still running, although they are surplus funds beyond the capital, are not *surplus profits* which can be legally divided among the stockholders, without leaving a sufficient surplus on hand to meet the probable losses which may accrue, instead of breaking in upon the capital of the company. The corporation should, therefore, at all times keep on hand, or properly invested, a surplus fund sufficient to meet the probable losses upon risks then assumed by the company and which have not yet terminated. And upon that fund, which I presume is the only one which existed in this case beyond the capital, the assured whose premiums have helped to constitute the fund have certainly an equal claim with any other creditors of the corporation.

The decision of the vice chancellor was unquestionably right, and it must be affirmed with costs.

SCOTT v. THE EAGLE FIRE COMPANY

7 Paige (N.Y.) 198 (1838)
Cases in Chancery, New York

The Eagle Fire Insurance Company was one of the corporations rendered insolvent by the great fire in New York, in December, 1835; and this bill was filed by some of the stockholders in behalf of themselves and others, claiming all the surplus funds of the company in the hands of the receivers, beyond the capital stock of the company at the time of the fire which produced the insolvency. It appeared by the bill and answer, that at the time of making the last dividend, a little short of six months previous to the great fire, the surplus fund beyond the capital stock and the dividend then made was about $73,000, if all the debts due to the company were good and collectable; at which time the amount of property remaining insured by the company was about ten millions of dollars. At the time of the fire this surplus fund had increased, by the receipt of new premiums, &c. to about $97,000; but the total amount of property at risk at that time was not stated in the pleadings. The cause was heard on bill and answer, before the vice chancellor of the first circuit. He decided that the complainants were not entitled to the funds of the company beyond the amount of the capital stock; but that the creditors of the corporation were entitled to have the surplus fund as well as the capital stock, applied in payment of their debts. The bill was therefore dismissed with costs. From this decision and decree the complainants appealed to the chancellor.

J. Anthon, for the appellants. The capital of a corporation being entire, the adventurers have no other fund but this to look to for the reimbursement of their losses. The stockholders are entitled from year to year to all the surplus funds remaining, over and above the capital, after the payment of all the losses arising out of the business of the year. No adventurer has a right to claim the application of the surplus profits, earned on the closed business of former years, to the payment of his loss on a contract of a subsequent year. If the risk of a current year, by an extraordinary casuality, terminate in losses exceeding the capital, the adventurers of that year (the capital being entire) must claim pro rata on that capital. A surplus on closing the operations of any given year being ascertained and declared, an omission to divide it does not make it part of the capital,

so as to subject it to the demands of future adventurers; but it remains a fund held in trust by the company for future distribution among the stockholders. A contrary rule would enable a corporation to increase its capital ad libitum, without the assent of the legislature. This conclusion is confirmed by the charter of the Eagle Fire Company, which points out a precise and specific mode of increasing the amount of the capital; and this can be done in no other way. The stockholders, therefore, who have either actually purchased this surplus or earned it by the risk of their funds, are the only persons entitled to it; and upon the account prayed for in the bill, the adventurers of the past year can only insist that the earnings of that year shall be retained to keep the capital pro rata entire. (4 Laws of New York, p. 564, 11
29th sess., ch. 152. *Wood* v. *Dummer*, 3 Mason, 311.) The company—quasi company—cannot make a contract pledging the surplus fund as well as the capital for the payment of the debts of the company. Its powers are limited by the charter to the legal capital, which it can alone bind by contract. The consent of the stockholders would not give such powers for the same reason. The directors are the mere agents of the stockholders, limited in their powers by the charter, and cannot bind them beyond the legal capital. If the stockholders are competent, by acquiescence or otherwise, to put their earned profits or any other portion of their profits at risk, it cannot be in the character of stockholders; the charter forbidding it. It can be done only in the character of underwriters, and then as they would be personally responsible, they would in their personal character receive the profits and be subject to the loss....

The Chancellor. The claim made by the appellants in this case is founded upon the erroneous supposition that it is the duty of the directors of an insurance company to divide all its surplus funds beyond its capital stock, periodically, among its stockholders; leaving such capital stock alone as the fund to which the creditors of the company, who become such by the loss of property insured, are to look for remuneration. But as I had occasion to say in another case, (*De Peyster* v. *The American Ins. Co. and others*, in Chan. 25th May, 1837,) the capital stock of an incorporated insurance company is not the primary or natural fund for the payment of losses which may happen by the destruction of the property insured. The charter of the company contemplates the interest upon the capital stock,

and the premiums received for insurance, as the ordinary fund out of which losses are to be paid. And the surplus of that fund, after paying such losses, is surplus profits within the meaning of the charter; which surplus profits alone are to be divided, from time to time, among the stockholders. The unearned premiums received by the company upon which the risks are still running, and which may therefore all be wanted to pay losses which may happen upon those risks, are not surplus profits which the directors are authorized by the charter to distribute among the stockholders. The capital stock of the company is a special fund, provided by the charter, to secure the assured against great and extraordinary losses which the primary fund may be found
12 insufficient to meet. And if it becomes necessary at any time to break in upon this special fund, to pay such extraordinary losses, it must be made good from the future profits of the company before any further dividends of those profits can be made. (1 R. S. 590, § 4.) The directors of an insurance company have therefore no right to divide all the interest or premiums on hand at the time a dividend is declared; but they should always leave a surplus fund, in addition to the capital stock, sufficient to meet the probable losses on the risks then assumed by the company and which have not then expired. And if any losses accrue upon such risks, whether more or less than the whole capital of the company, that surplus or contingent fund must be applied to satisfy such losses. The fact therefore that the amount of the losses in this case was more than all the funds of the company, including its capital, furnishes no reason whatever for taking the natural and primary fund for the payment of losses, and giving it to the stockholders, to the injury of the creditors of the company.

As the directors are bound to exercise a proper discretion in making dividends of surplus profits, if they abuse that power by dividing the unearned premiums without leaving sufficient to satisfy the probable losses, they may, in case of any extraordinary loss which is sufficient to exhaust the whole capital and more, make themselves personally liable to the creditors of the company. On the other hand, should they without reasonable cause refuse to divide what is actually surplus profits, the stockholders are not without remedy, if they apply to the proper tribunal, before the corporation has become insolvent. But after such insolvency it would not only be improper but it would be highly inequitable to take such surplus fund and divide it among the stockholders; leaving the insured, whose premiums had contributed to the increase of that fund, to sustain a loss. In this case the fund remaining on hand, after the last dividend, in July, 1835, was certainly not more than a prudent board of directors ought to have retained to meet the probable losses which might occur upon the ten millions of property then insured by the company; as it was less than three-fourths of one per cent upon the amount at risk. And before the time for making the next semi-annual dividend arrived, this extraordinary calamity, which was equally destructive to the interests of the stockholders of the company and of the assured, gave to the latter a preferable claim upon all the funds and property of the company.

For these reasons I am perfectly satisfied that the decision of the vice chancellor was right. The decree appealed from must therefore be affirmed with costs.

PEOPLE ex. rel. MCMASTER & HARVEY v. THE BOARD OF SUPERVISORS OF THE COUNTY OF NIAGARA

4 Hill. (N.Y.) 20 (1842)
Supreme Court of the State of New York

THE assessors of the town of Lockport, in the county of Niagara, assessed the *Canal Bank of Lockport*, a corporation under the general banking law, $140,000 for its personal estate. They also assessed the *Lockport Bank and Trust Company*, another corporation under the general banking law, $4800 for its real estate, and $102,000 for personal estate. The assessors of the several towns in the county through which the road of the *Lockport and Niagara Falls Rail-Road Compa-*
14 *ny* passes, assessed the company several sums of money for its real estate, which, in the aggregate, amounted to the sum of $141,200. At the annual meeting of the board of supervisors in October last, the officers of these companies applied to the board to have the names of the corporations stricken from the assessment rolls, and they presented affidavits, which they were afterwards permitted to amend by adding further affidavits. The cashier of the *Canal Bank of Lockport* made affidavit "that the said bank has *suffered a loss* of its capital from the depreciation of state stock and other causes, *to an amount exceeding the whole income or profits* of the bank for the present year." In the supplemental affidavit afterwards produced the cashier swore "that the said bank is not, and has not been for the year last past, in the receipt of any profits or income *over and above the ordinary expenses and losses* of the said bank during said year." Affidavits in nearly the same words were submitted on behalf of the other bank.

The first affidavit submitted on behalf of the *rail-road company* stated, "that the said company is not in the receipt of any profits or income; *all the receipts* of the company for the last year *have been absorbed in the necessary expenses, repairs, and improvements.*" The second affidavit on behalf of the company stated "that said company has not, during the year last past, and is not now, in the receipt of any profits or income whatever *over and above the ordinary expenses and losses* for said year." The person making this affidavit swore that the word "improvements" in the first affidavit meant nothing more than ordinary repairs.

On receiving these affidavits the board of supervisors struck the names of all three of the corporations from the assessment rolls.

The relators are taxable inhabitants of the town of Lockport, and, as such, are actually assessed the present year for real and personal estate. They served papers upon the board and gave notice of this motion for a *mandamus* to compel the board to restore the names of these corporations to the assessment rolls.

By the Court, Bronson, J. So far as relates to the question of taxation, there is no difference between banks created under the general law and those which have special charters. Both are corporations; (*The People* v. *Assessors of Watertown*, 1 *Hill*, 616;) and, like other moneyed or stock corporations deriving an income or profit, are liable to taxation
on their capital. (1 *R. S.* 414, *tit.* 4.) It is not a tax upon 15
income or profits, but upon capital. And the tax is to be levied upon the amount of the capital stock of the corporation *paid in, and secured to be paid in*, after deducting the amount expended for its real estate, which is taxed separately, and the amount of stock which may be owned by the state and by incorporated literary and charitable institutions. (*Id.* §§ 1, 2, 6, 10.) No respect is paid either to accumulations or losses of capital in the course of the business of the company; but the amount paid and secured to be paid as capital, is taken as the true sum to be inserted in the assessment roll. (*Bank of Utica* v. *City of Utica*, 4 *Paige*, 399.) It would have been a more just and equitable rule to take the amount of capital as it actually exists at the time of making the assessment. But as this would involve an enquiry into the private concerns of the corporation and the persons dealing with it, and as it would often be very difficult, if not impracticable, to arrive at a correct result, the legislature has thought proper to adopt another standard. That standard is so plainly laid down by the statute that, so far as I know, none of our moneyed corporations have heretofore claimed any exemption from taxation on the ground that a part of their capital had been lost; but they have from time to time applied to the legislature to reduce the nominal to the actual amount of their capital, as the only means of diminishing the burden of taxation.

These banks have not set up the loss of a portion of their capital as a ground for reducing the amount of their assessments; but it is urged in another form, as the ground for a total exemption from taxation. The loss of capital is used as a set-off against income or profits. The first affidavit laid before

the supervisors was, that the bank "has suffered a loss of its capital" from several causes "to an amount exceeding the whole income or profits of the bank for the present year;" and the second affidavit states the same thing in another form, to wit, that the bank has not during the last year been "in the receipt of any profits or income over and above the ordinary expenses and losses" of the corporation. This supposes that the supervisors may go into the question of profit and loss, and see how that account stands upon the operations of the bank for the last year. But I do not so read the statute. A tax is to be levied upon all monied or stock corporations "deriving an *income* or profit from their capital, or otherwise." (1 *R. S.* 414, § 1.) And the name of the corporation is only to be stricken from
16 the assessment roll when the president or other proper officer shall make affidavit, "that such company is not in the receipt of any profits *or income*." (§ 9.) It is undoubtedly true that "profits" and "income" are sometimes used as synonymous terms; but, strictly speaking, "income" means that which comes in, or is received from any business or investment of capital, without reference to the outgoing expenditures; while "profits" generally mean the gain which is made upon any business or investment when both receipts and payments are taken into the account. "Income," when applied to the affairs of individuals, expresses the same idea that *revenue* does when applied to the affairs of a state or nation; and no one would think of denying that our government has any revenue because the expenditures for a given period may exceed the amount of receipts.

This statute has plainly distinguished between the gains or clear profits of a corporation, and its income or receipts. Manufacturing and marine insurance companies, "whose *net* annual *income* shall not exceed five per cent on the capital stock," are allowed to commute for their taxes. (§ 11.) And turnpike, bridge and canal companies, "whose *net* annual *income* shall not exceed five per cent on the capital," are wholly exempt from taxation. (§ 12.) But there is no such qualification of the word "income" when applied to other corporations. They are subject to taxation when they are "in the receipt of any profits *or income*." It is not when the income exceeds the losses, but when there is *any income*, without regard to losses. If the legislature had intended clear gain or net profits, it can hardly be doubted that some other form of expression would have been used.

The 13th section goes still further to confirm what has already been said. After providing for the total exemption of certain corporations whose "net annual income" does not exceed a certain sum, the legislature go on in this section to point out the mode of ascertaining the fact on which the exemption rests. Two of the officers must make affidavit stating "the *income and profits*, and the total *expenditures* during the preceding year." We here find *profits* as well as income used to designate the *receipts* of the company, and put in opposition to *expenditures*. This shows the sense in which the terms "profits" and "income" in this statute are to be understood. The exception of particular corporations out of the operation of the general rule laid down by the statute, and making the question of taxation in the excepted cases turn on the amount 17
of *net* income, amounts to such a legislative construction of the word "income" in the preceding sections as forbids the exemption which is set up by these banks.

It may be thought unreasonable to impose taxes upon a corporation which is not in the receipt of any clear profits; but it is no more than happens to the owners of other property both real and personal. The owner is assessed and taxed on the value of his estate, notwithstanding the property may be so managed as to prove a charge upon the owner, instead of yielding any net profits....

As notice has been given of this application, and we entertain no doubt upon the question, a peremptory writ will be ordered. But the parties will be at liberty to put the matter in such form as will authorize a record to be made of our judgment, upon which a writ of error may be brought if the parties shall be so advised.

Motion granted.

GRATZ v. REDD

43 Ky. (4 B. Mon.) 178 (1843)
Chancery, Kentucky

CHIEF JUSTICE EWING delivered the Opinion of the Court.

THE Legislature of this Commonwealth, by act approved the 27th day of January, 1830, incorporated a company, with a capital of one million of dollars, to be raised by subscription, in shares of $100 each, to make a railway from Lexington to the Ohio river; fixed the tolls they were authorized to charge for passengers, transportation, &c., and authorized them to commence running their cars and charging tolls as soon as fifteen miles of
18 the road should be completed.

By the 22nd section it is provided, "that the President and Directors shall annually or semi-annually, declare and make such dividends as they may deem proper, of the *net profits arising from the resources of said Company, after deducting the necessary current and probable contingent expenses*, and divide the same among the stockholders in proportion to their respective shares." The corporation having completed the road to the extent of the fifteen miles and more, commenced running cars and taking tolls on that part. The Board of Directors, on the 20th of July, 1835, declared a dividend of 4½ per cent. on eighty dollars per share then paid in; and on the 7th January, 1836, a dividend of 2 per cent. on $90 per share then paid in, for the six months ending the 1st January, 1836, and on the 30th December, 1836, a third dividend of 4 per cent. per share for the year ending the 1st January, 1837. The first dividend declared was directed to be placed to the credit of stock due, and the second and third were divided in cash....

The complainant, Redd, having recovered two judgments in the Jefferson Circuit, against the Company, one for $741 60, with interest from the 28th October, 1838, and costs, the other for $288 60, with interest from the 10th day of October, 1838, and costs, and having executions returned, "no property found," filed his bill in the Chancery Court of Louisville, against Gratz and the Company, to subject the demand due from Gratz to them, for dividends improperly declared and paid to him, to the payment of his judgments and costs. He charges that all the property of the corporation is under mortgage to the Commonwealth of Kentucky and to the City of Louisville, for more than it is worth, and that the Company have nothing that is liable to execution: but that there is due from various stockholders, a large sum, for and on account of *dividends improperly* divided, at a time when there was *no profits to divide*, and sets forth and charges the various steps taken by the stockholders, at their meeting and adjourned meeting, and committee's reports, resolutions, submission and award, and the report of the

award to the directory, and their acceptance, sanction and approval of the same, and entry thereof on their books, and notification of each of the stockholders, to refund the amount so improperly divided; that Benjamin Gratz was one of the stockholders when those dividends were made and was present at the meeting of the stockholders when the investigation was ordered and when the report of the committee was received, and when the order of reference was made, and was in the Board when the report was made, and received and approved by the Board; that he had received $1,296 of these improperly declared dividends, on account of stock which he held in the company, which was liable to be attached and applied to the payment of his said judgments. He makes Gratz and the Company defendants, and calls upon them to answer and exhibit all the orders and resolutions on the subject of these dividends, and prays that Gratz *pay over* the amount due from him, in satisfaction of his judgments, 19
and for *general relief*....

The books also of the corporation, and all the accounts, orders, resolutions and steps taken and noted in the same, are *prima facie* evidence against all the stockholders, as the books of a private company would be evidence against each member.

Placing out of view the award, it may be questionable whether it was not the duty of the directory, upon the evidence afforded them, by the reports to, and resolutions of the meetings, and the collation and exhibition of the accounts in these reports, and the sanction given to them by the meetings, (though there was no direct order upon the stockholders to refund,) connected with the evidence afforded by the books, to demand a restoration of the dividends paid out, and to have taken some steps to coerce their restitution. Be this as it may, it is very evident, at the time when these dividends were declared and divided out, there was no profits to divide, unless, as is contended by the counsel for Gratz, the money paid in on forfeited stock should be credited to profits, or the annually accruing interest on the $150,000 borrowed, should be charged to cost of construction and not deducted from profits.

The stock subscribed was the capital of the Company subscribed and paid in for the construction of the road, and we cannot sanction the position, that the sum paid in on the stock ceased to be capital on the forfeiture of the stock, and by such forfeiture was converted into profits, to be divided among the stockholders as such. It was subscribed and paid in as capital, and treated and expended as such, and ought not to have been divided as profits. To distribute it out as profits before the work was completed, would be to squander a fund paid in, to be expended in the construction of the railway, and to which contractors and other creditors had a right to look for the payment of their demands, for work and labor done and to be done, in the construction, and for materials furnished and to be furnished. Though the fourth section of the charter, upon the failure of any subscriber to pay any installment for the space of sixty days after the same

shall be due and payable, authorizes the directory to forfeit the stock on which it is demanded, which may be sold for the benefit of the Company, yet it gives no authority to change the destination of the fund already paid in from its original object. Had a sale been made of the stock, and had it commanded a price, substituting the purchasers in the place of the former stockholders, the amount bid might have been carried to profits, or had a fair estimated value been fixed upon it, and that estimated value exceeded its par value, including the sum paid on it, that excess, perhaps, might have been carried to profits. But the stock was not sold, nor was any estimated value fixed on it, nor can we say that there was an excess to be applied to profits, nor was any so applied on the books of the Company, nor can we presume, from the state and condition of this Company, as it is now exhibited to us from its books, that the forfeited stock was worth, or
20 would have commanded in market one cent. Had it been worth any thing, the presumption is that it would not have been forfeited, and if forfeited for other causes, the presumption is, if it were not worthless, that while the Company was struggling to raise the means necessary to complete the work, that they would have readily resorted to the expedient of selling the forfeited stock, not only to obtain the benefit of the surplus, if it would have commanded a premium, but also to obtain the aid of the purchasers in their payments of the accruing and unpaid installments upon the stock so purchased. Be this as it may, it was not sold, but the fund paid was carried and set down to capital on the books, as it rightfully should have been, and not to profits, and the position that it should be credited to profits, is an after thought by Gratz or his counsel, not sustained by the cotemporaneous construction of the charter, and action of the Directors themselves, among whom was Gratz himself.

Nor can we sanction the position contended for, that the *interest annually accruing* upon the $150,000 borrowed under the authority and guarranty of the State, is chargeable to construction and ought not to have been deducted from and paid out of the annual profits, before a division was made. The money was borrowed in easement of the stockholders, and to relieve them from hasty and heavy calls upon their stock, which they might not have been able to meet without hardship and oppression, and the interest should have been paid and kept down out of the profits, if any, without withdrawing from or lessening the capital. A division of profits is not authorized by the 22nd section of the charter, until "all the necessary *current and probable contingent expenses*" have been deducted. This annually accruing interest account not only should have been charged to expenses and deducted from the profits before a dividend was declared or distribution made, but an additional sum, in strict propriety, should have been set apart, from year to year, as a sinking fund for the ultimate payment of the principal. If annually accruing interest be chargeable to and paid out of the capital, it would, in process of time swallow up the whole amount, leaving the Company with their debts unpaid, in bankruptcy and ruin, while the stockholders, for whose easement the power to borrow was allowed, are permitted to distribute among themselves the funds of the Company, under the false name of *surplus profits.*

If the money paid in on forfeited stock be set down to capital and not to profits, and the interest upon the sum borrowed be charged to expenses and deducted from the profits, together with other charges and deductions that should rightfully be made, there was then no surplus profits to divide, at either of the times that dividends were declared, as is apparent from the books of the Company and the exhibits in the case, as well as from the parol evidence adduced; and consequently, the sums paid out to stockholders, and credited on their stock, were paid out and credited, without the authority of, and against the express provisions of their charter, upon an erroneous basis and mistaken estimate of profits; and the sums so paid and credited must have been and were paid out of, and withdrawn from the capital. Indeed, according to the proofs now before us, taken from the books, and the uncontradicted reports made under the order of the Company, and tacitly or impliedly sanctioned by them, and which unobjected to, uncontradicted or explained, we must take as proof, if the interest be not charged to expenses there was no profits to divide, but the expenses, even in that case, exceeded the profits. But charging the interest to expenses, and there was a palpable excess of expenses beyond the profits, and an obvious encroachment upon the capital, to the full extent of a sum equal to the amount divided and distributed among the stockholders.

1st. The question arises, therefore, whether the complainant, a judgment creditor, with a return of "*nulla bona*" on his executions, may not, in Chancery, subject the fund so improvidently paid out or credited, to the satisfaction of his judgments. If the directory could reclaim and recover back the sums so erroneously paid and credited, then could the complainant, upon the return suggested, subject the amount so recoverable from Gratz or any other stockholder, to the payment of his demand as a *chose in action*, under our statute. And we can perceive no good reason why they may not recover it back....

And as Gratz may be proceeded against alone, for a breach of trust, in ordering trust funds to be paid out, or if even it be questionable whether he should be made liable for concurring in an order made by himself, in conjunction with others, by which a trust fund was directed to be paid out to third persons, without making the others parties, we cannot doubt when he concurs in the orders and *receives* the fund under the order, that he may be rendered responsible by a proceeding against him alone, and recovery had against him, at least to the extent of the fund so received.

BARRY v. MERCHANTS EXCHANGE CO.

1 Sandf. Ch. (N.Y.) 280 (1844)
Cases in Chancery, New York

[A contract creditor claimed that bonds and mortgages issued by the Merchants' Exchange Company were illegal because they increased the company's capital beyond that specified in the charter and also because they impinged upon the company's obligation to divide profits among its shareholders.]

THE ASSISSANT VICE-CHANCELLOR. — . . .

22 In reference to the accumulation of the profits of the corporation, and thereby increasing their solid capital. I do not find any provision of law which forbids that course. We know perfectly well that our banking institutions, (all of which were chartered with limited capitals previous to the General Banking Act of 1838,) in the days of their prosperity, very frequently accumulated a large surplus, and used it to increase their business. No one, so far as I have heard, ever questioned their right to do so; and the stock of those institutions was appreciated by the public precisely as they exhibited a greater or lesser amount of surplus property, beyond their capital and liabilities. The practice of monied corporations to accumulate their profits, has been recognized in our legislation relative to the banks, and has been before this court judicially in several cases. See *Bank of Utica* v. *City of Utica*, (4 Paige's R. 399; *Lowerre* v. *American Fire Insurance Company*, and *De Peyster* v. *The Same*, (6 ibid. 482. 486;) *Scott* v. *Eagle Fire Company*, (7 ibid. 198.)

The right to keep a surplus on hand, was not questioned in those cases, and in the insurance causes, it was declared by the Chancellor to be a duty in reference to outstanding risks. From the year 1830, to the present year, the custom of our banking corporations to accumulate their profits beyond their capital, has annually been brought before the legislature by the reports of the bank commissioners, which gave the condition of each bank, and exhibited such surplus in each instance where it existed; and during the current year the report of the comptroller exhibits the same details. Yet we have never heard of any doubt or question being raised as to the perfect right of these institutions to retain their profits as a surplus, if they preferred that course to dividing them. The legislature appears to have left this matter to the corporations themselves, wisely deeming that the natural desire of all men to enjoy the fruits of their property, would be a sufficient preventive against any inordinate or dangerous accumulation.

In the case of *Scott* v. *The Eagle Fire Co.*, *ubi supra*, the Chancellor says, if the directors without reasonable cause should refuse to divide what was actually surplus profits, the stockholders are not without remedy, if they apply to the proper tribunal. To this I may add, that they have in a great measure, the remedy in their own hands. They may eject the recusant directors at the next annual election, or if they fail to induce a majority of shareholders to join them in that proceeding, they may sell their stock and retire from the association.

In the charter in question, the corporation is authorized to receive the rents and profits of their exchange, and divide the same amongst the stockholders, at such times as they may deem expedient and proper. It is thus left entirely to the discretion of the trustees.

It is however said that this clause is mandatory, and that the permission to designate the times, for a division of profits, does not authorize a total omission to divide for a long period.

I cannot take this view of the clause in the charter. Whether the first time to be designated for a dividend of profits, shall be one year or twenty, is left to the corporation to determine. Nor is there any serious danger of inordinate accumulation, or of the growth of any overshadowing monopoly, by leaving corporations to pursue their own course in this respect. Few men would care to forego the receipt of an income from their stock, during their lives or for any long period, in order that in the next generation, their heirs may participate in the management of some gigantic corporation. The danger that the surplus may be squandered, or the control pass to unwelcome hands, is too manifest to induce the most ardent admrier of posthumous power and influence, to incur such hazard of his estate. And if there be any evils arising from such surplus accumulations, the legislature in their future action will apply the remedy.

Another argument which was made to bear upon both theories of the complainant's counsel, was pressed upon me with great force, viz. that the amount fixed as the capital stock of the corporation, was an absolute restriction upon the amount and value of the property both real and personal, which they may hold permanently.

Some modifications of this position, at once forced themselves upon the attention of the counsel. If the capital were the limit of the property of the corporation, they could make no dividends or profits, for those are beyond the capital. Again, in the ever varying and fluctuating values of all descriptions of property a corporation that was within its capital last year, may without a single new purchase or expenditure, be worth this year, twenty per cent. beyond its capital, by the increased value of the same property.

Hence the learned counsel were driven to rest their point upon a designedly permanent increase of property, beyond the capital of the Company. Still the rule encountered difficulties.

The object of corporators in all monied and business corporations, is to make greater profits than they can command by the separate use of the same amount of capital. They put in their money, the capital stock, for the very purpose of having it increase in value, and more rapidly than in private adventures. And we have seen, that unless positively enjoined by their charters, there is nothing to require them to divide the increase annually, or in any given time.

It was argued, that in this particular case, the design was one not referring to profits for ultimate division, but it was a permanent and solid investment of profits which never could be divided, and which became an essential and integral portion of the real capital of the Company. That the exchange was an unit, indivisible, and composed of the capital stock, and nearly as much more; the latter being added in anticipation of earnings or profits, and the whole incapable of partition or division.

On this subject of the capital stock of a corporation, the elementary treatises are comparatively barren.

It is the aggregate amount of the funds of the corporators, which are combined together under a charter, for the attainment of some common object of public convenience or private utility. This amount is usually fixed in the act of incorporation, although we have seen in the statutes of 1823, one exception to this practice. It is thus limited, in reference to the convenience of the intended corporators, and for the information and security of the public at large. To the corporators, it prescribes the amount and subdivisions of their respective contributions to the common fund; the voice which each shall have in its control and management; and the apportionment of the profits of the enterprise. To the community, it announces the extent of the means contributed and forming the basis of the dealings of the corporate body, and enables every man to judge of its ability to meet its engagements and perform what it undertakes. And when, as in most instances, the statute requires the stock to be paid in before the corporation can transact business, security to those contracting with it, is thereby superadded to the information of its resources. These objects for the public benefit, are sometimes defeated by fraud and deception, but they are such as the legislature have in view in limiting the amount of capital stock, and requiring a specified sum or proportion to be paid in.

One further consideration dictates the amount thus fixed. This is the probable and reasonable extent of the means requisite to the accomplishment of the end proposed, qualified in many cases by the unwillingness of the legislature to create these artificial beings with an undue amount of capital....

The capital stock of a corporation, is, like that of a copartnership or joint stock company, the amount which the partners or associates put in as their stake in the concern. To this they add upon the credit of the company, from the means and resources of others, to such extent as their own prudence or the confidence of such other persons will permit. Such additions create a debt; they do not form capital. And if successful in their career, the surplus over and above their capital and debts becomes profits, and is either divided among the partners and associates, or used still farther to extend their operations.

The proposition that a corporation is limited even in its permanent ownership of property, to the amount fixed as its capital, is entirely new, and has not the sanction of authority or reason. The custom of retaining the profits which I have before mentioned, has been long continued, and has worked in many of our corporations, and especially in banking institutions, an increase of their solid property and estate, as permanent as any that has been inferred in this case. Not that such increase has in those instances been so invested and mingled with the fruits of the original capital, as to become indivisible therefrom; but the increase has in many of the instances been as fixed and permanent as the capital itself, and with no purpose or probability of its being returned to the stockholders until the concern should be wound up voluntarily, or by the expiration of the charters.

. . .

But it was contended that the unrestricted power of borrowing, which the Company claims for effecting the purposes of its charter, virtually confers upon the corporation unlimited power. That the purposes of the charter would in this instance at least be no restraint, because they could embrace accommodations for every description of commercial business; and the extent of their credit would be equally ineffectual, for there would be no limit to that, except in the prudence of the lender; and finally, that no such extravagant authority was granted to this corporation expressly or by implication, and it is contrary to the spirit and policy of our laws and institutions.

This whole argument is, in my judgment, unsound. The danger of inordinate accumulation of property and consequent overshadowing power, is wholly fallacious. The whole extent of the corporate credit, is in truth, measured and controlled by its capital. Every addition to its means beyond its paid up capital, (leaving profits out of view,) must be by gift or contract, and if by contract, a debt ensues. If a corporation with a million of capital, succeeds in running into debt two millions it has no more solid property, and is intrinsically worth no more than before, unless the property obtained on credit is worth more than it cost, and then the increase of property is only such excess of value. And if worth less than cost, then the company has by the operation, sunk a part of its capital.

All experience shows that the financial management of corporations, is in general less judicious and safe than that of individuals. Hence losses are likely to ensue from expansions, upon credit; and the farther such credit is pushed by any corporation, the greater the danger that such losses will impair and finally consume its capital. The lenders of money are usually sagacious enough to protect their interests when dealing with corporations as well as with individuals; and few would lend money to a company which already owed debts greatly exceeding its whole capital stock, however flattering in appearance the investment might be. The laws of trade have placed an impassable barrier to the power of corporate borrowing, in the tendency of such institutions to make an improvident use of exuberant means, and in the caution and prudence of capitalists. It is utterly impossible for a corporation with a known limited capital to accumulate by means of its credit, the gigantic property and power which the imagination of the counsel portrayed. . . .

In this case, then, I am satisfied that the Merchants' Exchange Company were authorized by law to borrow money for the completion of their building, to the extent adopted by them, and to secure its re-payment by their corporate obligations, and by mortgages on their real estate. . . .

SAGORY v. DUBOIS

3 Sandf. Ch. (N.Y.) 466 (1846)
Cases in Chancery, New York

THE bill in this cause was filed, October 1, 1844, by Charles Sagory, as receiver of The New York Banking Company, against Cornelius Dubois, Jr., a stockholder in the company, to compel him to pay up the unpaid balance on the shares of capital stock owned by him....

THE ASSISTANT VICE-CHANCELLOR. . . .

The act to authorize the business of banking, (Laws of 1838, chapt. 260,) enabled any number of persons to associate and
26 establish banks, and expressly conferred on the institutions organized under it, subject to the prescribed limitations, all the powers usually exercised by the banks previously incorporated in this state. They were authorized to discount bills, notes, and evidences of debt; to receive deposites; to issue bank notes for circulation; to buy and sell bullion, coin, and bills of exchange; to loan money on real and personal security, and to exercise all incidental powers necessary to carry on such business.

The 15th section of the act provided, that the aggregate amount of the capital stock of any such association, should not be less than $100,000....

By the 20th section, every association by its original articles, might provide for an increase of its capital from time to time.

By section 26th, each association was required on the first Mondays of January and July in every year, to make and transmit to the comptroller, a statement upon oath, containing amongst other things,

"1. The amount of the capital stock paid in according to the provisions of this act, or secured to be paid."

"8. The amount of the losses of the association; specifying whether charged on its capital or profits, since its last preceding statement, and of its dividends declared and made during the same period."

"11. The amount which the capital of the said association has been increased during the preceding six months, if there shall have been any increase of the said capital," &c.

By the 28th section, "If any portion of the original capital of such association shall be withdrawn for any purpose whatsoever, whilst any debts of the association remain unsatisfied, no dividends or profits on the shares of the capital stock of the association, shall thereafter be made, until the deficit of capital shall have been made good, either by subscription of the shareholders, or out of the subsequently accruing profits of the association," &c....

The defendant contends, that his obligation by his subscription, was merely to take the twenty-five shares, which he has done; that he incurred no personal liability to pay for such shares; and that the only remedy which the association had, for his omission to pay the calls upon his stock, was to forfeit it to the use of the association, under the sixth Article.

I think this is altogether too restricted a view of the effect of his subscription for this stock.

The provisions of the General Banking Law, to which I have referred, demonstrate that the legislature had no intention to create banks without actual capital. For more than thirty years previous to the passage of that act, the business of banking had been a privileged pursuit in this state, variously guarded by penal laws, and its exercise conferred only by special acts of legislation. By the general banking law, it was designed to 27
throw the business open to the public, so far as to dispense with special charters; but in no respect departing from the system of prescribing and defining its limits, and preventing frauds and abuses upon the community, which had so long been a marked feature in our legislation. Hence the various restrictions as to circulating notes, the capital stock, &c., which are contained in the act of 1838. No institution could organize under it, with a less capital than $100,000. The privileges conferred, and the prior course of legislation show, that this was intended to be *actual capital*, and not nominal; a substantial reality, not a bubble. The exemption of stockholders from personal liability for the debts of the association, affords a further reason for the legislature's insisting upon a known and actual capital. The subsequent provisions confirm this view, so as to leave no room for a doubt. The certificate, which was to make known to the public the existence, sphere of operations, and resources of the bank, was to specify the amount of its capital stock, and the number of shares composing it, and by whom they were held. The capital stock might be increased from time to time, not by paying in upon the capital first subscribed and set forth in the certificate; but by an addition to such original capital; precisely as the Articles of the New York Banking Company prescribe. Then in the semi-annual statements which were to be filed with the comptroller, in order to keep the community informed of their progress and stability, each association was required to state the amount of its capital stock *paid in according to the provisions of the act, or secured to be paid.*

Now the act makes no provision in express terms, for the paying in of the capital. But the paying in or securing it, is a necessary consequence of the provisions, that the capital stock shall not be less than $100,000, and that the amount of it shall be determined upon and specified, in the certificate upon which it becomes organized.

The semi-annual statement is to show the amount of its losses, and to specify whether they have been charged on its *capital* or profits. Here again is evidence that the word capital, throughout, means not a name, but a thing; not a nominal sum paraded to a credulous public, but a sum fixed by the organic articles, and actually paid or secured....

The authorities to which I have referred, with the few exceptions stated, concur in maintaining the principle upon which I deemed the defendant liable to pay for his shares of stock, and are decisive by their weight and character....

Another question of moment arises in respect of the dividends
28 declared, and which were so arranged as to be cotemporary with the payments of three of the instalments called in on the capital stock, and were applied to the discharge of such instalments.

The 28th section of the general banking law, prohibits dividends by withdrawing the capital stock, or out of profits while the paid up capital is deficient, so long as there are any debts owing by the association. And the law relative to monied corporations, (1 Rev. Stat. 589, § 1,) makes it unlawful for such corporations to make dividends, except from their surplus profits.

The defendant was an active director of the New York Banking Company, and must be deemed chargeable with knowledge of the state of its affairs. According to the statutes, which I have just cited, his right to receive and apply the dividends in question, depends on the state of the institution, and the existence of surplus profits.

There is some doubt upon the testimony, whether the two first dividends did not exceed the profits actually earned when they were paid, but the point is not so clear as to authorize me to say that any part of those dividends was made by a withdrawal of the capital.

In regard to the third dividend, payable Nov. 1, 1840, it is clear to my mind that it ought not to have been made. The Hernando Rail Road and Banking Company, had failed long before that period, to meet its engagements with the New York Banking Company, and the balance against it on the books of the latter company, was at that time more than $112,000. The failure of the Hernando Company, had been communicated to the board of directors of the New York Banking Company, in April, 1840, and again on the 19th of October, 1840, when the dividend was declared. I have no doubt but that the directors *believed* what the president hoped, that there would be no ultimate loss from this debt, and that they declared the dividend in good faith; but I think it was improvident and improper, to divide their apparent surplus, when nearly a third part of their whole capital was locked up in a suspended debt of an uncertain, if not doubtful character. In support of this opinion, I refer to the chancellor's observations in *De Peyster* v. *The American Insurance Company*, (6 Paige, 486;) and *Scott* v. *The Eagle Fire Company*, (7 ibid. 198.)

The consequence is, that the credit which the defendant received upon his capital stock for the amount of the third dividend, is not to be regarded as a payment of such amount, and the same is still due and payable upon his subscription....

The decree will direct the defendant to pay to the receiver the unpaid balance of his twenty-five shares of stock, without any credit for the third dividend, and with interest from January 15, 1844. The amount can be ascertained and inserted in the decree, without going into the master's office.

STATE OF MARYLAND
v. BALTIMORE AND OHIO RAILROAD CO.

6 Gill. (Md.) 363 (1847)
Court of Appeals of Maryland

...By a resolution of the General Assembly of *Maryland*, passed at its December session, 1846, the Attorney General was directed to institute suit against the *Baltimore and Ohio Rail-road Company*, to recover the dividend of $15,000, which had been declared by that Com-
30 pany, payable in part in the bonds of said Company....

ARCHER, C.J., delivered the opinion of this court....

The State, being a stockholder, and refusing to receive the dividend thus declared by the Company, as it was declared, has instituted this action to recover the amount of *three per cent*. in money, considering the dividend in the same light, and as having the same legal effect, as if it had been declared in money, and not in money and bonds....

Thus is the power conferred, and thus is the duty imposed, of constructing a Rail-road. For this purpose a capital is provided, of $3,000,000; and this power, and this duty, are to be exercised in no other way, looking to this section alone, than by the means placed at the disposal of the Company, that is, by its capital, and the products of its capital. It was certainly a part of the contract of the Company, when they accepted their charter, that they would make and keep in repair the road, though it required their whole fortune, which consists of their capital, and of the earnings of their capital. These duties the Company undertook to perform, with the means placed by the charter at their disposal; subject, however, to the right, conferred by the 19th section, at the discretion of the President and Directors to divide the net profits....

The 19th section interposes no difficulty in the way of the above construction. That section we will advert to. It is in the following words:

"And be it enacted, That the said President and Directors shall annually, or semi-annually, declare and make such dividend as they may deem proper, of the net profits arising from the resources of the said Company, after deducting the necessary current and probable contingent expenses; and that they shall divide the same amongst the proprietors of the stock of said Company, in proper proportions to their respective shares."

There is clearly nothing in this section which is in any manner imperative on the Company to declare dividends of their net profits. Their duty is defined to make such dividend as they may deem proper from the resources of the Company. If, in the honest exercise of their duties, looking to the whole interest of the Company, they deemed that the net profits should be otherwise applied, to accomplish or further the objects of the act of incorporation, they were at liberty to withhold a dividend....

But it is urged, that if the net profits of the Company can be applied to the construction of the road, or to extraordinary works of repair there would be no profits left to secure the guarantee provided by the 9th section of the act of May session, 1836.

But we think the true construction of that section is, that this guarantee is to be satisfied out of the gross profits of the Company.

This section provides, that the interest on each instalment of stock subscribed shall, after the lapse of three years from the time of payment by the State, be paid out of the profits of the work. The term profits may mean gross profits or net profits. Which it means must be determined by its association, and by the whole clause. Now, in the same sentence, the terms clear annual profits are used. Then, in another part of the same section, and in the same sentence, on a contingency therein mentioned, the language is, that the State shall be entitled to receive a perpetual dividend of six per centum per annum, out of the profits of the work, as declared from time to time. So that the term profits, as used in the first part of the sentence, is used without limitation or qualification, and wherever afterwards it is used, it is qualified and defined to mean *clear annual profits*, or *as declared* from time to time, which declaration of profits, as declared from time to time, would be only from the *clear annual profits* by the charter. It then appears, that they have used the term as contradistinguished from *net profits*, or *clear annual profits*, or *profits declared from time to time*. And as this has been done, we think the inference is clear, that by the term profits, as first used in reference to the guarantee, they meant gross profits. This guarantee is in no manner impaired by the act of 1838, ch. 386.

32 The above views dispose of the various propositions contained in the prayers, except the question arising under the second proposition, as to the ability of the Company, at its discretion, to appropriate its net revenue, and agree to refund the same to its stockholders, or to make such appropriations absolutely to the purposes of the road.

We have before seen that the Company, in the honest discharge of its duties, may, under the charter, appropriate the net revenue of the Company to the purposes of the charter; it is, we think equally clear, that they may, having appropriated the net revenue of the Company to the purposes of the charter, designing at the time to repay them, agree to refund the same to the stockholders.

If designing to make a dividend of the net profits, they have used them for the purposes of the Company, intending at the time to return them to the stockholders, as was the case in the cause before the court, as is abundantly evident from the Twentieth Annual Report, which is in evidence before the court, we think there is nothing in the charter which would prohibit the Company from refunding the amount thus used by them to the stockholders. The character of the act ought to be determined by its intention.

The legislature would not, certainly, have designed, that if the Company have on hand $500,000 of net profits, and designing to divide the same, and should from any cause connected with the prosecution of the enterprise, have required the use of $100,000, that they must, in order to carry out their design of dividing the said $500,000 among their stockholders, abstain from the appropriation of any part of the net profits temporarily to that object, and resort to a loan for the purpose, keeping the net profits idle in their coffers, until the period of the declaration of a dividend should arrive.

We are satisfied they might agree to refund the net profits which they may have used, and might, under the powers granted to them by the charter, borrow money to supply the place of that which had been used, and that they might borrow from the stockholders as well as from any one else, and that they had a perfect right, with the consent of the stockholders, to treat the money thus used as a loan, and for this purpose, might pass to the stockholders, who were willing to receive them, their bonds.... 33

Now as to the second proposition, which asserts that the State can recover the whole amount of the dividend, although the Company had not cash on hand sufficient to pay the dividend, and did not intend to declare a cash dividend of three per cent., but of one per cent. only,--we remark that the plaintiff has certainly no standing in court, except upon the dividend. The relation of debtor and creditor cannot exist as between the Company and the stockholder in this respect, until the dividend is made. The plaintiff, by the institution of this action, affirms the dividend, and he must take it as it is....

LEXINGTON LIFE, FIRE AND MARINE INSURANCE CO. v. PAGE

56 Ky. 327 (1856) Kentucky

H. C. PINDELL, for appellees—This suit is brought by the Boston agents of the Lexington Fire, Life and Marine Insurance Company, claiming a balance due them on account of twenty thousand seven hundred and eighteen dollars and sixty-eight cents, for advances made by them in the payment of losses, and for commissions. The account is fully proved, and its correctness not controverted.

The object of the petition is twofold:

1. It submits to the court the validity of the assignment made by the company of its assets and effects to R. A. Buckner; charges that it is fraudulent, and prays that it be so declared, and that the assigned effects be subjected to plaintiffs' demands; but if it be adjudged valid, any benefits to which they may be entitled be secured to them according to the provisions of the deed

34

2. It is charged that dividends were improperly declared when there was not any profit out of which dividends could be declared; that it was a dividend of the capital stock; and praying that the stockholders be compelled to refund so much as may be necessary to satisfy the claim of plaintiff unless it be the opinion of the court that the right to reclaim such dividends passed to the assignee by the assignment. And in that case they pray that the assignee be required to reclaim them, and account in court for these and the other assets of the company....

The question as to the legality of the dividends declared will be first noticed.

The commissioner's report shows the condition of the company when the three last dividends were declared—May, 1848, November, 1848, and May, 1849. It appears that in calculations made semi-annually by the company to ascertain the amount of dividend, that the unearned premiums were estimated as assets; that the excess of the assets, so in part composed, above the sum of the capital stock, and [**425**] the liabilities other than those on unexpired risks, was treated as profit, and a large portion of it divided as such among the stockholders. The aggregate amount of premiums upon unexpired risks at each of the dividends does not appear in the commissioner's report, but the portion of that aggregate which it would have taken to re-insure the outstanding risks does, and even that greatly exceeds the profits at those periods, according to their mode of estimating them.

In May, 1848, when there was a dividend of five dollars per share, or fifteen thousand dollars in the aggregate, the excess of assets over capital stock and liabilities, other than those arising from risks, was thirty-three thousand nine-hundred and eighty-four dollars and ninety-one cents, and at that time it would have taken eighty-three thousand one hundred and fourteen dollars and ten cents to re-insure outstanding risks, excluding those on cargoes.

In November, 1848, when there was a dividend of three dollars per share, or nine thousand dollars in the aggregate, the excess of assets over capital stock and liabilities, was fourteen thousand one hundred and five dollars and twenty-two cents, and it would then have taken seventy-seven thousand four hundred and seventy-five dollars and eighty-nine cents to re-insure outstanding risks, excluding those on cargoes.

In May, 1849, there was a dividend of ten dollars per share, or thirty thousand dollars in the aggregate; the excess of assets over capital stock and liabilities, other than those arising from risks was forty-six thousand four hundred and twenty-seven dollars and fifteen cents, and at that time it would have required one hundred thirty-nine thousand four hundred and eighty-eight dollars and eighty-nine cents to re-insure the outstanding risks, not including risks on cargoes.

The commissioner says he is unable to report the cargo risks, and, of course, what sum would have been required to re-insure them. But by a supplemental report, it appears that from May, 1848, to May, 1851, the premiums received from cargo risks were considerably more than one-third of those received from all other sources. Cargo risks, however, differ from all others in this, that generally not being heard from between their commencement and termination, lapse of time after commencement does not lessen the cost of a re-insurance. So, that if the [**426**] amount of cargo risks at the time mentioned be any criterion, a very large allowance would have to be made for them to ascertain the true amount which would have been necessary to re-insure all the outstanding risks. Now, as the claims for premiums unearned were greater than the excess of assets above the debts and capital stock when added together, they must have specifically constituted the profits, if any existed, as well as part of the capital itself. And as those claims were not divided among the stockholders, but the dividends were generally made of stock notes, they were specifically dividends of the subscribed capital. Possibly this might not have been objectionable, if there had been substituted for the capital so divided actual profits in a form equally available to the company. But this should certainly be manifested by those seeking to establish the justice of such division. So far from this appearing, the contrary is shown by the commissioner's report and the correspondence with Ames. The claims which were substituted appear to be uncollectible, and the fact evinced that it was a cause of the nearly failure of the company. It is clear that no actual profits existed at the time the dividends were declared, but for several years before the failure an actual diminution of the capital.

Any attempt to demonstrate that the claims of an insurance company for premiums on risks, still running and undetermined, are not, in any sense of the term, *profits,* would be but obscuring by argument a self-evident proposition. It would not have been attempted, but for the almost unanimous denial of it by the defendants, including some gentlemen of the legal profession. It was stated as an axiom in the cases of *Scott* v. *The Eagle Fire Insurance Company,* 7 Paige, 198, and *De Peyster* v. *American Insurance Company,* 6 Ib., 486.

The word *profits* is defined by Webster as follows: "1. In commerce, the advance in the price of goods sold beyond the costs of purchase. 2. Any gain or [**427**] pecuniary advantage. 3. Any advantage; any accession of good from labor or exertion." Obviously the profit of business transactions is the pecuniary gain or advantage derived from them—the excess of all the moneys arising from them over all those expended in effecting them. If the expenditure exceed the receipts, there is no *profit;* and the fact that the amount of receipts is ascertained before the expenditures can not change the case. The commissioner's report shows enough to make it perfectly clear that the losses exceeded the amount of so many of the premium claims as were proportionate to the time the outstanding risks had to run; or, in other words, which, if collected, would have been sufficient to re-insure the outstanding risks at the rate at which they were taken. The sums which would have been required to re-insure, at the two first dates stated, were respectively eighty-three thousand one hundred and fourteen dollars and ten cents and seventy-seven thousand four hundred and ninety-five dollars and eighty-nine cents, and the losses sustained by the company before the next subsequent dates, only six months thereafter, were one hundred and twenty-seven thousand two hundred and sixty-six dollars and seventy-four cents and two hundred thousand one hundred and fifty dollars and forty-five cents. The amount of all the uncollected premiums in May, 1848, was one hundred and forty-eight thousand seven hundred and twenty-four dollars and fifty-four cents; in November, one hundred and thirty-nine thousand one hundred and nine dollars and sixteen cents; in May, 1849, two hundred and forty-three thousand eight hundred and eighty-five dollars and seventy-six cents. The report does not show the losses subsequently to the last dividend.

It can not be said that the losses were such that the company could not have anticipated them, and could, therefore, not be required to make such large deductions from their assets before treating the residue as profits; for whatever might have been the result. It could not properly be said that there were profits to divide while the risks were out, which might require the premiums received to meet the losses that might occur....

Judge SIMPSON delivered the opinion of the court:

[This opinion was delivered 23d January, 1856, but suspended
36 by a petition for a rehearing, which was overruled.—REP.]

On the 1st of November, 1851, the Lexington Fire, Life and Marine Insurance Company made an assignment of the whole of its effects to R. A. Buckner, in trust, to pay off the debts of the company according to the order therein specified.

In the spring of 1849, and previous to that time, the company had declared several semi-annual dividends of what was deemed by the board of directors to be its profits, some of which dividends were credited upon the notes which had been executed by the stockholders for the payment of their stock subscriptions.

This action was brought by Page & Richardson, who claim to be the creditors of the company, for advances made by them in the payment of losses [437] and for their commissions in acting as the agents of the company.

The plaintiffs, in their petition, presented their claim to relief in a double aspect. They attempted to impeach the validity of the assignment to Buckner on the ground of fraud; but if the deed be valid, they prayed that they might have the benefit of its provisions so far as they would operate in their favor. They also charged that the dividends which had been declared by the company were illegal, having been made when in fact there were no profits to divide; and prayed that the stockholders might be compelled to refund enough thereof to pay their demand, unless the right to reclaim them had passed to the trustee, in which event they prayed that he might be required to collect them and account for them as part of the assets of the trust. The insurance company, Buckner the assignee, and the individual directors and stockholders who declared and received the dividends, were all made defendants to the petition....

The next question that properly presents itself for consideration, is that which involves the legality or illegality of the dividends which were made by the board of directors.

By the seventh section of the charter by which the company was incorporated, it was enacted "that it shall be the duty of the president and directors, on the first Mondays of May and November in each and every year, to make a dividend of so much of the profits of said corporation as to them, or a majority of them, shall appear advisable."

The board of directors, in making the dividends in question, considered as profits the premiums on unexpired risks, and unless this was proper, the dividends which were made were not authorized by the charter inasmuch as independent of these premiums the means of the incorporation, over and above its liabilities, were insufficient for their payment. We think it very evident that these premiums could not be properly regarded as profits. Only so much thereof as might remain after paying the amount of such losses as should occur would, in reality constitute the actual profits on the insurance upon which they had been paid. This was the decision of the court in the cases of *De Peyster* v. *American Insurance Company,* 6 Paige, 486, and in *Scott* v. *Eagle Fire Insurance Company,* 7 Paige, 198, which were cases very similar to the present one. We can not, indeed, [**441**] very well perceive any plausible ground on which this position can be controverted. The losses must, in every case, be deducted before the profits, in any kind of business whatever, can be ascertained. This proposition is so self-evident, that argument to sustain or illustrate it is wholly unnecessary.

So much of these premiums might possibly have been regarded as profits, as the previous business of the company, for a series of years, would have demonstrated could be safely considered as a surplus that would remain after all losses were paid; but upon no imaginable hypothesis could it be right or admissible to treat the whole amount of premiums, which resulted from such risks that were still pending, as actual profits. The most safe, and, 37
indeed, only allowable principle to act upon in such cases, would be to exclude from the computation of profits altogether all such unearned premiums. Excluding such premiums, some of the dividends were made when there were no profits on hand to divide among the stockholders, and such dividends were obviously unauthorized and illegal. It is, however, difficult to determine, either from the commissioner's report, or any evidence in the cause, which of the dividends should be regarded as subject to reclamation. It is necessary to a correct decision of this question, that the condition of the company at the time each one of the dividends was made should appear. Two dividends might be made without there being on hand a sufficiency of profits to have authorized either at the time they were respectively declared, and still the last one might have been proper, if the first one had not been made. In such a case it would be manifestly wrong to treat both of the dividends as illegal in the hands of the stockholders. The last one might have been retained by the corporation to satisfy its claim against the stockholders for the first one, which was illegal; but when it has been paid over, a different question is presented. The question, then, is, which of the two is subject to [**442**] reclamation? The first one the stockholders have no right to retain because it was unauthorized, and therefore it is undoubtedly subject to reclamation. If, then, the corporation has a right to reclaim the last one also, it might be able to compel both of them to be refunded.

It is evident, therefore, that it is indispensably necessary, in order that the court may be able to determine how many and which of the dividends were illegal, that is, how many of them were subject to reclamation, if any, that all the dividends that have been made, and the condition of the corporation when they were made, should appear.

The next subject of inquiry is, supposing some of these dividends to be illegal, did the right to reclaim them pass to the trustee by the deed of trust which was executed by the corporation?

The solution of this question involves two matters of inquiry: First: Had the corporation a right to reclaim these dividends? And, in the second place, if the right existed, did it pass by the deed under the peculiar circumstances in this case?

The declaration of these dividends was undoubtedly made in good faith, although it was made under a misconception of what constituted the profits of the company, out of which the board of directors were authorized to make dividends. This court, in the case of *Gratz* v. *Redd,* 4 B. Mon. 191, intimated an opinion, although the question was left undecided, that the company could reclaim dividends which had been made under similar circumstances. It would seem, according to well-settled general principles, that if dividends were made under a misconception on the part of the directors of what constituted profits, and under a belief that there were profits to divide, when in fact they were none, they might be reclaimed, because the stockholders who received them were not entitled to them, and they had been paid over and received under the operation of a mutual mistake....

Wherefore, the judgment of the circuit court is reversed, and cause remanded, that a judgment may be rendered against the corporation for the debt due to the plaintiffs, and for further proceedings consistent with this opinion, whereby the amount of the trust fund to which the plaintiffs will be entitled may be ascertained, and its payment adjudged to them.

CARPENTER v. THE NEW YORK & NEW HAVEN RAILROAD COMPANY

5 Abb. Pr. (N.Y.) 277 (1857)
Supreme Court of New York

DAVIES, J.—The complaint in this cause is filed by the plaintiffs, alleging that they are stockholders in the corporation, and it is filed as well on their behalf as of all other stockholders who desire to avail themselves thereof, and who are willing to contribute to the expense of the action. The complaint alleges that by reason of the frauds of the transfer agent of the corporation, a larger amount of stock therein has been issued than was authorized by the act of incorporation; that such stock is so mingled with the original and genuine that it is impossible to distinguish the one from the other, and that in consequence of the refusal of the directors and the other stockholders to recognize the said stock, large claims have been preferred against the corporation, in consequence thereof; that other claims are also pending, and which the plaintiffs believe, to a considerable amount, will be established against the corporation; that the directors have omitted for several years, to declare any dividends, but that they have declared a dividend on February 16, 1857. The plaintiffs allege that the same is to be paid without any recognition of the rights of those claiming to be stockholders by virtue of the stock issued by said transfer agent, that the company have no surplus earnings from which to pay the same, and that its payment would be injurious to the credit of the company. Upon the facts stated in the complaint, a temporary injunction was issued restraining the payment of said dividend. The defendants now answer the complaint, and set forth that the plaintiffs are stockholders to the extent of fifty shares, but claim to be stockholders in a much larger number of shares; that such latter claim is denied by the directors and by the original, and as the defendants claim, the genuine stockholders of the corporation; that the company on April 1, 1856, presented of net earnings the sum of $88,793.57, and earned a surplus between that date and October 1, 1856, a further sum of $117,740.21, making a total surplus on hand, applicable to the payment of dividend, of $206,533.78; that the claims against the company, which can be legally established against it, cannot be large, and which the company will have adequate means to pay off and discharge. The defendants now move to discharge the order for a temporary injunction.

On motion to vacate an injunction order, on complaint and answer, if all the equities of the complaint are denied, the injunction cannot be sustained. In this case those equities are denied. The ground upon which this complaint could be maintained is, that the defendants were about to misapply the funds of the corporation, and intended to pay a dividend to its stockholders, when, in fact, there was no money earned for such a purpose. It cannot be doubted that in a proper case such a complaint may be entertained. The case of Carlisle *a.* The South-eastern Railway Company is an authority in point. In that case an act of parliament prohibited the company from declaring and paying dividends until certain roads had been made and completed. . . .

I do not suppose it would be contended that this court has any right to interfere with the internal management of the affairs of the company by its duly constituted board of directors, in reference to matters resting in their discretion. Such are the times and circumstances under which dividends shall be paid—whether or not they should be paid out of earnings while disputed claims are unadjusted and unascertained—independent of the allegations of the complaint that there were no surplus earnings out of which this dividend could be paid. The objections interposed by the plaintiffs to its payment are mainly that claims to a large amount are impending over the property, and that, if established, the payments thereof will greatly exhaust the capital, and that if the dividends are reserved, as they should be, a fund will be provided to meet the same. The defendants deny that any such claim can or will be established against them, and say that it would be unjust to the stockholders to deprive them of their share of the earnings of the road to create a fund to liquidate a debt which they say cannot and which may never
40 be established. In this view the great majority of the stockholders concur, as it appears from the answer that since the dividend was declared a meeting of the stockholders has been held, and the conduct of the directors in declaring the same has been approved of by them. A stockholder can only claim the intervention of this court to protect the corporate property when it is threatened with waste or misapplication.

For the reasons given by me a few days since in the case of Blatchford against the defendants,* the plaintiffs can only be regarded as stockholders to the extent of fifty shares. As such holders they are entitled to the aid of the court to protect their property against waste or misapplication. The directors and the trustees are the trustees of the common fund belonging to the stockholders of the corporation, who are the *cestui que trusts.* To protect such property, and see that it is legally and properly applied, is the duty of this court, when its aid is invoked in a proper case. From the facts before me I am bound to say that it appears that the directors have earnings on hand sufficient to pay this dividend, and that this court has no right or authority to require them to retain such dividend to create a fund to liquidate debts which may or may not be established. Such dividends, when declared, belong to the stockholders; and if the same can be legally paid, as I think they can in this case, it is not competent for an individual stockholder to prevent such payment.

The temporary injunction must, therefore, be dissolved.

FORD v. LOCUST MOUNTAIN COAL AND IRON COMPANY

25 Phil. Leg. Int. 268 (1868)

Opinion by SHARSWOOD, J.

The plaintiffs are certain stockholders of the corporation defendants, and they complain that instead of dividing the surplus profits among the stockholder, in the shape of dividends, they are about to adopt the policy of setting aside so much annually as will eventually sink the capital. 41
The answer sets out the contemplated action at large, and both parties are desirous of having the opinion of the court upon the lawfulness of the proposed measure.

The Locust Mountain Coal and Iron Company was incorporated by an act of April 5, 1842, upon the model of the act of May 25, 1839, entitled "An act to incorporate the Anthracite Iron Co." By this act the affairs of the company were to be managed by directors, one of whom to be the president, who shall be chosen by the stockholders annually on a day and in a manner prescribed; and by the tenth section "Dividends of so much of the profits of said corporation, as shall appear advisable to the directors, shall be declared twice in every year," * * "but they shall in no case exceed the amount of the net profits actually acquired by said company, so that the capital stock shall never thereby be impaired." The capital of the company consists in the land it owns. By the charter, having acquired land, it was authorised to divide the same into stock, and issue certificates accordingly at a certain rate per acre. The value of the stock depends on the value of the land. The value of the land consists in the coal. When that is exhausted the land will be scarcely of any value. In this way the value of the shares of the stockholders will be yearly decreasing, though by the division of the net receipts semi-annually, large dividends will necesarily be declared, a fictitious value will be given to the stock in the market, those who understand the operation of things will be enabled to sell at a large advance, and the unfortunate purchaser, after receiving his large interest for a few years, will suddenly and unexpectedly find his capital gone. It is against this result the directors desire to provide. Their plan, in its general features, is to retain out of the price received from the coal as taken out of the land, a small sum of money, and accumulate the same, till it shall amount to the par of the outstanding certificates of the capital stock. A careful estimate has been made by their engineer of the amount of coal in their ground, and a calculation based on this estimate as to when the entire coal will be exhausted.

The directors of this company are certainly invested with discretionary powers over this subject. They are to declare
42 dividends of so much only of the profits as shall appear advisable to them. Indeed it may well be doubted whether where a part of the capital is annually converted into money--as in this case by the sale of coal from which they derive their royalties, which constitute their annual receipts--such part can lawfully be distributed as dividends. The directors are expressly prohibited from making any dividend, which shall impair the capital stock, under a heavy penalty upon such of the directors as shall consent to such a dividend. But apart from this consideration, the exercise of such a discretion cannot be controlled by a court of equity, so long as it is honestly exerted, with no ulterior, personal or selfish ends, and with a view to subserve the true interests of the stockholders. However unwise the policy adopted may be in the estimation of the chancellor, he has no right to substitute his discretion for theirs. To do so would make him head manager of all the corporations within the reach of his process. In this case, too, the stockholders, at their annual meeting, February 4, 1867, passed a resolution approving of the creation of a sinking fund for the purpose of securing the par value of the capital stock of the company on the plan recommended by the board of directors. At this meeting a stock vote was taken, which resulted in 15,469 in favor to 3302 votes against it.

I do not doubt that it is perfectly lawful for the directors to establish such a sinking fund, and to set aside such portion of their receipts from time to time as they may deem necessary and proper....

As I am at present advised, let it be declared that the

directors of the Locust Mountain Coal and Iron Company, the defendants, have power, in the exercise of their discretion, to create a sinking fund to secure the par value of the capital stock of the company out of their annual receipts, but that they have not power to pay over or transfer any of the moneys or assets to any persons as trustees in trust for such a purpose, and let an injunction issue to restrain them from any such transfer or payment.

COMMONWEALTH v. THE OCEAN OIL COMPANY

59 Pa. St. 61 (1868)
Supreme Court of Pennsylvania

May 18th 1868. Before THOMPSON, C.J., STRONG, READ, AGNEW and SHARSWOOD, JJ.

Error to the Court of Common Pleas of Dauphin county:
44 Of May Term 1868, No. 64.

This case originated in the court below from an appeal by the defendant, The Ocean Oil Company, from the settlement of the Auditor-General and State Treasurer, made April 4th 1867.

The company made a return of $311,954.14, as their net earnings or income for the year ending November 1st 1866, on which they were taxed at the rate of 3 per cent., making $9358.74. They appealed from this settlement, alleging that no net earnings had been realized during that year, and that the return had been made by mistake.

On the trial, before Pearson, P.J., the Commonwealth having given in evidence the company's return; the defendants called David Boyd, who testified:

"On November 13th 1866, I was elected treasurer, and got the late treasurer to make the report. He did so, and I signed it; but discovered soon after that it was entirely incorrect. I wished to get it back but could not, and then appealed. I examined and found we had made no profits. We have since made two years' reports, and they were accepted. The amount paid in this case was $1,000,000. We declare dividends of oil, which are only a return of the investment to those who advanced. We have returned to shareholders some $600,000 or more, but our books will not balance till $1,000,000 is paid in. No net earnings are made. We pay a tax on our capital stock--$15,000 last year, $10,000 this year. The first well flowed some three hundred barrels per day, next one pumped seventy-five barrels per day. Flowing wells do not last over four or five months; pumping wells six months, generally.

"Paid $1,000,000 in stock for the land, and the holders realized over a million. The company actually paid a million. Some stock sold at $4, some $20 per share; original shares sold low--land had not been developed then."

Judge Pearson charged the jury:--

"If the oil were, practically speaking, inexhaustible,
the product, after deducting expenses, would be net 45
profits; but if you are satisfied that all of the oil will soon be extracted from this land, then the company divides not its net profits alone, but its capital. * * *

In assessing the actual profits in business of the character under consideration, we must look to probabilities, as demonstrated by experience. If you are satisfied from the evidence that this company is consuming and dividing its capital, which may soon be gone entirely, then all of the dividends declared are not net profits. If the oil will last for a few years to come the capital will be refunded to the stockholders, after which all that is made above expenses will be net income. But should the Commonwealth be obliged to wait for its taxes until that occurs? We think not, but that a jury should act on <u>reasonable</u> probabilities, as every man would do in assessing the value of this property as oil territory, taking into account the time that it will probably take to exhaust the capital and the profits which will be made in the mean time, you can then consider whether the whole sum returned was net earnings or income, or whether the company should be charged with one- half, one-third, one-fourth, or with what other quantity thereof, and render your verdict for such sum, with interest thereon, after three months from the date of settlement."

The verdict was for the Commonwealth for $3205.35.

The Commonwealth took a writ of error, and in several specifications assigned the charge of the court for error...

The opinion of the court was delivered, May 27th 1868, by

READ, J.--The capital of oil companies is generally nominal, and when therefore the capital of this company is called $1,000,000, it is very evident that this sum was not paid for the 4 acres of land, but that it was valued for the purposes of a division into stock at one million. "Some stock sold at $4, some $20 per share," says the treasurer, "original shares sold low--land had
46 not been developed then."

This company calling and returning its capital at one million, is taxed upon its capital stock at that sum, but by the Act of the 30th April 1864, Pamph. L. 218, the "net earnings or income" of said corporation are subjected to a state tax of "three per centum upon such annual net earnings or income, in addition to the taxes now imposed by existing laws."

The question therefore is, what is the meaning of "net earnings or income?" Does it mean, as it was construed by the treasurer in his report to the auditor-general, the product of the business after deducting expenses only? if so, then, the settlement by the auditor-general and state treasurer is correct.

But it is contended by the company, that the annual product must first be applied to the repayment of capital, and this would leave no net earnings or income to tax. The court below compromised between these two constructions, and held that there must be an application of so much of the annual product, as would repay the capital, in the probable number of years that oil would flow or be taken from the land, and then the surplus would be the net earnings or income subject to taxation. This mode requires the interposition of a jury wherever there is a difference of opinion between the company and the state authorities.

I can see no warrant for such a reading of the law. The income from the works of the company after deducting all expenses appears in this case by the testimony of the treasurer, to have been paid to the shareholders as dividends, and were no doubt advertised as such, thus enhancing largely the value of the stock in the market.

When a capital stock is created, and paid into a corporation, authorized to transact any business whether of banking, manufacturing or mining, and is divided into shares of a fixed amount, that capital is presumed to remain until its dissolution. The value of the stock and the shares into which it is divided, may rise or fall according to the success of the enterprise. In banks, for
instance, the profits may be largely remunerative, or if 47
unfortunate, the capital may be utterly lost. This is the theory of incorporated companies, the capital invested remains either really or nominally to their close.

The present company pays dividends which are of course its net earnings or income, and it is the net income, whether declared or not, the state intended to tax. This is the plain common sense meaning of the term, made familiar to every one since the formation of the internal revenue system. The theory of the company is, that the capital must be repaid to its shareholders, and then it has no capital left.

But if this company has paid $600,000, it must be different from all other such companies, if its shareholders have not been overpaid already. The court below were therefore in error in allowing a portion of the net earnings to be applied to the reduction of the capital stock.

Judgment reversed, and <u>venire</u> <u>de</u> <u>novo</u> awarded.

COMMONWEALTH v. PENN GAS COAL COMPANY

62 Pa. St. 241 (1869)
Supreme Court of Pennsylvania

May 17th 1869. Before THOMPSON, C.J., READ, AGNEW, SHARSWOOD and WILLIAMS, JJ.

Error to the Court of Common Pleas of Dauphin county: No. 90, to May Term 1869.

48 On the 11th of July 1867 the accounting officers of the Commonwealth settled an account against The Penn Gas Coal Company, as follows:

"For tax on net earnings or income, per Act of April 30, 1864 for years ending November 1st 1865 and 1866, as per report herewith filed:

1865.	Net earnings or income - - -	$173,079.72
1866.	do. do. - - - -	68,757.54
		241,837.26
Tax three per cent. due Commonwealth, -	-	7,255.11

The company appealed from the settlement, because the amount, $241,837.26, on which the tax is charged, exceeds the net income and includes a portion of the company's capital.

On the trial, November 23d 1868, the Commonwealth gave in evidence the settlement, and the report of the company on which the settlement is based, showing the net earnings or income to be $241,837.26, and claiming a deduction of $54,000 for "waste of capital for coal taken out;" three per cent. tax being assessed on total amount returned.

Pearson, P.J., directed a verdict for the Commonwealth for $8374.56, the amount of the tax and interest, subject to two points reserved; the first being: If the court shall be of the opinion that under the return made, the company is not taxable on its stock exhausted, then judgment to be rendered in favor of the Commonwealth for $6564.89.

The court rendered judgment on the reserved point for the Commonwealth for $6564.89.

The Commonwealth took a writ of error, and assigned the judgment for error....

The opinion of the court was delivered, July 6th 1869, by

49

READ, J.--We have carefully considered this case, and the reasoning of the learned judge in the court below, but we are unable to see that the case of The Commonwealth v. The Ocean Oil Company, 9 P.F. Smith 61, does not govern the one before us. All capitals of mining companies, whether of coal, iron, copper, or tin, or silver or gold, and so of quarrying companies, whether of stone, marble or slate, are nominal, like those of petroleum companies, and fixed by their promoters at such large figures, that, by applying the principle contended for by the appellees, the whole annual income would have to be retained to supply the loss of capital, which would dissapoint the stockholders of their dividends, and the state of her taxes. The difficulties pointed out in our former opinion, of adopting and applying any such principle to these companies make it necessary to establish one general invariable rule--that the net earnings or income are the product of the business deducting the expenses only, upon which basis the settlement was made by the Auditor-General and the State Treasurer.

Judgment reversed, and *venire de novo* awarded.

PITTSBURG AND CONNELLSVILLE RAILROAD COMPANY v. THE COUNTY OF ALLEGHENY

63 Pa. St. 126 (1870)
Supreme Court of Pennsylvania

The opinion of the court was delivered, January 3d 1870, by

THOMPSON, C. J.—The great question in this case is, whether the plaintiff in error, the Pittsburg and Connellsville Railroad Company, is bound by its contract with the county of Allegheny, to pay interest on the bonds of the latter, received by it in payment of stock subscribed by the county. The contract of the company was to pay interest equal to that falling due on the bonds, for thirty years, the period of the maturity of the bonds, and this suit was brought to recover unpaid interest falling due on the 1st January 1858, and intermediately up to and including the 1st January 1867. Of course, a decision of this question will not only settle the liability of the company for interest past due, but that which is by the terms of the contract to fall due....

An obvious reason why, without express authority, a contract like that we are considering could not be legally entered into by the railroad company, is, that to pay interest anterior to earnings by the company, would require a diversion of its capital from its legitimate, to a different purpose, from that for which it was ostensibly obtained, and which was the inducement for the subscriber to stock, to pay it in. In sixteen years and eight months the capital would all be sunk on this principle. In half that length of time—not an unusual period for the completion of a road the length of the Pittsburgh and Connellsville road, especially at the time when the contract under consideration was entered into, the half of the capital would be diverted to pay interest, if the plan were universal and applicable to all the stockholders. If it were not, it would be a fraud on shareholders who paid in their money, and did not receive interest. Nothing could be more completely *felo de se* of a project undertaken on this policy than such a rule. In almost all improvement companies, and especially in this by the 13th section of its act of incorporation, there is an express provision against an impairment of the capital by paying dividends not earned. It is true, interest and dividends possess ordinarily dissimilar characteristics; but in a case like this it is only in name, with the distinction, perhaps, that the principles of apportionment applies to the one and not to the other: 6 Wright 479. It is not necessary, however, to multiply words to prove what is most apparent—that a semi-annual payment of interest out of capital of a company before any earnings are made is the same injury as if paid as dividends; one is as much within the prohibition as the other, both being within the same mischief. Without express authority, or beyond the limits of authority conferred, we think the company had no power to bind its stockholders, who constitute the company, to pay interest to the county of Allegheny for a period of thirty years, or any other period....

The answer to the argument on this portion of the case is, that the legislature did authorize this railroad company so to contract. So far as this is true, and it must be granted that it is, to a certain extent, the answer is complete. In the presence of express authority, the transaction is not to be regarded as obnoxious to public or good policy, or to be set aside because foolish and unwise. Nor is such a provision in conflict with any constitutional prohibition against the grant of such authority. Let us see to what extent the power exists in this case....

Previously to this, on the 12th of April 1853, the legislature authorized the railroad company "to pay to the shareholders entitled to receive the same, interest at the rate of six per cent. per annum, on all instalments paid by them, which interest shall be charged to the cost of construction; and continue to pay the same *until the road shall be completed;*" and that until the period for which a dividend shall be declared, all the profits and earnings of the road shall be credited to the cost of construction. ...

This view of the Act of 13th April 1853 simplifies the controversy. The authority to pay interest is coupled with and inseparable from a period fixed in the act during which it should continue. That time is clearly defined by the words "until the completion of the road." These words qualify and limit the power to contract for interest; and are of the same binding force as those which authorize the company to pay interest. The company could contract so far by virtue of the authority given; beyond that the contract is *ultrà vires.*

MESERVE v. ANDREWS

106 Mass. 419 (1871)

CONTRACT. After the decision reported 104 Mass. 360, the case was recommitted to the auditor, who made the following report, to which he annexed an account computed as therein stated:

"The plaintiffs were pawnbrokers, and for several years
52 were lessees of a shop numbered 108 on Sudbury Street in Boston; and the defendant, who was engaged in the gift-enterprise business, as it is called, with their permission occupied a part of the shop. For this occupation he settled and paid down to January 1, 1865. He continued to occupy to March 1, 1865, eight weeks and a half. For this he has not paid. As he paid at his last settlement on January 1, at the rate of three dollars per week, and as there was no satisfactory proof of a new contract, or of a material change of occupancy, I have charged him for the eight and a half weeks, at the rate of three dollars per week.

"In February 1865 a new arrangement was made. The plaintiffs agreed after March 1 ensuing to assist the defendant in carrying on his said business, and to allow him to occupy a larger part of the shop. And the defendant agreed to pay the entire rent of the shop, except what should be paid by one Foster, the tenant of another part; to furnish the necessary capital; to defray all expenses incident to said business; and, as compensation for the assistance to be rendered by the plaintiffs, to pay them one quarter of the net profits of the business. The plaintiffs were to carry on their business as pawnbrokers, in the same shop. Pursuant to this agreement, the defendant was allowed to occupy such part of the shop as he chose, and the plaintiffs rendered such assistance in the management of the gift-enterprise business of the defendant as they were required to render. They expended money in fitting the shop for the defendant's better accommodation, and purchased and paid for sundry articles of shop furniture for use in his said business, and paid certain expenses necessarily incurred in the prosecution thereof. On April 30, 1865, the shop was burned, and with it were consumed certain articles of shop furniture and goods, which were a part of the defendant's stock in trade, and were used in his said business. On May 1, the plaintiffs procured another shop numbered 85 on the same street, and on that day both parties moved into it. In this shop the defendant continued carrying on his said business, with the plaintiffs' assistance, till May 15, when he removed to a shop on Court Street, and notified the plaintiffs that he had dissolved his connection with them.

"Upon all the evidence, I find that the net profits of the defendant's said business during the months of March and April were $1200; and that during the first fifteen days of May there were no profits and no losses.

"In March, a criminal prosecution was commenced against the defendant for carrying on his said business. He employed counsel, and expended considerable sums of money in his defence. In the course of the following year the proceeding was determined in his favor. There was no proof that the plaintiffs took any part in the defense, or were consulted about it, or undertook to be responsible for any part of the expenses. Nor did it appear in evidence that the criminal procedure arose or grew out of the acts or doings of the plaintiffs or the acts or doings of anybody with their knowledge or consent. But had the prosecution resulted adversely to the defendant, he would probably have abandoned his said business.

"In ascertaining the net profits of the said business of defendant, I have not taken into account the loss which he sustained as aforesaid by the fire, nor the moneys which he expended in his defence. The plaintiffs called on the defendant for a settlement, before instituting this suit."

Upon the return of this report, the parties submitted the case to the judgment of the superior court under an agreement "that the above report be taken as an agreed statement of facts, and if the court should be of opinion that the loss of the defendant by fire, or the sums expended by him, or any part thereof, in defending against prosecution, mentioned in the said report, ought to be deducted from the profits of the business reported by the auditor, then the case is to be recommitted to ascertain their losses and sums paid." The superior court ordered judgment for the plaintiffs without any deduction for either of the causes specified in the agreement, and the defendant appealed....

WELLS, J. This case, having been sent back for a more complete statement, (104 Mass. 360,) comes up again upon the amended report of the auditor as an agreed statement
54 of facts.

1. As to the costs and expenses of the criminal prosecution commenced against the defendant for carrying on his business, which was subsequently determined in his favor, the report now states: "There was no proof that the plaintiffs took any part in the defence, or were consulted about it, or undertook to be responsible for any part of the expenses. Nor did it appear in evidence that the criminal procedure arose or grew out of the acts or doings of the plaintiffs, or the acts or doings of anybody with their knowledge or consent." The report fails, therefore, to show that the plaintiffs were in any way chargeable for those costs and expenses; or that the prosecution was other than a mere personal affair of the defendant. It is not enough that it had reference to the carrying on of a certain kind of business by him; or that, as the report further states, "had the prosecution resulted adversely to the defendant he would probably have abandoned his said business." That alone does not show that the prosecution was a matter of joint concern; or that it should affect the profits of the business while it was carried on. The finding of the auditor upon this point is therefore affirmed.

2. As to the loss by fire, it now appears that the loss was of "certain articles of shop furniture and goods, which were a part of the defendant's stock in trade, and were used in his said business;" the business being designated as the "gift-enterprise" business. We suppose the "gift enterprise" to be some mode of conducting trade in merchandise. The profit and loss of trade in merchan-

dise is not confined to that which results from sales. Depreciation or advance in value of the stock unsold must also be taken into acccount. Depreciation may come from fluctuation of prices in the market, from deterioration in quality, or diminution in quantity, occasioned by the numerous causes incident to the business; among which, in our opinion, fire is to be included. Loss by fire, whether of goods constituting part of the stock in trade, or of shop furniture, should be deducted in making up the net profits for division.

The case will accordingly be recommitted for correction
of the report in this particular; unless the amount of 55
such correction shall be agreed on; and judgment will
then be rendered for the amount thus found to be due, if
anything.

<u>Ordered</u> <u>Accordingly</u>.

GRAY v. DARLINGTON

82 U.S. 63 (1872)
Supreme Court of the United States

ERROR to the Circuit Court for the Eastern District of Pennsylvania.

An act of Congress of March 2d, 1867,* provides that

"There shall be levied, collected, and paid *annually* upon the gains, profits, and income of every person, . . . whether derived from any kind of property, rents, interest, dividends, or salaries, or from any profession, trade, employment, or vocation, . . . or from any other source whatever, . . . a tax of five per centum on the amount so derived over $1000. . . . And the tax herein provided for shall be assessed, collected, and paid upon the gains, profits, and income *for the year ending the* 31*st of December next preceding* the time for levying, collecting, and paying said tax."

The same section also provides (with some exceptions not important to be mentioned), that

"In estimating the gains, profits, and income of any person, there shall be included all incomes derived from interest upon notes, bonds, and other securities of the United States, profits realized within the year from sales of real estate purchased within the year, or within two years previous to the year for which income is estimated, . . . and all other gains, profits, and income derived from any source whatever."

In this state of statutory law, W. Darlington brought the present action against W. C. Gray, collector of internal revenue, to recover the sum of $1000, alleged to have been illegally assessed and collected under the said law as gains, profits, and income of him, the said Darlington, for the year 1869. It appeared from the allegations of the declaration, that in 1865 the plaintiff, being then the owner of certain United States treasury notes, exchanged them for United States five-twenty bonds; that in 1869 he sold these bonds at an advance of $20,000 over the cost of the treasury notes, and that upon this amount the assistant assessor of the United States for the collection district in Pennsylvania within which the plaintiff resided, assessed a tax of five per cent., alleging it to be gains, profits, and income of the plaintiff for that year; that on appeal to the assessor of the district, and to the Commissioner of Internal Revenue, this assessment was affirmed, and was transmitted to the defendant, as collector of the district, for enforcement; and that upon the latter's demand, with notice that, unless paid, he would collect the same with penalty and interest, the tax was paid by the plaintiff under protest.

To the declaration, setting forth substantially the facts above stated, the defendant demurred. The demurrer was overruled by the Circuit Court, and judgment given in favor of the plaintiff for the amount paid by him, with interest and costs. The defendant brought the case to this court on writ of error, and assigned as error the overruling of the demurrer.

Mr. G. H. Williams, Attorney-General, and Mr. C. H. Hill, Assistant Attorney-General, for the plaintiff in error; Messrs. 57
Blair, Dick, and Darlington, propriâ personâ, contra.

Mr. Justice FIELD delivered the opinion of the court.

In 1865 the plaintiff, being the owner of certain United States treasury notes, exchanged them for United States five-twenty bonds. In 1869 he sold these bonds at an advance of twenty thousand dollars over the cost of the treasury notes, and upon this amount the assistant assessor of the United States for the collection district in Pennsylvania, within which the plaintiff resided, assessed a tax of five per cent., alleging it to be gains, profits, and income of the plaintiff for that year. On appeal to the assessor of the district, and to the Commissioner of Internal Revenue, this assessment was affirmed, and it was transmitted to the defendant, as collector of the district, for enforcement. Upon the latter's demand the tax was paid by the plaintiff under protest, and the present action was brought to recover back the money.

The question presented is whether the advance in the value of the bonds, during this period of four years, over their cost, realized by their sale, was subject to taxation as gains, profits, or income of the plaintiff for the year in which the bonds were sold. The answer which should be given to this question does not, in our judgment, admit of any doubt. The advance in the value of property during a series of years can, in no just sense, be considered the gains, profits, or income of any one particular year of the series, although the entire amount of the advance be at one time turned into money by a sale of the property. The statute looks, with some exceptions, for subjects of taxation only to annual gains, profits, and income. Its general language is

"that there shall be levied, collected, and paid *annually* upon the gains, profits, and income of every person," derived from certain specified sources, a tax of five per cent., and that this tax shall be "assessed, collected, and paid upon the gains, profits, and income for the year ending the 31st of December next preceding the time for levying, collecting, and paying said tax."* This language has only one meaning, and that is that the assessment, collection, and payment prescribed are to be made upon the annual products or income of one's property or labor, or such gains or profits as may be realized from a business transaction begun and completed during the preceding year. There are exceptions, as already intimated, to the general rule of assessment thus
58 prescribed. One of these exceptions is expressed in the statute, and relates to profits upon sales of real property, requiring, in the estimation of gains, the profits of such sales to be included where the property has been purchased, not only within the preceding year, but within the two previous years. Another exception is implied from the provision of the statute which requires all gains, profits, and income derived from any source whatever, in addition to the sources enumerated, to be included in the estimation of the assessor. The estimation must, therefore, necessarily embrace gains and profits from trade and commerce, and these, for their successful prosecution, often require property to be held over a year. In the estimation of gains of any one year the trader and merchant will, in consequence, often be compelled to include the amount received upon goods sold over their cost, which were purchased in a previous year. Indeed, in the estimation of the gains and profits of a trading or commercial business for any one year, the result of many transactions have generally to be taken into account which originated previously. Except, however, in these and similar cases, and in cases of sales of real property, the statute only applies to such gains, profits, and income as are strictly acquisitions made during the year preceding that in which the assessment is levied and collected.

The mere fact that property has advanced in value between the date of its acquisition and sale does not authorize the imposition of the tax on the amount of the advance. Mere advance in value in no sense constitutes the gains, profits, or income specified by the statute. It constitutes and can be treated merely as increase of capital.

The rule adopted by the officers of the revenue in the present case would justify them in treating as gains of one year the increase in the value of property extending through any number of years, through even the entire century. The actual advance in value of property over its cost may, in fact, reach its height years before its sale; the value of the property may, in truth, be less at the time of the sale than at any previous period in ten years, yet, if the amount received exceed the actual cost of the property, the excess is to be treated, according to their views, as gains of the owner for the year in which the sale takes place. We are satisfied that no such result was intended by the statute.

JUDGMENT AFFIRMED.

Dissenting: The CHIEF JUSTICE, and Justices CLIFFORD and BRADLEY.

[NOTE.—In view of the divided state of the court in giving judgment in the above case, it may not be uninteresting to the reader to know that from a letter, entitled to credit, in the possession of the Reporter, it appears that the point decided in the case, had been ruled in the same way in the Third Circuit, by the late Mr. Justice GRIER, in the case of *Bennet* v. *Baker, Collector*, tried on the 7th of April, 1865; the late honored Justice having been, says the letter, "very clear and emphatic in his opinion."]

RICHARDSON v. THE VERMONT AND MASSACHUSETTS RAILROAD COMPANY

44 Vt. 613 (1872)
In Chancery, Vermont

BILL IN CHANCERY. The bill charged that at the first meeting of the Vermont and Massachusetts Railroad Company, held November 21, 1844, in Boston, before the shares were fully taken, and in order to induce persons to become shareholders and members of said company, it was duly voted "that all subscribers" (for stock) "be allowed interest on all sums paid by them up to the time when the road shall be completed and put in operation." That in pursuance of said vote, interest was allowed to stockholders and paid until October 1, 1848; that the railroad of said company remained unfinished for six and a half months afterward, viz: until the 15th day of April, 1849; that the orators were shareholders in said company during said six and one half months, or the representatives of persons then shareholders therein, and as such became entitled to interest from said company upon their shares. . . .

The opinion of the court was delivered by

PECK, J. The corporation had authority to stipulate, as it did, that each stockholder should be entitled to interest on sums paid on stock subscriptions, while the road was in process of construction, till it should be completed and go into operation: payable whenever the surplus earnings should enable it properly to do so, that is, when the corporation should be pecuniarily in condition to warrant the payment of dividends. In the early stages of such undertakings, the use of money necessary for the construction of the road may be presumed to be worth the legal interest; and therefore he who pays early practically contributes more than he who pays the same sum late. This arrangement for the payment of interest, or interest dividends, so called, is equitable and just, as it is but a mode of distributing benefits among the stockholders in proportion to the aid they have respectively contributed to the common enterprise, and thus producing equality between them. Equality is equity as between the stockholders; and such payment, made only out of the surplus earnings not needed for the payment of debts of the corporation, nor for the prosecution of its business, does not interfere with the rights of creditors, nor contravene any principle of public policy. It is no more withdrawing capital from the corporation than would be the payment of ordinary dividends, to which purpose the fund would otherwise be appropriated. Nor is there any want of legal consideration to uphold the promise. In addition to the equality thereby to be produced among the stockholders, it is apparent that they paid in their money on the faith of this agreement; for it had its origin in the outset of the enterprise. . . .

It appears that the interest was paid to the stockholders from time to time up to October 1, 1848, and that the road was not completed till April 15, 1849, when interest ceased to accrue. The interest accruing from October 1, 1848, to April 15, 1849, remaining unpaid, the vote of the corporation, at the annual meeting

February 9, 1853, was passed for the issuing certificates to the stockholders for the amount of such unpaid interest, payable July 15, 1856, with a provision that if there is not sufficient money in the treasury on the 15th of July, 1856, to meet the whole amount of such certificates or dividend, the holders of such scrip shall receive *pro rata* so much as the treasurer is able to pay; and as soon thereafter as the treasurer is able to pay the balance due on such interest scrip, he shall give notice of the fact, &c. In pursuance of this vote the directors passed the vote of February 22, 1853, and the treasurer proceeded to issue the certificates accordingly. The orators seek to recover only according to the terms of these two last votes, and the adjustment made and certificates issued in pursuance of them. . . . We think therefore that the proceedings of the corporation, terminating in the issuing of the interest certificates, created an obligation upon the corporation to pay according to the terms and conditions of such certificates. 61
The policy as well as the validity of such contracts has been frequently recognized. *Waterman* v. *Troy & Greenfield R. R. Co.*, 8 Gray, 433; *Rut. & B. R. R. Co.* v. *Thrall*, 35 Vt., 536. In *Waterman* v. *Troy & Greenfield R. R. Co.*, the plaintiff failed upon the ground that the action was premature; the court very properly holding that the construction of the agreement, (which was similar to the vote in this case of November 21, 1844,) was, that the interest was not payable till the road was completed and in operation, and the corporation in receipt of income from its business. The conclusion to which we have come in this case is not in conflict with the decisions in Massachusetts, in suits at law between some of these stockholders and this defendant corporation, relative to this interest on payments upon stock subscriptions. *Wright* v. *Vt. & Mass. R. R. Co.*, 12 Cush., was commenced July 3, 1849, before the vote of February 9, 1853, fixing the time and prescribing the contingency upon which the payment should be made. SHAW, Ch. J., speaking of the vote of November 21, 1844, says: "supposing the original vote of the stockholders should be regarded as declaring a general right of the stockholders previously to paying in any instalment on the shares, that each should be entitled to interest, to be computed on his payments, from the time of each payment to the time when the railroad should go into operation and be in condition to earn income and pay dividends, this would be equitable, because it would put stockholders on an equal footing, whether they should pay earlier or later. It would encourage capitalists to advance their money early to meet the exigencies of the company before it could enjoy any income; and it seems right that the use of such capital should be paid for as a common charge on all." In that case it did not appear that the road was completed or put in operation at the commencement of the suit, or that the corporation was pecuniarily in a condition to pay; and the case turned on the point that the action was premature. The language of SHAW, Ch. J., in delivering the opinion of the court, is, that "whether the plaintiff might or not maintain an action to recover this claim when the road

should be completed and put in operation, we do not perceive how he could do it before that time, without some vote of the corporation fixing the time of payment, and making it payable in money." *Barnard et als.* v. *Vt. & Mass. R. R. Co.*, 7 Allen, 512; and *Cunningham et als.* v. *Vt. & Mass. R. R. Co.*, 12 Gray, 411, were commenced after the railroad was completed and in operation, and after the vote of February 9, 1853, and the issue of the interest certificates in pursuance of it; but the plaintiffs failed to recover, not because the defendant was not under obligation to pay according to that vote, but on the ground that the contingency of the possession by the defendant, of sufficient funds for that purpose, specified in that vote, was not shown. This objection to a recovery by the plaintiff, on which those cases turned, is obviated in this case by the admission in the answer, as well as
62 by the proof in the case, of abundant funds to answer the contingency and fulfill the condition on which the interest was to be paid.

The decree of the court of chancery is reversed, and the orators are entitled to a decree according to the prayer of the bill, with costs, except that on the seventy-five dollar stock and the fifty dollar stock interest should be cast upon the sum paid to the corporation therefor, instead of upon its nominal amount of one hundred dollars per share, and the interest certificates should be reduced accordingly wherever the stock can be identified and distinguished from the stock for which one hundred dollars was paid to the corporation. The cause is remanded to the court of chancery, with directions to enter decree for orators, as above indicated.

ST. JOHN v. ERIE RAILWAY CO.

10 Blatchf. 271 (1872)
Circuit Court of the United States
Southern District of New York

BLATCHFORD. The plaintiff is the holder of certificates for shares of stock in the Erie Railway Company, which certificates declare him to be entitled to so many shares "in the preferred capital stock" of the company. Each cer- 63
tificate contains these words: "Said stock shall be entitled to preferred dividends, out of the net earnings, if earned in the current year, but not otherwise, not to exceed seven *per cent. per annum*, payable semi-annually, after payment of mortgage interest of said company in full."...

The practical question involved in this case is, whether the holders of the preferred stock are entitled to a seven *per cent.* dividend annually, before interest is paid by the defendants on one million of pounds of sterling bonds issued by them in 1865, after the preferred stock was created, and before rent is paid by the defendants on any leases taken by them since January 1st, 1862, of roads which they operate in connection with their own....

The statement in the contract, the statute, and the certificates, that the "preferred dividends" are to be paid out of the "net earnings," sheds no light, one way or the other, for a solution of the question. The mortgage interest and the delayed coupons are also to be paid out of the net earnings. Net earnings are, properly, the gross receipts, less the expenses of operating the road to earn such receipts. Interest on debts is paid out of what thus remains, that is, out of the net earnings. Many other liabilities are paid out of the net earnings. When all liabilities are paid, either out of the gross receipts or out of the net earnings, the remainder is the profit of the shareholders, to go towards dividends, which, in that way, are paid out of the net earnings. That this is the meaning of the expression "net earnings," in the contract, is shown by the fact, that the contract states that the trustees are to receive the net earnings, and out of them pay the floating debt, and the delayed coupons, and by the further fact, that the contract, the statute, and the certificates state that the mortgage interest is to be paid out of the net earnings, by stating that the preferred dividends are to be paid out of the net earnings, "after payment," (that is, out of the net earnings,) "of mortgage interest."

It results, from these considerations, that the bill must be dismissed, with costs.

ST JOHN V. ERIE RAILWAY CO.

89 U.S. 136 (1874)
United States Supreme Court

APPEAL from the Circuit Court of the United States for the Southern District of New York.

St. John, the appellant, a citizen of Alabama and the owner of certain shares of preferred stock of the Erie Railway Company, filed his bill in the court below on his own behalf and on behalf of the other holders of the preferred stock, to obtain a judgment as to the rights of such stockholders, and to protect them against the alleged wrongful acts of the company. The court below dismissed the bill, and the complainant appealed to this court.

The case is stated in the opinion.

Mr. **Dorman B. Eaton**, for the appellant:

The holders of the old unsecured bonds and judgment debts of the New York and Erie Company made a contract with its stockholders, mortgage bond holders and trustees, that such bonds and debts should be converted into a new and unique form of security, which they called "preferred stock;" which stock should hold the same place and have the same interest as then belonged to the bonds and debts, that is, next after the existing mortgage debt of the Company....

There is nothing in the phrase "net earnings" which impairs our argument, or presents any practical difficulty. Net earnings, plainly means gross earnings, less the expense of operation, and has been so judicially declared. The defendant should have kept separate accounts of its newly leased roads, and been prepared to sustain its losses or demonstrate its profits. The plaintiff is entitled to have counted as gross earnings on the line, as it existed when his stock was created, all the money thereon received and earned, and from this can be deducted only the expenses of operating such line, including, of course, rents payable for any portion of it. Such accounts are easily kept. On that basis the plaintiff will take his chances of a dividend, as the contract provides, and will regard his prospects as greatly improved. The Company denies that right, and refuses such account and payment....

Mr. Justice **Swayne** delivered the opinion of the court:

The complainant is the holder of three hundred shares of the preferred stock. The Company paid the delayed coupons and a dividend of five per cent. on all the preferred stock for the year 1863, and seven per cent. annually thereafter, until the year 1868. Since that time nothing has been paid. After the issuing of the preferred stock, the Company took leases of several additional roads. Some of them have been profitable and some not. The new Company took the leases held by the old Company, with an obligation to pay the annual rents which the latter was bound to pay. These rents amounted in the year 1862 to $372,400. The annual rents of the additional leases taken by the new Company amounted in the year 1868, to $376,107. Subsequently to 1862, the Company borrowed $5,000,000, for which it gave sterling bonds bearing interest at the rate of six per cent. per annum, payable in gold. The interest paid upon this debt in 1868, was $388,494.68. The money was borrowed for the repair and equipment of the roads of the Company, and was expended accordingly.... 65

The complainant claims that his rights are to be determined by the state of things which existed when his stock was issued, and that they are in nowise affected by the leases taken and the bonds issued by the Company thereafter. Hence he contends that full dividends should have been paid before any part of the net earnings were applied in payment of the interest on the sterling bonds and the rents under the leases of other roads to the new Corporation....

The dividends were to be paid after the mortgage interest and delayed coupons were paid in full.

This clause was inserted, doubtless, out of abundant caution, to prevent the possibility of a claim being set up to the prejudice of the holders of the mortgage securities. Whether the restriction was necessary for that purpose, we need not consider. The preferred dividends were to be paid out of "the net earnings of the road." The lexical definition of net is "clear of all charges and deductions." Webster. "That which remains after the deduction of all charges or outlay, as net profit." Worcester. The popular acceptation of the term is the same. There is no controversy between the parties on this subject. Such net earnings must have been earned in "the current year." There are these four specific limitations. There are no others. It is not said that the preferred dividends shall be paid next after the mortgage interest and delayed coupons, nor after, nor *pro rata* with anything else, nor before anything else except dividends upon the common stock. Beyond the four restrictions named, the matter is left to be regulated wholly by the principles of law and discretion of the Company....

The complainant insists that the "net earnings" must be the net earnings of things as they were when the preferred stock was issued. We find nothing in the case, express or implied, to warrant this view....

The business of the road was a unit. If it had been disintegrated as proposed by the complainant, we apprehend it would have been found that the correlations of the main stem and the branches were such, and that the expenses and charges incident to the entire business and those of the several parts were so interwoven and blended, that an accurate ascertainment of the net profit of the main line and any of the auxiliaries, taken separately from the rest, would have been impracticable. An ancillary road may be short and yield but little income, yet by reason of its reaching to coal fields, or from other local causes, its contributions to other roads of the series may be very large and profitable. Whether in this case the partial computation insisted upon could or could not have been made, the process was one upon which the Company was neither bound nor had the right to enter.

We hold that the computation by the Company for the year 1868 was made upon the proper basis, and that the complainant is concluded by it. We are of the opinion that the rents for that year, accruing under leases taken by the Company after the issuing of the preferred stock, and the interest upon the sterling bonds for that year, were properly paid, and that there were no net earnings earned in that year which could be properly applied in payment of preferred dividends. These views are fatal to the complainant's case. We have carefully examined all the authorities referred to by his learned counsel. None of them are in hostility to the conclusion at which we have arrived.

The decree of the Circuit Court is affirmed.

TUTT v. LAND

50 Ga. 339 (1873)
Supreme Court of Georgia

Land filed his bill against Tutt alleging that complainant and defendant formed a copartnership in the drug business, in the city of Augusta, on July 1st, 1868, which continued until October 31st, 1870, the terms of which were reduced to writing. That complainant was to receive one-quarter of the profits and defendant three-quarters; that the defendant, at the dissolution, agreed to account with him for his share of the large profits which had been made, but had failed to do so; that defendant is indebted to complainant about $10,000.00, and refuses to account. Prays discovery, relief, etc....

At the January term, 1872, the following order was passed: "It appearing that there are questions of complicated account in the above cause, it is ordered, that Joseph B. Cumming be, and he hereby is, appointed auditor, to investigate the matters upon said accounts, and all matters touching the allegation in cross-bill of defendant, with power to subpoena witnesses , administer oaths and hear testimony on any disputed fact or facts, and with other powers usually and customarily conferred on masters in chancery in like cases."

On June 1st, 1872, the auditor filed his report in the clerk's office. It was in substance, as follows:...

1st. The deduction of ten per cent. on account of depreciation of merchandise, to be taken from the profits as claimed by defendant, is not allowed. This item is $4,098.17.

2d. The deduction from value of fixtures, on account of depreciation, to be taken from the profits, as claimed by defendant, is not allowed. This item is $2,170.99.

3d. The auditor finds that no interest is chargeable against complainant on account of capital put into the business by the defendant, and disallows the deduction claimed from the profits on that account. This item is $1,489.48.

4th. The auditor disallows the deduction from the profits, claimed by the defendant, on account of the keep of a house which had belonged to the partnership, from November 5th, 1870, to March, 1871, for the reason that the house was turned over in November, with the other assets of the firm, to the defendant, and became, from that time, his property. This item is $85.87.

5th. The auditor allows the deduction from the profits of
68 the amount paid the book-keeper, Connor, for extra services in winding up the partnership accounts. This item appears to have been paid to him by the defendant, in good faith, for such services. It amounts to $700.00....

The articles of copartnership under which the complainant and defendant did business, were, in substance, as follows:

1st. Form partnership in the firm name of "William H. Tutt and Land."
2d. Tutt contributes $29,815.00 in stock.
3d. Land devotes time, labor and skill to business.
4d. Profits shall be divided as follows: three-fourths to Tutt and one-fourth to Land.
5th. Profits shall only be reckoned after deducting all expenses of the business, among which is included the sum of $2,500 00 per year to be paid to Tutt for rent of store....

TRIPPE,JUDGE....

The contract of partnership was, that one partner should furnish the stock of goods then on hand, and the other should render his skill, services, etc. It was further agreed that the first should have three-fourths of the net profits, and the second the remaining fourth. Under such a contract the partner furnishing the capital is not entitled to interest on the stock when a division of the profits is made. We can see no reason for such a claim. Such partner gets all the profits by the contract that are made on three-fourths of what he puts in the concern. The other fourth was intended as a set-off to the skill, time and services of the other partner, and the profits thereon to be his compensation. To hold as claimed by plaintiff in error, would give that other partner the net profits on one-fourth, less the interest thereon. Such was not the contract. Net profits of an adventure do not mean what is made over the losses, expenses and interest on the amount invested. The term includes simply the gain that accrues on the investment, after deducting the losses and expenses of the business. If but two or three per cent. is realized on the amount put in, it may be a poor business, but still there would be net profits, even if the legal rate of interest were ten per cent. or greater....

The goods and fixtures constituted the stock furnished by 69
Dr. Tutt. At the dissolution he claimed that there was a depreciation of the stock, and that he should be paid for it. It was not pretended that the value was lessened by reason of damage or injury from accident or other special cause. Had it so been, there might, probably be force in the question whether it was not a claim under the head of losses, and therefore properly chargeable to the firm. But it appeared that it was only the ordinary, natural depreciation that may occur in all things. At the time the partnership was formed, the value of the stock was ascertained, inserted in the articles, and it was agreed that Dr. Tutt should keep that sum in the business for the use of said firm during the continuance of the partnership, "and that the said sum of money or its equivalent in stock of goods is to constitute the capital to be used and employed," etc. We do not think that under this contract the partner who furnishes the stock, can, at the dissolution, claim for the ordinary, natural decrease in value of the goods. That is a risk or incident which attaches to his property, and is doubtless an item considered and passed upon by the party who invests his capital in that form, when he enters into such a contract. If A and B were to form a partnership for farming purposes, A to furnish the land, and horses and mules for ploughing, and B his skill, labor and superintendence, and the profits to be divided equally or in any given ratio between them, could A, at the end of two years or other period, when the dissolution might take place, claim compensation for the decreased value of his horses or mules on account of their increased age, or for the wear and waste of his land from time and cultivation, etc? It would scarcely occur to the mind of any one that such a right ex-

isted on the part of A, unless it was so specified "in the bond." Another item in this contract settles this question, as well also as the question of the right of Dr. Tutt to claim interest on his original capital. That item is: "It is agreed between the parties that the said gains, increase and profits shall only be reckoned, after deducting all *expenses of the business*, among which expenses is included the sum of $2,500.00 per year to be paid to the said W.H. Tutt for rent of the store on Broad street, supplied by him to the partnership for carrying on the business." The proper construction of this item excludes the idea of his claim for such interest, and for the ordinary depreciation of the stock he contributed. As well might it be asserted for the depreciation by time and use of the house, for that was also supplied by him to the firm....

Judgment affirmed.

MAIN v. MILLS

16 Fed. Cas. 506, Fed. Cas. No. 8,974 (1874)
United States Circuit Court
Western District of Wisconsin

BLODGETT, District Judge (charging jury). The controverted questions of fact to be passed upon by you are comparatively few. It is conceded that on or about the 16th of April, 1860, defendant Mills and one James L. Hill united under the general banking law of this state in the organization of a bank by the corporate name of the Bank of Madison, with a capital stock of $25,000, of which each held one-half; that said bank commenced the transaction of the usual classes of business carried on in this city by banking corporations and bankers, and continued in said business until the 7th day of October, 1873, when it was adjudicated bankrupt in this court on its own petition; that up to about the middle of January, 1869, defendant continued to hold half the stock of said bank and acted as its president; that during the time aforesaid, said bank paid the defendant dividends on his stock as follows: January 1, 1865, $6,084.66; January 1, 1866, $1,630.37; July 1, 1866, $1,740.28; January 1, 1867, $3,003.65; July 1, 1867, $815.55; January 1, 1868, $2,088.14; July 1, 1868, $1,565.57; January 1, 1869, $1,014.91; and that dividends to the same amount were declared and paid to said Hill, who held the other half of the stock at the same time. It was also admitted that about the middle of January, 1869, defendant sold to said Hill his stock and interest in said bank at a price much below par. But I think it may be taken as an admitted fact that the stock was treated between the parties to this transaction, Hill and Mills, as of little intrinsic value at that time; that the defendant retained the presidency of the bank until January, 1871, although the evidence tends to show that his connection with it was merely nominal after he sold his stock.

It is also admitted that during the time the bank continued in business, regular reports of its financial condition were made as required by law to the bank comptroller of this state, and filed in the office of the secretary of state, and that these reports are mostly, if not all, signed, and purport to be sworn to, by the defendant as president.

The plaintiff has also given evidence tending to show that at the time these dividends were paid the capital stock of the bank had become so impaired by losses from bad debts and mismanagement that no actual profits were made from the business of the bank; that at the time when each of these dividends was paid the current losses of the bank by hopelessly bad and suspended debts were such as to have absorbed and sunk all the profits of the business, so that in fact no dividend was really earned and payable to stockholders.

Upon the facts thus admitted to be true or claimed to be proven, plaintiff insists that he is entitled to recover from defendant the dividends which he has from time to time received from January 1, 1865, to January 1, 1869, inclusive. To this the defendant interposes by way of defense: (1) A general denial of the plaintiff's right under the law to recover upon the facts set forth in the complaint; (2) a denial of those facts, which puts the plaintiff upon proof of such as have not been admitted on the trial; (3) that as to part of said dividends the right of action accrued more than six years before the commencement of the suit, and is therefore barred by the statute of limitations.

It is the province of the court to instruct you upon some of these questions of law which arise upon the facts which you may find in the case. There is, perhaps, at this day no better established rule of law than that the capital stock of a moneyed corporation, whether it be a banking, insurance, mining or manufacturing company, is to be treated and deemed as a trust fund for the purpose of securing the payment of the debts of the corporation. In banks the capital stock stands as a guaranty to the extent of its amount, for the payment of the creditors of the bank. Theoretically under your law this stock and a certain degree of personal liability of the stockholders is pledged, first to secure the payment of the circulating notes of the bank, and after that to the general creditors. But it being admitted that there is no circulation in this case, the general creditors may be said to be the parties directly interested in this fund.

The officers of such a corporation have no right to make dividends to stockholders unless there are profits to be divided, over and above all losses, because the necessary result of so doing is to deplete the capital fund. The capital stock being, as I said, a trust fund, the first duty of the officers of the bank is to keep this fund intact and unimpaired. If there are gains and losses, the gains should be set off against the losses so far as may be necessary to keep the capital fund whole. All net profits above what are requisite for that purpose, may, as a general rule, be rightfully divided to stockholders. And while it is not necessary for me to say in this case how far in my opinion a stockholder who is not an officer might be protected in the receipt of dividends, I will say that officers, who know and are bound to know the condition of the affairs of the bank, have no right to take dividends unless legitimately earned and on hand.

Applying these general principles to the case before us, you see that it becomes an important inquiry for you, and really the only material and important issue of fact for you to determine in this case, whether the bank had gains or profits which it rightfully could divide to its stockholders at the time the dividends in question were made.

You have heard the testimony bearing upon this branch of the case. The plaintiff has put in proof, which as he claims, shows that at the time each of these dividends was declared the losses, or suspended debts which ultimately proved to be losses, greatly exceeded the gains then on hand, and he therefore insists that those dividends were wrongfully made to the defendant and should be returned by him, because he, being an officer of the bank, was bound to know that these debts were either hopelessly lost, or so precarious and uncertain of collection that the bank had no right to consider them as part of its living available assets.

The defendant, on the contrary, insists that at the time these dividends were paid no serious losses had been sustained; that while some paper was suspended or overdue, and some accounts overdrawn, yet the debtors were all substantially solvent and good for their indebtedness to the bank. And it is for you to say whether the proof satisfies you that at the time any or all these dividends were paid the bank had made or had not made gains over and above its losses which authorized the making of the dividends.

If you are satisfied from the evidence that at the time these several dividends, from January 1, 1865, to January 1, 1869, were made, or either of them, the losses of the bank did at the time exceed the gains, so that in fact there were no profits over and above losses, then you should find for the plaintiff as to such of said dividends as you are satisfied from the evidence were made when there were no profits over and above losses to divide.

But in passing upon this testimony you must view it as far as possible from the standpoint of the transaction itself, and not in the light of subsequent revelations. The proper inquiry is, would a sagacious, prudent banker, in the light of all the facts disclosed to you in the evidence, have considered Darwin, Parkins, and the other persons whose names appear in the testimony as debtors of the bank, as solvent, and the debts of the bank against them as good and collectible at the time these dividends were made?

From the nature of the business the assets of a bank must all the time be represented by what is due to it from its debtors. The officers of a bank cannot collect in all its bills receivable on some special day, and then say, Now we will make a dividend. We know we have no bad debts because no body owes us, and therefore we have a right to divide our surplus. This rule would be impracticable, and if acted upon would prevent any dividends being paid. But there is a constant demand for the exercise of sound judgment and sagacity as to the standing and value of its paper. The bank officer is not only bound to be honest, but he is bound to possess the requisite ability for the ordinary exigencies of the business he undertakes. He is not expected to be infallible, nor to make no mistakes, but he must use the caution of an ordinarily prudent man engaged in such business. Your own good sense and experience in life will teach you that it does not necessarily follow, because a man has overdrawn his account at a bank or has not paid his note at maturity, that the debt is therefore bad and should be charged up to profit and loss. It may be the overdraft is allowed because the bank officer knows, or thinks he knows, that the drawer is abundantly good, although it is probable that a banker who habitually, to any considerable extent, allowed overdrafts and overdue papers to remain unadjusted would soon lose his reputation as a safe and competent man in the business, and deservedly lose the confidence of the community. As I said before, you must as nearly as possible put yourselves in the place of the managers of this bank at the time these dividends were paid, and decide as well as the proof will enable you whether these debts now claimed to have been losses then, ought to have been so considered at that time by this bank officer and stockholder. Ought these debts to have been classed as doubtful or desperate at the time? If they ought, common prudence would have dictated the withholding of a dividend at such times. And if made at such times an officer of the bank occupying the responsible position in its affairs which was occupied by the defendant, would have no right to excuse payment of a dividend, because he is bound to know all the facts about its affairs which are disclosed by its books and records, or can be ascertained on close inquiry. He cannot be heard in a court of justice to say he did not know these things, because it is his duty to know them, and the law will conclusively presume he did know them. From what I have said as to the facts you must find, in order to sustain the plaintiff's case, you will readily infer that unless those facts are found by you from the proof the defendant is not liable. . . .

The bank, as a corporation, is bound to keep its capital stock intact, and the banking law has many provisions intended to secure that result. If there is any reduction of the capital funds, the bank can bring suit to recover back such funds, from those who have appropriated them wrongfully, and in case the bank refuses or neglects to do so, a creditor or person aggrieved may bring such suit, but the cause of action accrues to the bank and the statute begins to run when the misappropriation is made. . . .

The fact that Mills and Hill were the only stockholders and only officers in this bank, does not change the legal aspect of the questions raised in this case. A bank corporation is just as much an artificial body, and has the same rights and duties, with two stockholders, as though it had a hundred stockholders. The ownership of the stock in a bank, under the law of this state, is a fact of which any person can, by due inquiry, obtain information. The law requires lists of stockholders to be filed semi-annually in the office of the state bank comptroller and in the office of the register of deeds of the county where the bank is situate, so that all depositors can ascertain, not only who the stockholders were, but how many there were. The reports were only admissible to show the act of defendant in representing the stock as remaining intact, and also as tending to show the extent to which he participated in the actual management of the bank affairs.

Much testimony has been admitted on the trial of this case which, perhaps, was not necessary to elucidate the issues on which you are to pass. I have already called your attention to these issues, and it is enough to say that you ought not to consider in this case any testimony which does not tend to prove those issues.

Verdict for amount of dividends paid out after January 1, 1868, with interest.

EYSTER v. CENTENNIAL BOARD OF FINANCE

94 U.S. 500 (1876)
Supreme Court of the United States

MR. CHIEF JUSTICE WAITE delivered the opinion of the court.

This case presents the single question whether, in the distribution of the moneys remaining in the treasury of the Centennial Board of Finance at the close of the affairs of that corporation, as provided for in sect. 10 of the act of June 1, 1872, the appropriation of $1,500,000 made by Congress in the act of Feb. 16, 1876, must be paid into the treasury of the United
74 States before any division of assets is made among the stockholders in satisfaction and discharge of the capital-stock.

It is very apparent that the object of Congress, in all its legislation with reference to the Centennial Exhibition, was to enable the people of the United States to commemorate "the completion of the first century of their national existence" by an exhibition "in which the people of the whole country should participate," and which should have the sanction of the government. In that sense, the object was national; but it is equally clear, that, until the act of 1876, it was expected that the entire expense would be borne by the people without assistance from Congress. Certainly, no pecuniary liability whatever was assumed by Congress. That is declared in the most positive terms.

The acts of 1871 and 1872 did nothing more than provide the necessary organizations through which the people might operate under the auspices of the government. That of 1871 authorized the appointment of the board of commissioners, which was afterwards, by the act of 1872, incorporated as the "United States Centennial Commission." The duty of this board was to prepare and superintend the execution of a plan for holding the exhibition. That of 1872 was specially intended to provide a way by which the people could procure the necessary funds. It was so expressly declared in the preamble; and for that purpose the Centennial Board of Finance was incorporated, with apt provisions for subscription to and sale of its capital stock, and for the control and management of its affairs. The proceeds of the stock, together with the receipts from all other sources, were to be used by this corporation for the erection of buildings with their appurtenances, and for all other expenditures required in carrying out the objects of the act of 1871. Then, by sect. 10, it was provided, "that, as soon as practicable after the said exhibition shall have been closed, it shall be the duty of said corporation to convert its property into cash, and, after the payment of its liabilities, to divide its remaining assets among its stockholders, *pro rata*, in full satisfaction and discharge of its capital stock."

Afterward came the act of 1876, which made the appropriation now under consideration, "to complete the . . . buildings and other preparations," and directed its payment to the president and treasurer of the Centennial Board of Finance for that purpose, but which contained a proviso, "that in the distribution of any moneys that may remain in the treasury of the Centennial Board of Finance after the payment of its debts, as provided for by the tenth section of the act of Congress approved June 1, 1872, incorporating the Centennial Board of Finance, the appropriation hereinbefore made shall be paid in full into the treasury of the United States before any dividend or percentage of profits shall be paid to the holders of said stock;" and "that the government of the United States shall not, under any circumstances, be liable for any debt or obligation of the United States Centennial Commission or the Centennial Board of Finance, or any payment in addition to the foregoing sum."

The whole controversy arises upon this proviso. On the one hand, it is contended that it requires the repayment to the United States of the full amount of their appropriation before any distribution can be made to the stockholders; and, on the other, that the stockholders must be reimbursed for their stock subscriptions before any payment is made to the United States. It becomes necessary, therefore, to ascertain the intention of Congress in this particular, and for that purpose the acts of 1871, 1872, and 1876, being *in pari materia*, are to be examined and construed together.

There is no doubt but that the act of 1876 appropriated public moneys for the completion of the centennial buildings and other preparations. Neither is there any doubt that, under certain circumstances, the Centennial Board of Finance was required to pay back to the treasury of the United States the full amount of the appropriation. The corporation assumed such an obligation by taking the money upon the conditions imposed. If this did not create a debt, technically so called, it certainly did create a liability. The act of 1872 provided for a division of the assets of the corporation among the stockholders, only after the payment of all liabilities; and, unless the contract entered into otherwise directs, it would seem to be clear, that, so far as that act is concerned, the United States must be paid in full before the stockholders can claim any distribution among themselves.

In the act of 1876, the language is somewhat different. By that the United States are to be paid out of the moneys that remain in the treasury of the company, after the payment of the debts. If this were all, the intention would be manifest. The liability of a corporation to its stockholders on account of their stock is not a debt. The shares of a stockholder represent his proportion of the property of a corporation; and, upon the winding up of its affairs, the assets remaining after all liabilities are discharged are for division among the stockholders, according to their respective interests. The payment to stockholders upon such a division is for a dividend of the property
76 divided, not for a debt owing by the corporation. The United States, then, even under this act, are entitled to a preference over the stockholders, unless the words "before any dividend or percentage of profits shall be paid to the holders of such stock" change the condition of the parties. This will depend much upon the signification of the term "profits" as here used

In construing statutes, some effect should, if possible, be given to every word employed to express the legislative will. Nothing should be rejected, if it can be avoided; and nothing can be added, except by implication from what is expressed. As in the act of 1872 stockholders are not to be paid any thing until all liabilities are discharged, and in that of 1876 the United States are to be reimbursed before any profits can be divided, and no provision is made for the redemption of capital stock, except upon a division of the profits, it is apparent that, if such a redemption is to be made before the liability of the United States is satisfied, something must be supplied in the statute, by implication, that has been apparently omitted. The presumption is, however, that every thing has been expressed which was intended; and, if an effect can properly be given to the word "profits" that will harmonize the two statutes, without a resort to implication, it should be done.

The capital stock of this corporation was not employed in, but to prepare for, the business of the contemplated exhibition; and the receipts of the exhibition, over and above its current expenses, are the profits of the business. These were the only profits anticipated. They are, in fact, the net receipts, which, according to the common understanding, ordinarily represent the profits of a business. The public, when referring to the profits of the business of a merchant, rarely ever take into account the depreciation of the buildings in which the business is carried on, notwithstanding they may have been erected out of the capital invested. Popularly speaking, the net receipts of a business are its profits. So here, as the business to be carried on was that of an exhibition, and its profits were to be derived only from its receipts, to the popular mind the net receipts would represent the net profits.

Giving that signification to the word in this case, we encounter no difficulties. The statutes are complete, and there is nothing to supply. Every thing is in harmony, and no strained construction is required. All accounts are easily adjusted, without resort to unusual proceedings.

When a corporation is to be wound up, there is not, ordinarily, a necessity for an account of profits. After the liabilities are paid, the remaining assets belong to the stockholders, and all that need be done is to make the proper division. For 77
that purpose, it is quite immaterial whether what remains is profit or capital. In either case, it belongs to the stockholders, and is to be distributed among them *pro rata*. Such a division produces a dividend, — that is to say, a part or share of the thing divided. If the division is of profits, then the dividend is of profits; if of capital, then of capital. The dividends declared by a corporation in business usually are, and, except under special circumstances, always should be, from profits. Hence, the word frequently carries with it the idea of a division of profits; but that is not necessarily its only meaning. Its special signification, in any particular case, is always dependent upon the character of the thing divided.

By the act of 1872, the assets were to be reduced to cash, liabilities paid, and the remainder divided among stockholders. The words "in satisfaction and discharge of its capital stock" add nothing to, and take nothing from, what precedes; and the whole of that part of sect. 10, taken together, provides for nothing more than what would have been done without it. If there had not been a word upon the subject, the law would have disposed of the property in precisely the same way, and the stockholders could have compelled a settlement upon that basis.

The act of 1876 requires the payment of debts, and then the reimbursement of the United States before a distribution of profits to stockholders. Not a word is said about restoring capital: in fact, there is no mention of capital at all. The act of 1872 is not repealed. On the contrary, it is left in full force in every particular, save that the new liability incurred to the United States is made payable after those contemplated by the act of 1872 are satisfied in full. In this, the United States made a concession to creditors, but not to the stockholders.

Neither was any thing taken from stockholders: they retain all the rights which the act of 1872 gave them. ...

We think, therefore, that Congress did not intend, by the act of 1876, to change the order of distribution as provided by that of 1872, except by giving a preference to other liabilities over that to the United States, and that the word "profits" was used in 1876 to represent the net receipts of the business of the exhibition to be had in the buildings erected and upon the grounds prepared for its accommodation by means of the capital of the Centennial Board of Finance. In this way "profits," in the act of 1876, and "remaining assets," in that of 1872, have substantially the same meaning; and the two statutes are relieved from all discrepancies, without doing
78 violence to the language of either.

If the impaired capital is made good out of the profits, it will be for the purposes of distribution only. Indirectly, therefore, a division of the capital unimpaired would operate as a dividend of profits, because, before the stockholders could be paid in full the receipts of the business must be applied to supply the deficiency arising from depreciation. Such a dividend is prohibited.

The decree of the Circuit Court must be reversed, and the cause remanded, with instructions to enter a decree directing the payment of the sum of $1,500,000 into the treasury of the United States by the Centennial Board of Finance before any division of the remaining assets of that corporation is made among the stockholders, and it is *So ordered.*

MR. JUSTICE STRONG dissented.

GRANT v. HARTFORD AND NEW HAVEN RAILROAD COMPANY

93 U.S. 225 (1876)
Supreme Court of the United States

ERROR to the Circuit Court of the United States for the District of Connecticut.

This action was brought by the Hartford and New Haven Railroad Company against Henry A. Grant, collector of internal revenue for the first district of Connecticut, to recover the sum of $2,785.65 income tax, and $139.28 penalty, paid to him under protest in January, 1868. The controversy arose upon the question of the company's income for the two fiscal years ending Aug. 31, 1867. During that period they expended from their earnings $55,712.60, in constructing over the Farmington River at Windsor a new stone bridge, to be used in place of a wooden bridge which was deemed insecure; and they charged the amount to current expenses. The assessor of internal revenue for the district insisted that this sum should have been charged to account of construction, and was fairly to be regarded as "*profits used in construction*," within the meaning of the one hundred and twenty-second section of the act of June 30, 1864; and, therefore, he made a special assessment of the amount. The company having appealed to the commissioner of internal revenue without effect, this action was brought.

A jury having been waived, the cause was tried by the court, which found specially an agreed statement of facts. From this it appears that the amount charged to current expenses during each of the two years in question (including together the said sum of $55,712.60) was not greater than the proper ordinary current expenses and depreciation of the entire property; and that the company returned the entire balance of their gross earnings over and above said expenses, in the shape of dividends and surplus, and paid the regular tax thereon.

Judgment having been rendered in favor of the company, the collector sued out this writ of error. . . .

MR. JUSTICE BRADLEY delivered the opinion of the court.

The company having returned the entire balance of their gross earnings over and above current expenses, in the shape of dividends and surplus, for the period in question, and paid the regular tax thereon, we do not see why this was not a full compliance with the law. The object of the law was to impose a tax on net income, or profits, only; and that cannot be regarded as net income, or profits, which is required and ex-

pended to keep the property up in its usual condition proper for operation. Such expenditure is properly classed with repairs, which are a part of the current expenses. If a railroad company should make a second track when they had but a single track before, this would be a betterment or permanent improvement, and, if paid out of the earnings, would be fairly characterized as "profits used in construction." The works of the company would have an additional value to what they had before, with an increased capacity for producing future profits. This kind of expenditure is what Congress meant to reach, when, in the one hundred and twenty-second section referred to, it imposed a tax not only on the dividends of every railroad, canal, and turnpike company, but also on "all profits of such company
80 carried to the account of any fund, or used for construction."

The counsel for the government insists that this bridge was a betterment, because it was much more valuable than the old wooden bridge. But the assessor did not include the excess merely: he assessed the whole expenditure bestowed upon the new bridge, without making any allowance for the old one. His idea seems to have been, that all earnings used in new constructions are made taxable by the act, without reference to betterments, or to their being substituted for other constructions. Indeed, his assessment is not for "*profits* used in construction," but for "*earnings* used in constructing new Windsor Bridge, $55,712.60." In this view he was decidedly wrong. Earnings expended on a new structure may or may not be profits. Whether they are or not depends on other things to be taken into the account besides the mere fact of such expenditure. Had the assessment been merely for the increased value of the new bridge over the old one when in good repair, the case might have admitted of very different consideration.

Judgment affirmed.

UNITED STATES v. SCHILLINGER

14 Blatchf. 71 (1876)
United States Circuit Court
Southern District of New York

Johnson, J. The question on this writ of error is, whether the defendant was liable to an income tax for the year ending December 31st, 1871, upon the amount of certain promissory notes. These notes were received by him during the year 1871, upon a sale of certain patent rights, in part payment of the price thereof. They did not become due until some time in the year 1872, and then they were paid. In my opinion there is no ground for this action. The tax was imposed for the years 1870 and 1871, and no longer, upon the gains, profits and income of every person residing in the United States. (*Act of July 14th*, 1870, § 6, 16 *U. S. Stat. at Large*, 257.) In the absence of any special provision of law to the contrary, income must be taken to mean money, and not the expectation of receiving it, or the right to receive it, at a future time. In this case, the defendant changed his patent rights for promissory notes payable in the future. Their value was uncertain; they might or might not be paid; but, until they were paid, they were not income, but only the ground of expecting income. The notes were no more taxable as income than would have been other patent rights, if the defendant had received them in payment of those he sold. There are in the next section of the statute, sec. 7, provisions which confirm this construction. It makes interest received or accrued upon all notes, bonds and mortgages, or other forms of indebtedness bearing interest, whether paid or not, if good and collectible, subject to the income tax. The purpose of this is evidently to prevent a man escaping the income tax, by abstaining from taking that which is due him. On the same principle, had these notes been due, and had the defendant allowed them to remain unpaid, there might have been room to contend that their amount should be regarded as income; but, not being due, when the income had become fixed for the year, they were no part of the defendant's income.

The judgment was in accordance with the law and must be affirmed.

Roger M. Sherman, (*Assistant District Attorney*,) for the plaintiffs in error.

David L. Williams, for the defendant in error.

WHITNEY ARMS CO. v. BARLOW

68 N.Y. 34 (1876)
Court of Appeals, New York

APPEAL from judgment of the General Term of the Superior Court of the city of New York affirming a judgment in favor of defendant, entered upon an order dismissing plaintiff's complaint on trial

This action was brought against defendants, as trustees of the American Seal Lock Company, a corporation organized under the general manufacturing act (chap. 40, Laws of 1848), to enforce the statutory liability to pay the debts of the corporation imposed by said act upon the trustees (§ 12), in case of failure on its part to make, file and publish an annual report. The case is reported on a former appeal in 63 New York, 62....

On October 6, 1871, said corporation entered into a contract with plaintiff, of which the following are the material portions, so far as this case is concerned:

"The Whitney Arms Company hereby agree to manufacture for, and deliver to, the American Seal Lock Company twenty thousand (20,000) circular railroad locks, as per sample furnished them, on the following conditions, viz.: one thousand (1,000) of said locks to be completed and ready for delivery in six weeks from the date of this instrument, ten thousand (10,000) by December 1, 1871, and the balance to be ready for delivery as fast as practicable thereafter, and the entire contract of twenty thousand (20,000) locks to be completed and ready for delivery on or before the sixth (6th) day of January, 1872.

"All of the above locks to be packed in boxes (containing one hundred each) by the Whitney Arms Company, marked 'American Seal Lock Company, 744 Broadway, New York,' and delivered to the depot of the New York and New Haven Railroad Company, or on board of steamboat, at the option of American Seal Lock Company, and a railroad receipt or bill of lading mailed to American Seal Lock Company, at their office in New York city.

"The American Seal Lock Company agree to receive from the Whitney Arms Company the twenty thousand (20,000) locks as heretofore specified, and to pay for them in sixty days from date, of each five thousand locks delivered, or sooner, if they receive their pay from the United States government on their vouchers, but in no case shall be delayed more than sixty days from date of each five thousand locks delivered, the price of each lock to be sixty (60) cents."

Plaintiff claimed a delivery under the contract, of some 700 locks, before January 19, 1872.

Further facts are set forth in the opinion....

ALLEN, J. The report made and filed by the American Seal Lock Company, in 1873, is the same in all respects as that made by the same company in 1872, which, upon a former appeal in this action,* we adjudged sufficient in form and substance, and a full compliance with the requirements of section 12 of chapter 40 of the Laws of 1848. It follows, therefore, that the corporation was not in default after the 19th of January, 1872, for not making the report required by law to 83
be made by manufacturing corporations within twenty days from the first day of January in each year, and the defendant and the other trustees are not liable for debts contracted by the company during the years 1872 and 1873, after the making and filing of the report on the day named....

The only question remaining is, whether there was evidence to go to the jury tending to establish an indebtedness existing against the Seal Lock Company, on the 19th day of January, 1872, the day on which the report of the company was filed, and which terminated the default before then, incurred by the company, and relieved the trustees from liability for debts thereafter created. The plaintiff argues, that there was evidence for the jury of the delivery of at least 100 locks in December, and before the 19th day of January, 1872, for which the company was a debtor; that by such delivery, under the contract, a debt was created for which the defendant was liable.

The counsel for the plaintiff presented the question by two requests to the court, both of which were refused.

First. That a verdict should be directed for the amount of goods proved to have been delivered before the report filed in 1872; and, second, that it be submitted to the jury to determine how many goods were delivered prior to that time. The requests assumed that by the delivery of the goods an indebtedness was created. But if there was any delivery of goods it was under the contract, and there could be no liability except according to the terms of the agreement. At the time of filing the report in January, 1872, the plaintiff was in default so far as is disclosed by the evidence, and had not then delivered the number of locks entitling it to demand payment of any sum, and could only entitle itself to demand

payment for those delivered, by the delivery thereafter of over 4,000 in addition to those now claimed to have been delivered, and the acceptance thereof by the Seal Lock Company. By the terms of the contract an obligation to pay only arose upon the delivery of 5,000 locks, and then the obligation became perfect, an indebtedness existed, although the purchasing corporation was entitled to a credit of sixty days for the payment thereof. There was no debt payable, either presently or in the future, by the Seal Lock Company, until 5,000 locks had been delivered, and that had not been done at the time of the filing of the first report. There was an executory contract under which a debt might accrue upon performance, but until performance it was but an executory
84 and contingent obligation, which, if performed by the other party might grow into a debt. It was not an existing indebtedness. The act is, in its nature, to some extent penal and the liability of the trustees cannot be extended by implication to contracts and contingent and conditional obligations not clearly within the terms of the act. This construction of the statute is recognized by the counsel for the plaintiff by the limit of the claim to a recovery for the locks actually delivered before the filing of the report. When the plaintiff should, under the contract, part with its property, and not before, it might become a creditor of the Seal Lock Company, with all the rights incident to that relation. . . .

A fortiori the evidence would not have sustained a verdict against the defendant as trustee upon the statutory liability resulting from the failure of the corporation to report.

The judgment must be affirmed.

All concur.

Judgment affirmed.

DAVIS v. FLAGSTAFF SILVER MINING COMPANY OF UTAH

2 Utah 74 (1877)
Supreme Court of Utah

BOREMAN, Justice, delivered the opinion of the Court:

The appellant, the Flagstaff Company, was incorporated in England, to acquire, hold and operate mining and smelting properties in Utah. The respondent sued the company, alleging the purchase of ores from it, and the non-delivery thereof; also, that he had advanced money to said company, and that a contract was entered into by and between the company and himself, whereby he acquired a lien upon the properties of the said company in Utah, and he asked the enforcement of said contract, and that a receiver be appointed. The other defendants were made parties because they were supposed to hold liens against the property of the said company.

The court below entered a judgment appointing a receiver, and requiring defendants to surrender possession of the property to the receiver, and enjoining them from interfering with the receiver in his holding, working and disposing of the property;

It appears that the respondents, by arrangements with the directors of the said company, had loaned the company very large sums of money, which was to a great extent, if not entirely, used in paying dividends. Subsequently the character of these loans was sought to be changed, and thus was created what are now offered as "ore contracts." . . .

The use of the money to pay dividends was in violation of the acts of Parliament, called the "Company's Acts." By these acts, this corporation is prohibited from declaring any dividends "except out of the profits arising from the business of the company." Dividends paid out of borrowed money were not paid out of "profits." Thus the company had no grant of authority for using the borrowed money to pay dividends, but it was in fact expressly prohibited from so doing. . . .

In the instance before us, we have no doubt that the respondent was fully aware of the corporate powers of the company. He was one of the incorporators of the company and one of its first directors. He owned and bought and sold large amounts of its stocks. He was a stock broker and manipulator of stocks. He went to London with letters that gave him "a good position" (to use his own language), and he says that "In London, the way of operating is very different from here, *decidedly old fogyish. They did not understand bulls and bears on the stock exchange.* A man would go a bear a thousand or two pounds there, and make as much disturbance about that as a man in America would a million." It was right in the line of his business to know the powers of these stock corporations. The large dividends from the borrowed money increased the market value of the stocks, the public supposing that the company was doing a legitimate business, and paying dividends out of "profits." Such people "did not understand bulls and bears on the stock exchange." A shrewd manipulator of stocks could afford to run the risk of losing money loaned to a company to be used to pay dividends, when he knew that he could receive it all back, and much more, too, by the sudden rise in the price of the stocks.

The evidence shows that the directors at that time were acting in entire harmony with the respondent, and willing always to comply with his wishes. The respondent did not
86 propose to lose the money advanced, and hence the claims were put into the shape of "ore contracts." A change of shape did not change the substance, however. Being based upon fraudulent and void loans, they were necessarily also fraudulent and void.

But let us assume that no loans ever were made, and that the ore contracts were original and not based upon prior transactions between the parties. The receipt of forward payments for ores to be delivered in future, as specified in these contracts, was beyond the powers of the corporation. The company has no grant of authority to thus bulk its expected productions and involve the company to its ruin by subsequent inability to comply with the terms of the contract.

Money arising from such forward payments for ores, could not legally be used to pay dividends. Such money was not "profits arising from the business of the company." The money might be termed *anticipated* profits, but we nowhere find any authority for the company declaring dividends out of any profits except such as are realized out of the business—"arising out of the business" of the company. And it is against public policy to allow corporations to thus deal so as to deceive and defraud the people. An unscrupulous directory or company might have no ores, and yet sell ore for ten, twenty or more years ahead of the production thereof, and use the money thus acquired in declaring one or two dividends of enormous size. Those knowing the inside workings of the company could sell off all their stocks at enormous profits, and leave the company bankrupted and in the hands of those who were deceived and defrauded into buying the stocks. Courts cannot look with any favor upon claims for such powers in corporations.

These ore contracts were the basis of the alleged contract of December 13, 1873, "Exhibit A," upon which this action is brought. As the ore contracts were invalid, and not within the power of the corporation to make, it follows that no action of the company could give them vitality. . . .

We, for the reasons stated, do not think that respondent has a claim upon the company for the enforcement of this contract, "Exhibit A," sued upon, nor is he entitled to damages for its breach or non-fulfillment. . . .

The judgment and order of the court below are reversed with costs, and the cause is dismissed.

UNION PACIFIC RAILROAD COMPANY v. THE UNITED STATES

99 U.S. 402 (1878)
Supreme Court of the United States

1. The act entitled "An Act to aid in the construction of a railroad and telegraph line from the Missouri River to the Pacific Ocean, and to secure to the government the use of the same for postal, military, and other purposes," approved July 1, 1862 (12 Stat. 489), after providing for the issue of patents for land and of bonds to the Union Pacific Railroad Company and other companies from time to time, as successive sections of their respective roads should be completed, requires the companies to perform all government transportation of mails, troops, &c., and to credit the compensation therefor on the government loan; and then adds, that "after said road is completed, until said bonds and interest are paid, at least five per centum of the net earnings of said road shall also be annually applied to the payment thereof."...

APPEAL from the Court of Claims..

This is a suit by the Union Pacific Railroad Company to recover compensation for services rendered to the United States prior to 1874, and during a portion of that year 1874, and the whole of the year 1875. A counter-claim is set up for five per cent of the net earnings of the company, under the provision of the sixth section of the act of July 1, 1862 (12 Stat. 489), that "after the said road is completed, until said bonds and interest are paid, at least five per centum of the net earnings of said road shall also be annually applied to the payment thereof."..

MR. JUSTICE BRADLEY, after stating the case, delivered the opinion of the court....

II. The question next arising is, What are the "net earnings" for five per cent of which the company became liable to account, and in what manner are they payable?

In the first place, they are the "net earnings of the road;" that is, the net earnings of the road as a railroad, including the telegraph. They have nothing to do with the income or profits of the company as a holder of public lands. The proceeds of this source of income are no part of the earnings of the road. These earnings, however, must be regarded as embracing all the earnings and income derived by the company from the railroad proper, and all the appendages and appurtenances thereof, including its ferry and bridge at Omaha, its cars, and all its property and apparatus legitimately connected with its railroad.

In the present case, but little difficulty is presented in determining what are the proper earnings of the road, except in

one particular. The company insists that the compensation accruing to it for services performed for the government, under the sixth section of the act of 1862, should not be estimated amongst the earnings of the road, in taking an account of net earnings upon which to calculate the five per cent in question. That compensation is not receivable by the company, — does not come into its hands, — at least was not receivable by it according to the act of 1862, but was directed by the sixth section to be applied to the payment of the subsidy bonds. After giving this direction, the section proceeds to add, that after the road is completed, " until said bonds and interest are paid, five per centum of the net earnings of said road shall also be annually applied to the payment thereof." It is contended that the net earnings here referred to are intended to be exclusive of
said compensation for government service, no part of which the 89
company was to receive. It must be admitted that there is some force in this view. But the majority of the court is of opinion that the plain letter of the statute cannot be thus varied by construction. The compensation accruing by means of services performed for the government is unquestionably earnings of the road and telegraph; and as there are no words in the act which go to show any intention to except this portion of earnings from the other earnings of the road in estimating the amount of net earnings, the conclusion arrived at is, that no such exception can be made. The fact that by a subsequent law the company is allowed to receive in money one-half of the compensation referred to, removes to a great extent the practical difficulties that have been suggested in this behalf.

There is another item in the table of earnings set forth in the eighteenth finding of the Court of Claims which may require consideration. We refer to the seventh item, entitled " company freight." If this means freight for the transportation of the company's own property over its own road, it ought not to be put down as a receipt, unless the same amount is also embraced amongst the expenses on the other side of the account. How this fact may be we have not before us the means of knowing. The evidence which the Court of Claims has in its possession will enable it to determine this matter. We merely decide that if the item appears only as a receipt or earning, and is of the character we have supposed, it ought to be excluded from the account.

Having considered the question of receipts or earnings, the next thing in order is the expenditures which are properly chargeable against the gross earning in order to arrive at the "net earnings," as this expression is to be understood within the meaning of the act. As a general proposition, net earnings

are the excess of the gross earnings over the expenditures defrayed in producing them, aside from, and exclusive of, the expenditure of capital laid out in constructing and equipping the works themselves. It may often be difficult to draw a precise line between expenditures for construction, and the ordinary expenses incident to operating and maintaining the road and works of a railroad company. Theoretically, the expenses chargeable to earnings include the general expenses of keeping up the organization of the company, and all expenses incurred in operating the works and keeping them in good condition and repair; whilst expenses chargeable to capital include those which are incurred in the original construction of the works, and in the subsequent enlargement and improvement thereof.
90 With regard to the last-mentioned class of expenditures, however, namely, those which are incurred in enlarging and improving the works, a difference of practice prevails amongst railroad companies. Some charge to construction account every item of expense, and every part and portion of every item, which goes to make the road, or any of its appurtenances or equipments, better than they were before; whilst others charge to ordinary expense account, and against earnings, whatever is taken for these purposes from the earnings, and is not raised upon bonds or issues of stock. The latter method is deemed the most conservative and beneficial for the company, and operates as a restraint against injudicious dividends and the accumulation of a heavy indebtedness. The temptation is, to make expenses appear as small as possible, so as to have a large apparent surplus to divide. But it is not regarded as the wisest and most prudent method. The question is one of policy, which is usually left to the discretion of the directors. There is but little danger that any board will cause a very large or undue portion of their earnings to be absorbed in permanent improvements. The practice will only extend to those which may be required from time to time by the gradual increase of the company's traffic, the despatch of business, the public accommodation, and the general permanency and completeness of the works. When any important improvement is needed, such as an additional track, or any other matter which involves a large outlay of money, the owners of the road will hardly forego the entire suspension of dividends in order to raise the requisite funds for those purposes; but will rather take the ordinary course of issuing bonds or additional stock. But for making all ordinary improvements, as well as repairs, it is better for the stockholders, and all those who are interested in the prosperity of the enterprise, that a portion of the earnings should be em-

ployed. We think that the true interest of the government, in this case, is the same as that of the stockholders; and will be subserved by encouraging a liberal application of the earnings to the improvement of the works. It is better for the ultimate security of the government in reference to the payment of its loan, as well as for the service which it may require in the transportation of its property and mails, that a hundred dollars should be spent in improving the works, than that it should receive five dollars towards the payment of its subsidy. If the five per cent of net earnings, demandable from the company, amounted to a new indebtedness, not due before, like a rent accruing upon a lease, a more rigid rule might be insisted on. But it is not so; the amount of the indebtedness is fixed and unchangeable. The amount of the five per cent and its 91
receipt at one time or another is simply a question of earlier or later payment of a debt already fixed in amount. If the employment of any earnings of the road in making improvements lessens the amount of net earnings, the government loses nothing thereby. The only result is, that a less amount is presently paid on its debt; whilst the general security for the whole debt is largely increased.

We are disposed to agree, therefore, with the judge who delivered the concurring opinion in the court below, that the twenty-seventh item of expenditure, as stated in the table of expenses in the eighteenth finding, entitled "expenditures for station buildings, shops, &c.," is a charge that may properly be made against earnings, since, as the fact is, such expenditures were actually paid therefrom, and were not carried to capital account. Should the company ever attempt to make a stock or bond dividend in consideration of such expenditure, the government would be entitled to demand its due proportion thereof by way of payment on account of its debt. But as long as such expenditures are fairly and in good faith charged to account of earnings, we see no good reason for disallowing the charge.

Of course, the allowance of this item will supersede the deduction of fifteen per cent from the seventh item of earnings; which item, however, is subject to the observations that have already been made upon it.

Expenses of the same kind as those included in item 27, which are contained in other items, and were disallowed by the Court of Claims, are to be allowed in like manner as those in item 27, including the expenses for issuing bonds.

We agree with the Court of Claims in its rejection of the expenditures contained in items 17 to 30 in the table referred to, excepting item 27. All payments of interest on the bonded indebtedness of the company should be charged to capital interest account, and not to current expenditures. Though payable out of earnings before any dividend can be made to stockholders, they cannot be deducted for the purpose of ascertaining the "net earnings" of the road, as that term is to be understood in the sixth section of the act. The bonded debt incurred for the purpose of construction and equipment is but another form of capital, analogous to preferred stock; and the interest accruing thereon is in the nature of a dividend on such capital. It has nothing to do with, and cannot affect, the amount of the net earnings of the road.

So the expenses of land and town-lot departments, and taxes on lands and town lots, are expenses properly belonging to the
92 land department of the company's property. They are entirely distinct from its expenses as a railroad company; and form no proper charge, in the accounts, against the earnings of the road.

The other items disallowed by the court require no particular remark. Their irrelevancy in the account of net earnings is obvious....

The decree will be reversed with instructions to enter a decree in accordance with this opinion; and it is

So ordered.

PEOPLE v. VAIL

57 How. Prac. (N.Y.) 81 (1879)
Supreme Court of New York

WESTBROOK, *J.*—The defendant was the president of the Merchants and Mechanics' Bank of Troy. He is charged by an indictment, found by the grand jury of Rensselaer county, in November, 1878, with having committed perjury in the quarterly report made in behalf of the bank to the superintendent of the banking department, in September, 1878, in two particulars: first, in stating that the "largest aggregate of loans to any one individual, firm or corporation" was $49,221.55; and, second, in declaring the "aggregate of loans upon paper, made, accepted, or indorsed by directors individually, and as members of firms," was $42,004.21. 93

By chapter 218 of the Laws of 1843, and section 3 thereof, as amended by chapter 419 of the Laws of 1847, the quarterly report of the bank, "which report shall be made on the oath of the president and cashier" must "contain a true statement of the condition of the bank * * * making such report, before the transaction of any business on the morning of the day * * * next preceding the date of such report in respect to the following items and particulars, to wit: Loans and discounts * * * due from the directors of the bank, or banking association, making the report," &c., &c.

By statute (2 *Edmond's ed., p.* 701., *sec.* 1), when an oath is one of the character upon which the present alleged perjury is predicated, such oath or affirmation must be one "required by law," and it is claimed by counsel for the accused that the law prescribing what the bank report must contain, does not authorize the superintendent of the banking department to demand answers upon the points on which perjury has been assigned, and that, consequently, the indictment must fall. The point taken renders the examination of each of the alleged perjuries necessary.

First, could the bank be required to state in its report the largest loan to "any one individual, firm or corporation?" The counsel for the defendant argue it could not, and that all that the law requires is the gross aggregate of loans and discounts, and that no particulars thereof can be ordered. If this position is sound, is the letter of the statute, to say nothing of its spirit, complied with? The act is imperative ("shall" is the word used) in requiring the report to "contain a true statement of the *condition* of the bank" as to its "loans and discounts." A mere statement of the total of all "loans and discounts," without any thing more, would not give "a true statement of the condition of the bank" in that particular.

The whole sum might be loaned to a single individual, who was utterly insolvent, and in that case, with a report giving only the general aggregate of all loans, the light, which the public ought to have, and which the law evidently contemplates, would be withheld. Without deciding how much of a detailed statement as to its "loans and discounts" a bank may be required to make, we are clear in our judgment, that the superintendent of the banking department may call upon an institution to state in its report, in a general way, the largest loan made to "any one individual, firm or corporation," and that such information is necessary to show its "condition." The history of banking institutions, which have been wrecked by large loans to single individuals, or corporations, or firms, shows how vital the information sought actually was. It is possible that inquiries might be made, which would be so searching and thorough as to be beyond the intent of the statute, which was designed to secure a report for publication, but we cannot but think, that the act both in its letter and spirit requires something more than a mere statement of the sum total of all its "loans and discounts." Something which will show the "condition" of the bank in that respect, and the maximum of a loan to a single individual, firm or corporation, certainly is within the plain requirements of the law.

Second. Had the superintendent of the banking department the right to require the report of the bank to show the "aggregate of loans upon paper made, accepted or indorsed by directors individually or as members of firms?"

If the answer to this question depended upon the same provisions of the section of the act, upon which it has been already adjudged that the former requirement was warranted, we should hold that the superintendent had not transcended his power. The "condition" of the bank as to its "loans and discounts" would be but very imperfectly known, by a statement of the total of its loans, and the largest sum owing by an individual, firm or corporation, unless information was also imparted as to the indebtedness of directors. This is so palpable, and the evil to be guarded against, the absorbtion of an entire bank capital by one or more of its officers, so frequent, that no argument is needed to show the wisdom of demanding this information.

The section, however, still more plainly calls for just the

statement which was made. It requires the sum "*due* from the directors of the bank or banking association making the report" to be given therein. Language plainer than this could not have been employed. It cannot be plausibly argued, if the objects and purposes of the act be considered, that the word "*due*" is used in its narrow sense so as to require a statement only of such liabilities as had matured. It ought to have no such interpretation, for the public would then never know how officers were using the institution. The word, evidently, is used in its larger sense to signify and cover liabilities by the directors to the bank, whether matured or not. This (*see Webster's Dictionary*) is the general meaning of the word. And if this interpretation be given to it in the law, we can see the wisdom of the provision, which is not 95
apparent if its meaning be limited to obligations and liabilities which have matured and are immediately payable.

Our conclusion is clear, that the motion to quash cannot be granted. A trial may show the indictment to be untrue, but on this application its allegations must each and all be regarded as verities. The defendant is charged with making willfully false statements under oath, in regard to two matters, upon which the superintendent of banking required information. The application to quash is made upon the assumption, that the officers asked more than the law allowed. We are clear that he did not, and hence the motion cannot prevail....

In conformity with the stipulation the clerk will enter upon the minutes, as of the day of the argument, a denial of the motion to quash the indictment giving the defendant an exception to the decision ordering it.

Opinion concurred in by justices BUTTS and SLADE.

VAN DYKE v. McQUADE

86 N.Y. 39 (1881)

APPEAL from judgment of the General Term of the Superior Court of the city of New York, entered upon an order made the first Monday of May, 1879, which affirmed a judgment in favor of plaintiff, entered upon the report of a referee.

This action was brought by plaintiff, as receiver of the Yorkville Savings Bank of the city of New York, against defendant, as one of its trustees, to recover the amount of interest or dividend paid to depositors on the ground that, at the time the said dividends were declared and paid, there were no net profits, earnings or income out of which any dividend could lawfully be paid.

The material facts are stated in the opinion. . . .

DANFORTH, J. . . .

The respondent contends that this case may be supported under the provisions of more than one positive law. . . .

If, however, either of the statutes referred to ever had any force as applied to savings banks, they became as to those banks inoperative after the passage of the act of 1875, entitled "An act to conform the charters of all savings banks or institutions for savings to a uniformity of powers, rights and liabilities, and to provide for the organization of savings banks, for their supervision, and for the administration of their affairs." (Laws of 1875, chap. 371.) . . .

A more serious question and the only one, I think, of any difficulty is presented by the remaining proposition of the respondent's counsel, by which he seeks to bring the defendant within section 33 of this act. It is thereby made the duty of the trustees of such corporation to regulate the rate of interest or dividends so that the same shall not exceed six per cent per annum, permits them to classify their depositors, prohibits the payment of interest on deposits beyond the time of deposit, declares that "no dividends or interest shall be declared, credited or paid, except by the authority of a vote of the board of trustees duly entered upon their minutes, whereon shall be recorded the ayes and nays upon such vote, and whenever any interest or dividends shall be declared and credited in excess of the interest or profits earned and appearing to the credit of the corporation, the trustees voting for such dividend shall be jointly and severally liable to the corporation for the amount of such excess so declared and credited." . . .

The action is upon the theory that interest could be paid the depositors only from "net profits;" that payment except therefrom would not only be a misapplication of the funds of the bank, but a violation of the statute. (§ 33, *supra.*) This view was sustained by the referee, and is upon this appeal reasserted by the respondent's counsel. So far as this stands upon the common-law duty of a trustee, it is unnecessary to add to the suggestions already made as to his duty in providing for and declaring a payment of interest; but the plaintiff's claim cannot be assented to as a proposition of law or as one which, standing by itself, would be a rule of action. It would be different if fraud intended or attempted had been shown (*Ex. Pet. Co.* v. *Lacey*, 63 N. Y. 422), but
there is nothing of that kind in the plaintiff's favor, and we 97
agree with the remarks of Lord Justice SELWYN in *Stringer's Case* (L. R., 4 Ch. App. 477), that "if we were to lay down as a rule that there must be actually cash in hand to the full amount of the dividend declared, we should be laying down a rule which would be inconsistent with what I understand and believe to be the custom of all companies of this description, and also inconsistent with mercantile usage; and we should be laying down a rule which would open the door to and encourage a very great amount of litigation, because there are very few dividends indeed which would not be open to more or less question if such a rule as that were laid down." Nor do I think the statute (§ 33, *supra*) stands on such rule or contemplated the accumulation of net profits as the only source from which interest might be paid the depositor; and it is this which concerns us at this point of our inquiry It should be observed that such term, "net profits," is not used in the statute. The words are "interest or profits earned and appearing to the credit of the corporation." There is a difference between interest or profits "earned" and interest or profits "received." In any just transaction they must be earned before they are due, and when due they are earned, although not received, and are none the less earned, although never received. The statute uses these different words. In section 38 the report of the corporation must among other things state "the whole amount of interest received or earned and the amount of dividends credited to depositors." Now when we find in section 33 that the trustee does not overstep his statutory duty so long as he declares no interest or dividends beyond interest or profits "earned," it should be held that if by comparing the amount of interest earned with the dividend it appears the latter falls short of the former, he cannot be subjected to the penalty. He may inquire what interest has been earned, and does not

incur this penalty in declaring a dividend upon it as a basis, although it has not been actually received. We might, perhaps, take judicial notice that interest is usually made payable upon investments on the 1st of January and 1st of July, and as the interest is to go to the depositor at the same time and to be previously declared, the amount becoming due the bank would necessarily be looked to. But the defendant need not rely on that necessity. The referee has found that the interest actually received by the bank exceeded all interest or dividends declared or credited by it; and in regard to the particular declaration of interest I am considering (that of July, 1876) it appears that it was in the aggregate $475.96, while the earnings were $1,434.21, during the six months then ending. But
98 the referee, deducting the expenses, finds the net income insufficient, or that there is none. It would seem also, from the items required to be stated in the report, that the statutory scheme contemplated the dividend might lawfully be paid from the whole amount of interest or profits received, without first deducting the expenses. It must show, the statute says, "the whole amount of interest received or earned;" not calling for diminution by expenses; and then, the amount of dividends credited to depositors. The one is placed in juxtaposition with the other and no intermediary item. There is no finding, and upon the facts there could not be one, that the dividend was in excess of the profits earned. The term "net profits" or "interest" is quite different. It describes the remainder of income after deducting expenditures. In *The People* v. *Sup'rs of N. Y.* (18 Wend. 606), a case relating to taxation, and in which different statutes embodying the words "income or profits," with and without modifying words, are dealt with, NELSON, J., says: "It is apparent that the legislature in using the phrase "any profits or income" did not intend to convey the same idea as that indicated by the words "net income." Income and profits on one side, and expenditures on the other, furnish data from which may be ascertained "net income" or "net profits" —phrases well understood in common affairs, explained and applied by law writers (Story on Partnership, § 34) and by the courts, and recognized by the statutory words "clear profits" or "surplus profits."...

But for the reasons before mentioned the judgment of the General Term and that entered upon the report of the referee should be reversed and a new trial granted, with costs to abide the event.

ANDREWS, MILLER and FINCH, JJ., concur; FOLGER, Ch. J., and EARL, J., dissent. RAPALLO, J., absent from argument.

Judgment reversed.

LITTLE MIAMI & COLUMBUS & XENIA RAILROAD CO. v. UNITED STATES

108 U.S. 277 (1883)
Supreme Court of the United States

MR. CHIEF JUSTICE WAITE delivered the opinion of the court.

This was a suit begun by the United States on the 29th of March, 1875, to recover of the Little Miami and Columbus and Xenia Railroad Company a tax of five per cent. on alleged profits of the company "carried to the account of any fund or used in construction," provided for by the act of June 30th, 1864, c. 173, sec. 122, 13 Stat. 284, amended by the act of July 13th, 1866, c. 184, 14 Stat. 139. A jury was waived and the trial had by the court. The case comes here on a finding of facts. From this finding it appears "that during the period covered by the petition, viz., from the 1st day of July, 1864, to the 30th day of November, 1869, inclusive, the defendant, in good faith, regularly made returns of earnings, profits, income, and gains, and of profits carried to the account of any fund, or used for construction, arising or accruing to it during said period, intended and believed by it to embrace all such profits, incomes and gains, and all such profits carried to the account of any fund, or used for construction, which by law it was bound to return; which returns were received and accepted, and for the amount of which assessments from time to time were made of the taxes payable thereon, which taxes were regularly paid by it to the officer lawfully authorized by law to collect the same." In addition to this it also appears "that over and above the amount so returned, on which taxes were paid as aforesaid, the defendant did in fact make additional earnings, which by it were carried to the account of some fund, or used for construction during said period, amounting in all to the sum of $168,707.22, on which no tax has been paid."

The finding also shows that during the year 1869 the defendant carried to the debit of profit and loss on its books, various items amounting in all to $184,395.06. In this way the books show no profits between July 1st, 1864, and November 30th, 1869, beyond the amount on which taxes were paid in the regular course of business. Of the sum so charged up, one item of $51,155.44 was for loss and depreciation on book accounts and other choses in action, acquired by the company prior to July 1st, 1864, and which had been standing on the books until 1869 at their par value; another item of $22,000 was for the depreciation in the value of bonds purchased after July 1st, 1864; another item of $106,014.62 was for the depreciation in the value of what was known as the "street connection track," and another item for $5,225 was for losses on a purchase in 1867 of shares of capital stock in a cotton-press company.

Upon these facts, so found, the company claimed that, in ascertaining the amount of profits liable to taxation, there should be deducted from the earnings during the period for which the tax was claimed these several items of loss and depreciation, but the court ruled, as a matter of law, "that for the purpose of taxation the defendant is not entitled by law to make the deduction as claimed," and gave judgment for five per cent. on the whole sum of $168,707.22.

In our opinion there was error in this ruling. The tax in
100 question is not upon *earnings* "carried to the account of any fund or used for construction," but upon *profits*. Earnings used to pay interest or dividends are taxable, whether actual profits or not, but earnings used for construction, or carried to the account of a fund, are not to be taxed, unless they represent profits of the company in its business as a whole, that is to say, the excess of the aggregate of gains from all sources, over the aggregate of losses. The law evidently contemplated an annual statement of accounts, and in this way an annual striking of balances between gains and losses. When, in such statements, it appeared that a part of the excess of gains over losses had been used for construction or added to some fund, then a tax was to be paid on what had been so used or appropriated. This was part of the system adopted for the taxation of the "profits, income, or gains" of railroad corporations, which, as was said in *Railroad Company* v. *Collector*, 100 U. S. 595, it was the object of this statute to provide. A tax was put on dividends, interest paid in the ordinary way, and *profits* used for construction or carried to some fund. This was a classification of the income of the corporation for the purposes of taxation.

In the present case there has been no assessment of a tax, but the United States have sued to recover such sum as, upon an investigation of the accounts of the company, it shall appear ought to have been paid. The burden of proof is upon the government. No more can be recovered than is shown to be due. In presenting the evidence no attempt seems to have been made by the United States to state annual accounts and ascertain the amount to be paid on that basis. The court has found that between July 1st, 1864, and November 30th, 1869, earnings to the amount of $168,707.22 had been used for construction or carried to the account of some fund, but it has also found that between the same dates the company lost $22,000 by depreciation in its investments in bonds, and $5,225 by depreciation in the stock of a cotton-press company. In the view we take of the law, these sums should have been deducted from the earnings as ascertained before fixing the amount of profits on which the tax was to be paid. It is not stated with certainty in the finding at what dates the losses actually occurred which are represented by the items of $51,155.44, depreciation in the value of book accounts and choses in action, and $106,014.62, depreciation in the value of the street connection track. For this reason we are unable to decide whether these losses, or any part of them, should be deducted. As the omission to make the finding sufficiently specific in this particular undoubtedly arose from the fact that the court ruled as a matter of law that no deductions could be made on account of losses of this character, we will remand the cause, so that further inquiry may be had on that point. This we have authority to do under section 701 of the Revised Statutes, which allows a cause to be remanded for "such further proceedings to be had in the inferior court as the justice of the case may require."

The judgment of the circuit court is reversed and the cause remanded, with instructions to deduct from the amount of earnings, as ascertained upon the former trial, the items of $22,000, *depreciation in the value of bonds, and* $5,225, *depreciation in the value of cotton-press stock, together with such other sums included in the items of* $51,155.44, *depreciation in book accounts and choses in action, and* $106,014.62, *depreciation in value of the street connection track, as, upon further hearing, shall be found to represent losses accruing to the company between July* 1*st*, 1864, *and November* 30*th*, 1869, *and to render judgment only for such an amount of tax as shall appear to be due upon that basis.*

WILLIAMS v. WESTERN UNION TELEGRAPH COMPANY

16 Jones & Spencer (N.Y.) 349 (1882)

By the Court.—Freedman, J.—This action is brought by the plaintiff as a stockholder of the Western Union Telegraph Company against the said company, its directors, and the Union Trust Company, to obtain an adjudication determining that a certain agreement made by the Western Union Telegraph Company with the American Union and the Atlantic and Pacific Telegraph Companies, is void, and for relief
102 not only against the agreement and its execution as being beyond the powers of the telegraph companies, but to the extent of reaching the personal liability of the directors of the Western Union Telegraph Co. The Union Trust Co. was made a party defendant because it had been selected as a trustee for carrying out the agreement. The agreement is dated January 19, 1881, and it provides for the purchase by the Western Union Telegraph Co. of the property, rights, and franchises (except the franchise to be a corporation) of the American Union and the Atlantic and Pacific Telegraph Co.'s at the price of $15,000,000 for the property, &c., of the American Union, and $8,400,000 for the property, &c., of the Atlantic and Pacific Telegraph Co., payable in the capital stock of the Western Union Co. As no stock of that company was on hand to make payment with, it was provided in the agreement that the capital stock of the company should be increased as follows, viz.:

"The Western Union Telegraph Company shall take such proceedings as it may be advised to cause its capital stock to be increased by an addition to its present outstanding stock of $38,926,590, represented by shares of $100 each, and shall issue and deliver the same to the said Union Trust Company for distribution as follows: $15,526,590 to holders of its present shares, the same being to represent its investment of earnings in the purchase, construction and equipment of additional lines, wires and general plant since the first day of July, 1866, and the remaining sum of $23,400,000 for the acquisition of new lines, property and connections in the manner above provided.

"In addition to the new stock above provided to be delivered to Western Union Company shareholders, the amount of $58,855.50, parcel of the present capital stock of said company, owned by it and now in its treasury, shall be distributed in like manner to its shareholders."...

In the next place, in order to overcome the objection that there was no formal exercise of the discretion and judgment of the directors as to what was the value of the investments at the time of the agreement in question, it was shown that on March 26, 1881, a meeting of the board of directors of the Western Union Telegraph Co. was duly held, at which a resolution was unanimously passed fixing the actual value of the property on hand and representing the investments at the time of the making of the agreement, and at the time of the said meeting, exclusive of interest and exclusive of the shares of the capital stock of the Atlantic and Pacific Telegraph Co. then owned by the Western Union Co., to be worth much more than the sum of $15,526,590, and formally declaring a dividend payable in certificates of stock to the extent of the sum last named.

In the third place, considerable additional evidence was given which, it was claimed, clearly established that the value thus fixed and determined upon was, at the times named, and still is, in point of fact fully equal to the nominal value of the certificates so proposed to be divided. The learned judge who tried the case, came to the conclusion that the evidence supported the claim, and he found the fact accordingly. ... The case made at the trial being as stated, unless the finding can be disturbed that the value on hand representing investments of past earnings, exclusive of interest and of the shares of the capital stock of the Atlantic and Pacific Co. then owned by the Western Union Co. on January 19, 1881, was in point of fact fully equal to the nominal aggregate value of the certificates proposed to be divided among the then shareholders of the Western Union Co. the present appeal presents the naked question of law, whether the said agreement of January 19, 1881, is contrary to law.

The examination of this question involves an inquiry into the power of corporations generally, and of telegraph companies in particular, and especially into the power to declare and pay so-called stock dividends....

Ordinarily, the law requires that additional stock to be issued by a corporation shall be paid for. This power of disposition the directors are to use in trust. They are trustees and are bound to use the power not only as directed specifically by statute, but under the general obligation of trustees to *cestui que trusts*. The duty of the trustees is to dispose of the shares in such a manner that value shall be returned for them to the corporation for its business purposes. Such would be the intent of any statute conferring in general terms the power to increase the capital to an amount in dollars, and such is, as was pointed out by the learned Chief Judge in determining the motion for an injunction, the implication contained in the act of 1875.

The terms of the agreement of January 19, 1881, do not provide or contemplate, nor was provision made in any other way, that the distribution of the new shares among the company's own shareholders should be made upon equivalent value being returned or promised to be returned by the shareholders, nor, indeed, upon any new value to the company. The agreement is sought to be upheld upon the theory that the shares to be distributed represent the company's investments of earnings in the purchase, construction, and equipment of additional lines, wires, and general plant since July 1, 1866, and that, as these earnings are or were due to or should have been divided among the shareholders, an acceptance of stock that represents them will be a release by the shareholders of the earnings, and is the
104 same in effect as if there had been a severance of the earnings from the other property of the corporation and a delivery to the shareholders, and a return to the company in the shape of capital. This theory would, upon the facts of this case, be open to no objection, so long as the scheme involved in it has the requisite sanction of a certain proportion of shareholders, if there were no statutory obstacle to it. But in its advocacy the respondents are confronted with the following statute of this State, viz.: "It shall not be lawful for the directors or managers of any incorporated company in this State to make dividends, excepting from the surplus profits arising from the business of such corporation; and it shall not be lawful for the directors of any such company to divide, withdraw, or in any way pay to the stockholders, or any of them, any part of the capital stock of such company, or to reduce the said capital stock, without the consent of the legislature, &c., &c." (2 *Rev. St.* 5 ed. p. 599, § 2; 7 ed. p. 1530, § 2.)

It seems too clear for argument that in the face of that statute, the issue of the stock to the shareholders of the Western Union Co. cannot be upheld as a dividend from surplus profits, because the profits were no longer on hand. They were converted into other property. Even if such other property remained, and still is, of equal value, it nevertheless took the place of the profits. It became capital. Unless otherwise provided by the charter or by-laws of a corporation, the profits and surplus funds of a corporation, whenever they have accrued, are, until separated from the capital by the declaration of a dividend, a part of the stock itself, and will pass with the stock under this name in a transfer or bequest (Iron Co. *v.* Commonwealth, 55 *Penn.* 451; Brundage *v.* Brundage, 1 *T. & C.* 90; Phelps *v.* Bank 26 *Conn.* 269).

If such other property deteriorated in value, the further objection would be that to that extent vanished earnings are sought to be replaced by paying out capital....

On the other hand, it seems to be equally clear, from what has already been said, that in that case, after such increase and re-divison was made, the $15,526,590 of stock, constituted part of the capital stock of the Western Union Co., in the treasury of the company, and as such could have been sold in the market, on account of, and for the benefit of the company. They therefore represented and constituted property, and not mere paper. Consequently, when the Western Union Co. attempted to distribute that part of its capital stock among its own shareholders, without any new consideration, the attempt involved a division, withdrawal and payment of part of the capital stock without the consent of the legislature, within the prohibition of the statute....

Even if the assumption be continued that the property repre- 105
senting the investments of past earnings was really worth $15,526,590, and that in view of that fact, no valid objection to the agreement will lie under chapter 568 of the Laws of 1870, and that in other respects the agreement as a whole is not in essential particulars in excess of the authority conferred by said chapter,—as to which matters I express no opinion and which it becomes unnecessary to determine,—yet the construction to be given to the statute forbidding the declaration of dividends except from surplus profits, and prohibiting the division, &c., of capital without the consent of the legislature, being as stated, and no such consent having been found to exist, the plaintiff has demonstrated that the proposed gratuitous division of $15,526,590 of stock among the shareholders of the Western Union Co., is wholly illegal....

ARNOUX, J.— . . .

1st. Was the agreement to issue stock as a dividend to represent the accretions to the capital of the Western Union Telegraph Company legal?...

Now conceding that there had been net earnings that had been converted into capital, and that the law permitted the increase of stock, this, under the law as laid down by Pierce, afforded no authority to the board of Directors of the Western Union Telegraph Company to issue the stock in question. They did have the power to sell any surplus property belonging to the corporation, and when such sale was made, to distribute the cash proceeds among its stockholders. But the transaction attempted was very different from this, and the temptation to play fast and loose with the stockholders, to put their earnings into stock at one time to the prejudice of those holders who depend upon their income, and to declare a stock dividend at another time, when the directors or their friends have sufficient control, is too great for many men to resist or to be overlooked and not prevented by the courts.

There is another evil that the courts must recognize. It is not only the watering of stocks, so called, but the increase of capital by withholding dividends from the stockholders, to build up the corporation beyond its original purpose, so that, from insignificant beginnings, such corporations increase to gigantic proportions, wielding enormous influence for evil in the hands of unprincipled men. The statutes against limitations and perpetuities demonstrate our State's hostility to any such accumulations, and it is equally contrary to public policy to have such overgrown and despotic corporations in our midst. The opposition to such corporations is extending throughout the land, and is concreting into an anti-monopoly league.

We are, therefore, led to the conclusion that it was not lawful for the directors of the Western Union Telegraph Company to declare a stock dividend to represent accumulated earnings of the company....

WILLIAMS v. WESTERN UNION TELEGRAPH COMPANY

93 N.Y. 162 (1883)

EARL, J. . . .

The actual value of the investments of the surplus earnings of the defendant, the Western Union Telegraph Company, as they existed January 19, 1881, was estimated by the directors of the company; and it was their judgment that the amount of the stock to be distributed among the stockholders of the Western Union *179] Telegraph Company represented no more than *the investments of the surplus earnings of the company since July 1, 1866; and such surplus earnings were worth the sum of over $15,526,590. . . .

The stock dividend was claimed to be in violation of chapter 18, part 1, title 4, section 2 of the Revised Statutes, which provides as follows: "It shall not be lawful for the directors or managers of any incorporated company in this State to make dividends excepting from the surplus profits arising from the business of such corporation; and it shall not be lawful for the directors of any such company to divide, withdraw, or in any way pay to the stockholders, or any of them, any part of the capital stock of such company, or to reduce the said capital stock without the consent of the legislature; . . . . These provisions were intended to prevent the division, distribution, withdrawal and reduction of the property of a corporation below the sum limited in its charter or articles of association for its capital, but not to prevent its increase above that sum. The purpose was to prevent the depletion of the property of the corporation thereby endangering its solvency. All the other provisions of the section show very clearly that such was the intention. Careful provision was made that the whole amount of capital stock should be paid in, and hence there was a prohibition against *188] *receiving a note or other evidence of debt in payment of any installment actually called in and required to be paid; and in case the directors violated any of the provisions of the section they were made individually liable to the corporation and to its creditors, in the event of its dissolution, to the full amount of the capital stock of the company so divided, withdrawn or reduced. All these provisions show that it was the purpose of the legislature, by means of them, to create a property capital for the corporation, and then to keep that

intact so as to secure the solvency of the corporation and its responsibility to its creditors. The "capital stock" in this section does not mean share stock, but it means the property of the corporation contributed by its stockholders or otherwise obtained by it, to the extent required by its charter. While the term "capital stock" is frequently used in a loose and indefinite sense, in this section and in legal phrase generally it means that and no more. In *State* v. *Morristown Fire Association* (3 Zabr. 195), GREEN, Ch. J., said: "The phrase 'capital stock' is very generally, if not universally, used to designate the amount of capital to be contributed for the purposes of the corporation. The amount thus contributed constitutes the 'capital stock' of the company." In *Burrall*
108 v. *Bushwick R. R. Co.* (75 N. Y. 211), FOLGER, J., defined "capital stock" as "that money or property which is put in a single corporate fund by those who by subscription therefor become members of a corporate body." In *Barry* v. *Merchants' Exchange Co.* (1 Sandf. Ch. 280), Vice-Chancellor SANFORD said: "The capital stock of a corporation is like that of a copartnership or joint-stock company, the amount which the partners or associates put in as their stake in the concern." By loss or misfortune, or misconduct of the managing officers of a corporation, its capital stock may be reduced below the amount limited by its charter; but whatever property it has up to that limit must be regarded as its capital stock. When its property exceeds that limit, then the excess is surplus. Such surplus belongs to the corporation and is a portion of its property, and, in a general sense, may be regarded as a portion of its capital, but in a strictly legal sense it is not *a portion of its capital, and is always regarded as [*189
surplus profits. The very section we are considering contemplates that there may be a surplus, and that such surplus may be divided. The surplus may be in cash, and then it may be divided in cash; it may be in property, and if the property is so situated that a division thereof among the stockholders is practicable, a dividend in property may be declared, and that may be distributed among stockholders. All such dividends diminish and deplete the property of the corporation, and that section was designed to prevent dividends of property which tended to deplete the assets of the company below the sum limited in its charter as the amount of its capital stock. But stock dividends never diminish or interfere with the property of a corporation, and hence are not within the purview of that section. After a stock dividend a corporation has just as much property as it had before. It is

just as solvent and just as capable of meeting all demands upon it. After such a dividend the aggregate of the stockholders own no more interest in the corporation than before. The whole number of shares before the stock dividend represented the whole property of the corporation, and after the dividend they represent that and no more. A stock dividend does not distribute property, but simply dilutes the shares as they existed before; and hence that section in no way prevented or related to a stock dividend. Such a dividend could be declared by a corporation without violating its letter, its spirit or its purpose. It is, therefore, clear that the directors of the Western Union Telegraph Company did not violate that section by the stock dividend which they de-
clared; and if that dividend was illegal it must be because it 109
was condemned by some other statute, or by some general principle of law or by public policy....

There is no public policy which in all cases, condemns such
*190] dividends. Shares having been legally brought into existence may be distributed among the stockholders of a company. By such distribution no harm is done to any person, provided the dividend is not a mere inflation of the stock of the company, with no corresponding values to answer to the stock distributed. It may be that a distribution of stock gratuitously to the stockholders of a company based upon no values, a mere inflation, or, to use a phrase much in vogue, a watering of stock, would be condemned by the law. But when stock has been lawfully created and is held by a corporation, which it has a right to issue for value, then a stock dividend may be made, provided that the stock always represents property. It is conceded that the directors of the Western Union Telegraph Company could have issued this stock for money to be paid into its treasury. It could have issued it for property to be received by it for the purposes of its legitimate business. But here it is found that over and above its capital it possessed property actually worth upwards of $15,000,000, and we know of no law that is violated, and no public policy that is invaded by issuing to the stockholders stock to represent that amount of property rather than in any mode to divide it up and distribute it among them. If it can issue stock in payment of property to be obtained by it as part of its capital for its legitimate uses, why may it not issue stock to its stockholders in payment for property in effect purchased of them and added to its permanent capital, and which they relinquish the right to have divided? So long as every dollar of stock issued by a corporation is

represented by a dollar of property, no harm can result to individuals or the public from distributing the stock to the stockholders. . . .

It is true that this dividend largely increases the capital stock of the company, but that is not against the policy of our laws. That cannot be against the policy of the law which the law expressly permits. There is no limit to the capital which business corporations in this State may have, and there is no limit in the law beyond which they may not increase their capital. All that can be required in any case is that there shall be an actual capital in property representing the amount of share capital issued. . . .

We are, therefore, of opinion upon the facts, found at Spe-
110 cial Term, that the stock dividend was authorized by law and, therefore, valid. . . .

JENNERY v. OLMSTEAD

36 Hun. (N.Y.) 536 (1885)
[affirmed on opinion below
105 N.Y. 654 (1887)]

Appeal by the defendants from a judgment for $952.06 damages and $413.16 costs against them and in favor of the plaintiff, entered in the Saratoga county clerk's office on the 6th day of October, 1883, upon the verdict of a jury.

This action was brought upon a bond given by the defendant Olmstead as principal, and Clement as surety, to the Saratoga Savings Bank, conditioned for the faithful performance by Olmstead of his duties as president and general actuary of said bank. The Saratoga Savings Bank was an institution doing business at Saratoga Springs, incorporated under chapter 626 of the Laws of 1867. On the 19th day of August, 1867, the defendant Olmstead was elected president and general actuary of this bank, the resolution fixing his compensation providing "that as compensation for his services in that capacity he receive such sum or sums from the net profits of the institution as such profits, after paying all incidental expenses, may warrant, not to exceed $1,000 per annum." On the day following Olmstead's election he qualified by giving the bond upon which the action is brought, and entered upon his duties as such officer, and continued to act as such until January 14, 1873, and continued in charge of the bank until February 10, 1873. Previous to or on the 1st day of January, 1873, Olmstead drew out of the funds of the bank $931.85, which he charged to himself on that day as cash, and on the 10th day of February, 1873, the further sum of $424.99, also charged to himself on that day as cash.

The action was once before tried, when the plaintiff recovered $1,038.88, with costs. This was affirmed by the General Term, but reversed by the Court of Appeals, that court holding, in opposition to the views of the Supreme Court, that although no provision was made in the contract of employment for annual rests, yet a reasonable construction of the resolution was, that if profits were earned in any one year, Olmstead was entitled to them as salary, irrespective of losses occurring in subsequent years of his administration; and that as the trial court had found that there was at one time during his service a surplus of $648.43, he was entitled, on the proof as it then stood, to deduct that amount from any sum which it might be found that he had subsequently taken. The Court of Appeals held further, that the $424.99 taken by Olmstead, February 10, 1873, could not be recovered in this action, for the reason that after January 14, 1873, Olmstead's relation to the bank was changed from that of president and general actuary, which offices he held when the bond was given, and became that of a mere custodian, and that any breach of duty in that capacity was not covered by the terms of the bond. Upon the trial it was conceded by the defendants that no profits were made by the bank in any year but 1869, and proof was offered by them to show that July 1, 1869, the bank had a surplus of $648.43.

M. Hale and *E. F. Bullard*, for the appellants.

E. T. Brackett, for the respondent.

112 Peckham, J.:

The chief question in this case is whether the bank made any profits in the year 1869, from which, under the agreement between the parties, the salary of the president could be paid. The defendants contend that there were profits to the amount of $648.43, while the plaintiff claims that there were none. The method by which the sum above mentioned is arrived at is by taking the difference between the purchase-price and the market value of certain government bonds then owned by the bank (the value of the bonds having in the meantime appreciated), and calling that appreciation in value profits. The method pursued by the plaintiff was to take the actual cost of the bonds, add to that the accrued interest on the coupons yet unpaid, and call the total the value of the bonds By this means a difference in the value of the bonds was made in the sum of $503, being that amount less than made by the defendants.

Both plans, it is perceived, take it as proper to obtain the value of the bonds, although unsold, as a means of deciding upon the profits. I agree to the correctness of neither plan. It is not a proper way to ascertain the fact of profits to estimate the value of bonds yet unsold and upon finding the estimated value to exceed the price paid, to call the difference profits. It is not profits in any true sense of that term. If the bonds were actually sold at such price, the transaction would then be completed and the profits actually realized instead of merely estimated.

It does not appear that defendant's counsel treats the method pursued by defendants as showing actual, realized profits, but he terms them estimated profits, and argues that the contract meant estimated profits instead of actual realized profits, for otherwise he claims that every piece of property of the bank would have to be sold annually in order to determine whether profits were made, which he very sensibly states would be absurd. The trouble with this mode of reasoning lies in the confusion of property with profits. To take an inventory of all the property of the bank and to place a valuation on it, and from it to deduct its liabilities, is perfectly proper in order to arrive at the financial standing of the bank as to solvency, and if solvent, how much beyond it the institution may be deemed to be.

Here was a savings bank without capital stock, and with but one resource at first from which to obtain money, viz., deposits, upon which it must pay interest. The means of profit to it were simply the possibility of so investing these moneys as to obtain a greater return for them than the bank was to pay by way of interest, and in a possible sale of securities or property purchased at a greater price than was paid for them or it. It could not have been contemplated by the parties to the contract that the president should have a right to demand the sale of any property at any particular time for the mere reason that a sale would then result in a profit, and thus possibly insure him a salary for that year.

The purchase and sale of stocks, as a business and for a profit, is not contemplated as pertaining to a savings bank; and in this case, by the very terms of the charter, only certain securities could be invested in, and could only be sold by the concurrence of a majority of the trustees. The investment in government bonds is assumed to partake of the character of a permanent investment; and in order to determine the profits of the year it is not necessary either to sell the securities or to estimate their value. The profits are, as I have said, the amount of money received by the bank from its investments, by way of interest, over and above the amount of interest it has to pay its depositors, together with the amount of any money it had received by the sale of property over and above its cost to the bank. If such a sale had been made, then a profit had arisen, but if not, then no profit had accrued simply from the fact that the property, if sold, would have resulted in a profit. It is as yet an uncompleted transaction, and with not the slightest right on the part of the president to demand its completion in order that he may earn his salary. As I have said, such right could not have been contemplated by the parties to this contract; and in case of non-sale, there exists no right to estimate what the profits would have been if the property had been sold and call that a profit made in that year. Suppose the property were soon after sold at a loss, the result would show that there had been no profit, but an actual loss, yet the president had received his salary on the basis of a profit. There is no reason, therefore, that I can see why the contract should be read as if it had said that the salary of the president should be based upon the estimated profits of each year.

It is plain that the same rule does not obtain to the full extent in the case of a loss, for a loss may be sustained without a sale of the property. It may deteriorate permanently and plainly in value, or may be burned up or stolen. In brief, if anything happen by which the bank sustains plainly and permanently a depreciation in, or total obliteration of, the value of property, such depreciation or obliteration must be regarded as a loss sustained, and such loss must be deducted from the profits before a net profit can be arrived at.
114 This is wholly distinct from adding a possible profit by the sale of property, if then sold, to the actual realized profits otherwise made, and at the same time keeping the property.

In the one case property has been permanently depreciated in value, or actually destroyed, and the amount of such depreciation or destruction is an actual realized loss, while in the other it is simply a fact that if the property were then sold a profit would be made, but as it is not, *non constat* that when sold a loss may not be met with.

It is claimed that profits are substantially realized by this appreciation in the value of government bonds, if the bonds are unsold, just as much as if they were sold. If unsold, it is said that the value of the bond is as well known by a simple reference to the reports of the stock market as it would be by an actual sale, and that if sold, all that is got in exchange is another article, whose value may also fluctuate from time to time, and hence there is no sense in demanding an actual sale of the bond before asserting a realization of a profit. Nevertheless the bond unsold is only called worth so many dollars, according to the market price thereof, whereas the bond when sold has actually brought so many dollars, and these dollars are in money, which is a standard of value, made so by law, and that money is now on hand.

It can now be determined as a fact whether a profit had been made, notwithstanding the other fact that in long periods of time the standard of value itself varies in its own intrinsic value. I therefore, in order to see what profits were made in the year 1869, reject wholly from the account the appreciation in the market price of the government bonds on the day the balance was struck. That appreciation was the sum of $648.43, and without that there was no profit.

The court erred, therefore, in leaving it to the jury to say whether there were profits in 1869 or not. The error did not harm the defendants, for the judge should have decided, as matter of law, that there were no profits, at least so far as this bond transaction was concerned.

The Court of Appeals has only held that as it appeared there were profits in 1869, the President was entitled to take his salary for that year out of them. The question now discussed has not been in any way passed upon by that court. The evidence in the case is, that when the term of service of the president expired, in looking over the books it appeared that the assets of the bank were less than its liabilities by $931.85, and more than that sum the defendant Olmstead had drawn for himself. *Prima facie* it would appear as if the bond he gave had been violated by his drawing money under such circumstances, when to draw it left the bank insolvent. He therefore attempted to explain it. One explanation was that this deficit only appeared by striking out this estimated profit by the appreciation in government bonds, and taking the method adopted on the part of the plaintiff relative to that subject and above described. But we hold such item ought to be struck out, and the defendant shows no justification thereby in drawing from the bank the amount above stated. As to the other amounts claimed they seemed to have been submitted to the jury fairly by the judge, and I do not see that from the testimony there was any such question in regard thereto as to show any error on the part of the judge by such submission. The condition of the bond signed by the defendants was that Mr. Olmstead should "well, truly, honestly and faithfully" perform his duties as actuary, etc.

The defendants claim no breach of the bond had been proved, because at most the drafts made by defendant Olmstead were made by reason of a mistaken construction on his part of his rights under the contract, and that there was no dishonesty or fraud in the matter.

His bond held him to a faithful performance of his duties. It surely cannot be said that he faithfully performed them when he took moneys which he had no right to take, although he took them under a mistaken belief that he had such right. It is not a mistake in bookkeeping, or in figures, or any other mere mistake resulting in his doing what he did not intend to do. He intended the very act he did, viz.: the drawing of this money, although by reason of his erroneous construction of the law he thought he was entitled so to do. In so doing he did not faithfully perform his duties. He may have thought he did, and he may have intended to, but the fact remains that he did not, and his failure resulted, as I have said, from no mistake which would in law operate as an excuse.

If, upon consultation with the trustees, there had been a mutual agreement as to the value of the property, and that it need not be sold, but an amount agreed upon as profits without such sale, then the defendant might have drawn the amount provided it did not exceed $1,000. No such case is here presented. But in regard to the Dorner lot this method seems to have obtained. This court, upon a former appeal, decided in regard to that matter, and it must be regarded as a final disposition of the question so far as we are concerned.

It may have been erroneous to call a witness on the stand and ask him what the books prove as to any disputed fact. But the only issue as to what the books showed was not regarding their contents.
116 All agreed as to that. It was only as to how to treat the value of these bonds. And that question was fully discussed and no mistake made as to the contents of the books by either side.

Upon certain facts, substantially undisputed, the simple question was whether profits had or had not been made, and nothing in the books obscured or threw light upon that question, which was not fully known and discussed by both sides. Under these circumstances no harm was done in allowing the general question.

I think there were no errors upon the trial which resulted in any injury to defendants, and the judgment should be affirmed, with costs.

BOCKES, J.:

I concur for affirmance. I do not think there is any error in the record of which the defendants can complain.

LEARNED, P. J. (dissenting):

The contract between the bank and Olmstead was that, in compensation for his services, he should "receive such sum or sums from the net profits of the institution as such profits, after paying all incidental expenses, may warrant, not exceeding $1,000 per annum."

When the case was before this court on a former appeal, the court thought that, in estimating these profits, the whole period of five years, during which Olmstead was in the employment of the bank, should be taken into account without making annual rests, and reducing the profits of one year by the losses of a subsequent year. It was, however, held by the Court of Appeals (90 N. Y., 363) that this was not the true construction of the contract; that the contract was to pay the sum of $1,000 "in annual payments out of the profits of the preceding year if earned;" that if profits were "earned he was entitled to be paid, and the bank could not charge against the profits of one year the losses of a succeeding year." The decision necessarily implies two things: First. That the profits of each year can be, and should be, determined at its end. Second. That when so determined they are not to be affected (as to this contract) by subsequent losses.

Now, as this institution was a savings bank, the duty of which was to invest its money, and keep it invested in securities, it is not to be supposed that the parties to the contract contemplated a sale every year of the securities of the bank, in order to determine what the profits of the year had been. It must have been contemplated that, without any such sale, the parties could annually ascertain how much the nets profits of the year had been.

Without making such a sale, there is no way of determining the amount of profits except by a comparison of the assets with the liabilities. And it seems to be agreed upon, on both sides, that such a comparison was proper and necessary, in order to carry out the contract as interpreted by the Court of Appeals. For it must be noticed that the question is one *under the contract;* that is how, *under the contract*, is it to be ascertained whether the net profits in any given year "warrant" Olmstead's receipt of any salary? By using the word "warrant" the parties meant that the payment of Olmstead's annual compensation should not reduce, at the time of payment, the assets below the liabilities. The only way to determine what the net profits would "warrant," at the end of any year, was to ascertain the value of the assets and to deduct therefrom the liabilities. This would show the total net profits. Deducting from that sum the net profits of the preceding year (if any remained after paying Olmstead), the residue would be the net profits of the year in question.

Olmstead was appointed August 19, 1867. We judge that nothing was shown as to the profits of the first year.

On July 1, 1869, there is a statement which shows an excess of assets over liabilities of $648.43. The Court of Appeals say that there is no evidence that any of this was lost before August 20, 1869. It does not appear how much of this was made in 1868 and how much in 1869. But it is assumed by the Court of Appeals, and by the learned justice at the circuit, that this sum is to be taken as the net profits of the year ending August 20, 1869; unless errors or improper calculation should be shown, as hereafter mentioned.

Now, in regard to this statement, the important question arises as follows: Among the assets were $6,000 in United States six per cent bonds. They cost $6,540, according to the statement. They were inventoried in the statement at their market value at that time, viz., $7,170. The plaintiff claims (in order to deprive Olmstead of part of his compensation for that year), that the bonds should be estimated thus:

Cost of bonds	$6,420 28
Accrued coupons, $180 gold, worth	246 15
Total	$6,666 43

118

By this estimate the value of the bonds is reduced by $503.57, and, of course, the net profits are reduced by the same sum.

The plaintiff admits that the net profits are to be ascertained by a comparison of assets with liabilities, but he insists that in making that comparison the bonds should be estimated at just what they cost. Suppose, however, that the bonds, since their purchase, had depreciated to fifty per cent of their cost, would it have been just to estimate them still at cost and to allow Mr. Olmstead compensation on that basis? This would be to pay him a salary out of supposed net profits, when, in fact, the bank might not be able to pay its liabilities. A depreciation in market value is no more real than an increase in market value. If these bonds had fallen to fifty per cent in the market, Olmstead could not have had them estimated in the statement at the cost price.

The Court of Appeals have distinctly said that the bank, under this contract, cannot charge against the profits of one year the losses of a succeeding year. They must have anticipated the suggestion made by the plaintiff's counsel, viz., that the bonds might subsequently depreciate, so that in the end there would be in this investment no profits. And they have said that the subsequent losses shall not, under the contract, take away the right to compensation.

If the net profits are to be determined (as the plaintiff admits) by deducting liabilities from assets, why should the bonds be estimated at what they cost? The question is, what are "the net profits of *the institution;* and those are determined by finding out how much more it has than it owes. Suppose Olmstead, on the 20th of August, 1869, had sold these United States bonds; he would have received for them $7,170. And the plaintiff admits that in that case the net profits of the institution would on that day have been just what Olmstead now claims them to have been. Then suppose that the next day Olmstead had bought the same amount of bonds for $7,170. The bank would then be in precisely the same condition in which it actually was without any such sale and purchase. It could not be denied that if he had done this "the net profits of the institution" would have been $648.43. Is it a sound construction of the contract to say that by such a sale and purchase he would have become entitled to compensation to which he is not entitled? 119

We must remember that the question is only as to a mode of determining compensation for services. Are not Olmstead's services shown to be valuable when an investment which he made has increased in value? Does not the actual condition of the bank at the end of each year furnish the basis to which the parties had reference in their contract? What difference whether the assets of the bank are in cash on hand or in investments? The point is, how much are the assets?

As to the Dorner lot, the resolution is not very clear. The learned justice was right in holding that the parties could agree as to its value for the purpose of estimating profits, and was also right in holding that the resolution did not have the effect of such an agreement.

But it may be remarked that if an agreement between the trustees and Olmstead as to the value of property would be material in determining net profits *without any sale*, it would seem that proof of actual value would be equally effectual.

Another point which has not been argued may be suggested. In estimating net profits the plaintiff deducts the dividends paid to the depositors. The bank could declare such rate of dividend as it chose. If these dividends were to be deducted in order to determine the net profits, it would seem that under this construction the bank might make dividends which would consume all the profits and leave nothing with which to compensate Mr. Olmstead.

I think the defendant was entitled to have the bonds estimated at market value. This would make a difference in defendant's favor of $503.57. If plaintiff stipulates to deduct that I think judgment should be affirmed; otherwise, reversed.

Judgment affirmed, with costs.

PARK v. GRANT LOCOMOTIVE WORKS

40 N.J. Eq. 114 (1885)
Court of Chancery, New Jersey
[affirmed on opinion below
45 N.J. Eq. 244]

VAN FLEET, V. C. This suit is brought by the complainants, as stockholders of the Grant Locomotive Works, to compel the payment of a further or greater dividend than that which the directors of the corporation have declared. The complainants sue, not only for themselves, but for all other stockholders standing in the same right that they do. In February, 1875, a suit was commenced in this court against the Grant
120 Locomotive Works, to wind it up as an insolvent corporation. A receiver was appointed, and the corporation enjoined from exercising any of its powers. The debts of the corporation at that time far exceeded in amount the value of its assets. There can be no doubt that it was hopelessly insolvent. Some of its creditors were secured by mortgage, and others were merely simple contract creditors. In June, 1875, an agreement in writing was made by all persons having an interest in the corporation, either as creditors or stockholders, the design of which was to restore to the corporation the property then in the hands of the receiver, in order that it might be enabled to resume its business. The agreement provides—*First*, for the clearing of the property of the corporation from incumbrances, by the cancellation of the mortgages thereon; and, *secondly*, that its creditors, both secured and unsecured, shall receive stock in payment of their debts. No new stock was to be issued, but the stock already issued, and then held by the stockholders of the corporation, was to be assigned to the creditors, subject to a condition which will hereafter appear. The stock thus to be assigned consisted of 3,000 shares of $100 each, making a total of $300,000. The fourth and fifth paragraphs of the agreement were intended to define the rights of the general or unsecured creditors after they became stockholders, and the questions now in dispute grow mainly out of their provisions. The following is their language:

"*Fourth.* That each certificate of stock assigned to each general creditor shall be stamped on its face: 'This certificate of stock is held as security for the payment of $——, without interest, and is to be assigned to David B. Grant on the payment of the above amount.' All dividends paid on this stock shall be credited to account of such payment, and indorsed thereon.

"*Fifth.* That all the net profits of the company, after the payment of taxes, insurance, and the necessary amount for the proper maintenance of the property of the company in its present condition and capacity, shall be divided annually among the stockholders."

This agreement was subsequently brought to the attention of the court by petition, and the court, on the application of all parties in interest, by decree, on the fourteenth day of June, 1875, directed the receiver to surrender to the corporation the property in his possession; that the franchises and privileges of the corporation be restored to it; and that the receiver be discharged from further duty under the order appointing him. This decree was carried into effect. The corporation took possession of the property and resumed its powers, and on the first of July, 1875, commenced business again. The complainants' debt against the corporation slightly exceeded $59,000, and they received, as the quota of stock to which they were entitled under the agreement, 203 shares. The assets of the corporation were worth, on the first day of July, 1875, according to a valuation then made by its officers, $600,000, divided as follows: Real estate, $30,000; buildings, $110,000; machinery, $160,-000; merchandise, $225,000; debts due, $75,000.

The fairness of this valuation seems to have been assented to by all parties. This is made manifest by the fact that a valuation of the property of the corporation is, by the agreement, made the standard by which the net profits were to be ascertained. The agreement, it will be re- 121
membered, provides that all the net profits, after the payment of taxes and insurance, "and the necessary amount for the proper maintenance of the property of the company in its present condition and capacity," shall be divided annually. It is obvious that it would be impossible to ascertain with certainty what the net gains of any business were, at any time during its progress, where the thing put in as capital consisted of merchandise or something else than money, unless the money value of the thing contributed as capital was fixed definitely, at the very outset of the business. In view of the provisions of the agreement, I regard it as entirely clear that the valuation made by the officers was made for the purpose of fixing definitely and unalterably the amount of the capital of the corporation. There is no dispute that their valuation was just and fair. The net profits must therefore be calculated on the basis or by the standard thus prescribed.

No division of net profits was made until February 12, 1883. On that day the directors declared a dividend of 12 per cent. The sum thus distributed, in its aggregate, amounted to $104,714. The directors, about the first of January, 1883, caused a balance-sheet to be made up, showing the financial condition of the corporation on the thirty-first day of December, 1882, and sent copies of it to the stockholders. According to this statement, the net profits realized up to December 31, 1882, exceeded by nearly two-thirds the sum which the directors ordered to be distributed in dividends on the twelfth of February, 1883. The net profits shown on the face of this statement or balance-sheet are a little over $260,000, but the complainants contend that they are in truth $50,100 more, and that their actual amount is $310,100. The value of the assets of the corporation, as given in this statement or balance-sheet, is $50,100 less than the sum at which they were estimated by the officers of the corporation on the first of July, 1875, and thus the net profits are made just $50,100 less than they would have been if the assets had been put down at the same valuation that they were given on the first of July, 1875. The change was made in this way: The value of the buildings and machinery was reduced, the buildings $22,000, and the machinery $32,000, total $54,000; and the value of the real estate was increased $3,900, making the difference $50,100.

The complainants insist that this reduction was wrongful as to the stockholders, and that the court should, on the facts before it, declare that the amount of the net profits divisible under the agreement, in the year 1883, was $310,000. The decision of this question must be controlled by the contract. The subject is one that it was competent for the parties to regulate by contract. The contract unquestionably imposes very important limitations upon the power of the directors. In cases where the power of the directors of the corporation is without limitation and free from restraint, they are at liberty to exercise a very liberal discretion as to what disposition shall be made of the gains of the business of the corporation. Their power over them is absolute so long as they act in the exercise of an honest judgment. They may reserve of them whatever their judgment approves as necessary or judicious for re-
122 pairs and improvements, and to meet contingencies both present and prospective. And their determination in respect to these matters, if made in good faith and for honest ends, though the result may show that it was injudicious, is final, and not subject to judicial revision. But the directors of this corporation have no such power. The contract takes it from them. The disposition of the net profits is not to be governed by the discretion or judgment of the directors, but by the rule prescribed by the contract. The contract prescribes the standard by which the rights of the stockholders to the profits are to be measured; and the directors in disposing of them have no right of judgment, but must perform their contract obligations. The purposes to which the net profits must be applied are limited and defined by the contract; they are to be used to pay taxes and insurances, and to keep the works of the corporation in the condition and up to the capacity they had on the first of July, 1875, and the balance must be distributed to the stockholders. The obligation created by the contract in this respect is plain and imperative. The directors have no power and no right to apply them to any other purpose, and if they should do so they would violate their contract. No part of them can be reserved to be employed as working capital. The stockholders have already contributed all the means for that purpose that their obligation requires them to furnish. The $50,100 in question was not reserved to be expended in repairs and improvements, in order to put the works of the corporation in the condition and bring them up to the capacity they had in July, 1875. Had the directors set apart a fund out of the net profits to be used for those purposes, it is quite evident, I think, that their action, in that regard, would have been within the fair scope of their power. The amount necessary to be expended in any year, for such purposes, I suppose, can never be fixed in advance with anything like certainty or precision, and the contract should therefore be construed as having submitted the decision of that question, to a very large extent, to the discretion of the directors. It may not be entirely accurate to say that any action taken by the directors on this subject, in good faith, would conclude the stockholders, and wholly exclude judicial inquiry as to whether or not their action had violated the contract; yet this I think may be safely said: that if a court should be called upon to

review the action of the directors in that regard, it would be bound, in deciding the question whether the contract had been violated or not, to adopt the same standard of judgment as that which should have governed the action of the directors, and not to adjudge that the contract had been violated unless it was made clearly to appear that the stockholders had been deprived of some right plainly secured to them by the contract.

There is nothing, however, in the action of the directors which gives either pledge or indication that the $50,100 will be appropriated for purposes authorized by the contract. The book of minutes of the corporation contains no record of their action. All they have done is to mark down the value of the buildings and machinery. This was done, they say, because they believed that seven years' wear and tear had depreciated them to the extent that their value was reduced, but the proofs show that during that period nearly $100,000 had been expended in 123
their maintenance. It is manifest, I think, that the stockholders have a right, under the agreement, to have this matter dealt with in a manner very different from that in which it would appear it has been dealt with. If the buildings or machinery are out of repair, or need to be renewed, so that some part of the net profits must be expended to put the works of the corporation in the condition and to raise them to the capacity they had in July, 1875, the stockholders have a right to have the judgment of the directors as to how much shall be expended for each of those purposes; and if net profits are reserved, they also have a right to know for what purpose they are reserved, in order that if the purpose is one not authorized by the contract they may challenge the action of the directors, and, if it is, that they may know how the net profits have been disposed of. Although there is no express provision of the contract so declaring, yet I think, when the contract is examined with a view of ascertaining what were the principal objects of the parties, there can be little doubt that one of them was that the works of the corporation should be constantly kept up to the capacity they had in July, 1875. On that part of the contract being fully performed, rested the main hope that either its present or ultimate purpose would be accomplished. And I regard it as entirely clear that the stockholders have a right to have that part of the contract faithfully kept. On the case as it now stands, the complainants are, in my judgment, entitled to a declaration that the amount of net profits shown by the balance-sheet of December 31, 1882, was $310,000, and that the reduction made in the valuation of the buildings and machinery was erroneous.

The remaining and more important question is, were the stockholders entitled, under the contract, to a larger dividend in 1883 than that which the directors declared? They distributed nearly $105,000. This left of the $310,000 nearly $205,000. If this balance consisted of money or of securities which could easily and readily be converted, without loss, there can be no doubt that the directors were bound by the contract to divide it. The proofs show that on December 31, 1882, the corporation held railroad securities, consisting of notes and bonds, which had been taken in payment for locomotives, for a little over $212,000. They

had been taken at par. These were, of course, included in the statement of December 31, 1882, and represented in part the sum shown on that statement to be net profits. None of them were then due, and none became due until February 10, 1883. After that date portions of some of them fell due every month, and portions of others every quarter. The one having the longest period to run will not mature until January 1, 1888. The securities were not sold at the New York Stock Exchange, and had no market value. The proof is that they were absolutely unsalable. They were taken, as already stated, in payment for locomotives. The corporation was created for the purpose of manufacturing and selling locomotive engines and other machinery. The contract under which the corporation resumed business imposes no limitation upon the power of the directors to make contracts in carrying on its business.
124 Their authority, in that respect, is full and complete. They are competent to make any contract which may be necessary or fit and proper to enable the corporation to accomplish the purposes of its creation. Ang. & A. Corp. § 256; Field, Corp. § 746.

The question of the expediency of making a contract which is within the capacity of the corporation is committed absolutely to the judgment of its managers, by whom alone it can act, and so long as they keep within the power conferred upon the corporation, and act in good faith, with honest motives and for honest ends, their contracts are valid, and conclude the proprietors of the corporation. *Elkins* v. *Camden & A. R. Co.*, 36 N. J. Eq. 241. It would seem, therefore, to be entirely clear that the directors, in accepting these securities in payment for locomotives, did nothing which was not clearly within the power committed to them. The true statement of the case, then, would seem to be this: Profits have been made, provided the securities which the directors have rightfully taken in the proper prosecution of the business of the corporation are paid or can be collected, but not otherwise. If it should turn out that part of the securities can be collected and part cannot, or cannot otherwise be converted, the part not paid or converted will in no sense be entitled to be regarded as profits.

The words "net profits" define themselves. They mean what shall remain, as the clear gains of any business venture, after deducting the capital invested in the business, the expenses incurred by its conduct, and the losses sustained in its prosecution. If, as in this case, merchandise is sold, and securities payable at a future day are taken in payment, it is entirely proper—nay, if accuracy is desired, it is indispensable—that, in making a statement of the condition of the business, the securities should be put down as part of its assets; and they must, as a general rule, if the statement shows that profits have been made, represent the profits either wholly or it part. And if subsequently, in attempting to collect them, losses are sustained or expenses incurred, the sum shown as profits will be reduced just to the extent of such loss or expense. Now, the agreement in this case requires that the net profits shall be distributed annually to the stockholders; but it is quite obvious, I think, that what the parties meant by the words "net profits," as here used, was not the whole sum appearing as "net profits" on any annual statement, if such sum represented securities taken by the corporation in the ordinary course of its business, which were not yet due, and which could not be converted except at a price much less than that which the corporation had given for them; but what they meant was net gains which had been actually realized, or which could be quickly realized without loss, by a sale of the assets representing the profits.

Two fundamental objects are apparent on the face of the contract. They are—*First*, that the creditors who hold the stock of the corporation as security for their debts shall be paid out of the net profits of its business; and, *second*, that the persons who assigned their stock as security for the debts of the corporation shall, as soon as the debts are paid, have their stock returned to them. The directors are bound, in conducting the business of the corporation, to have regard to both of these objects, and, if possible, so to manage its affairs that both may be ultimately accomplished. If the directors were to attempt to sell the securities of the corporation, which they had taken at par, and which were maturing at short dates and at frequent intervals, at merely nominal prices, or at prices far below their face value, they would attempt to do what, in my judgment, would constitute a flagrant breach of duty against both classes of *cestuis que trust*,—both those who have the present interest and those who have a prospect of having an ultimate interest. To divide the securities in kind is an impossibility. The only other method open then is by a sale of them, and that, according to the proofs, is also an impossibility, or, if not, it can only be effected at a loss which would be ruinous to all concerned.

My conclusion is that the complainants were not entitled to a greater dividend in 1883 than that which the directors declared.

BARRY v. MISSOURI, KANSAS & TEXAS RAILWAY CO.

27 Fed. 1 (1886)
United States Circuit Court
Southern District of New York

WALLACE, J. The complainant is the owner of coupons and scrip certificates representing $43,462 of unpaid interest owing by the defendant the Missouri, Kansas & Texas Railway Company upon bonds secured by an income mortgage created by it April 1, 1876. He has filed this bill on behalf of himself, and all other owners of coupons and certificates who may desire to join, to compel an accounting by the railway company of its earnings and operating expenses since the making of the mortgage. The bill prays for an injunction against the appropriation of the earnings contrary to the rights of the income
126 bondholders, and for a decree for the payment of the income applicable to the interest. The defendant the Union Trust Company of New York is the trustee named in the income mortgage, and the bill avers that this corporation is made a defendant because it asserts that no duty is imposed on it in respect to the matters involved in the suit, and has refused to bring suit after request on behalf of the complainant and others similarly situated. No relief is sought against the trustee, and it has not answered or appeared in the suit....

It appears by the proofs in respect to the surplus earnings of the company that during the period beginning April 1, 1876, and ending January 1, 1885, there was charged by the company against earnings in its net income account, among others, certain disputable items, amounting in the aggregate to $3,784,336. If these items are not properly chargeable against the income, the result would be that surplus earnings arose during that period of time to the amount of $2,073,662, being net profits from the business of the company applicable to the payment of the interest upon the bonds beyond the payment of interest on prior incumbrances and the expenses of maintaining and operating the property. Of these items, one of $255,275 is for unpaid indebtedness which had accrued against the company before the income mortgage was created; another of $1,593,665 is for the difference between the face of the income bonds and the sum realized upon them (80 cents on the dollar) by the company; another of $1,398,935 is for interest on prior incumbrances which the company has not paid, and which the complainant alleges the company is under no obligation to pay; and the other items are likewise for interest for which the complainant alleges the company was not liable.

Respecting the disputed items for interest, it appears by an agreement forming part of the income mortgage that this mortgage was created in order to fund unpaid interest upon existing mortgages of the company, and to pay off certain other mortgage bonds and the creditors at large of the company. The holders of the first mortgage bonds, the holders of junior mortgage bonds, and the creditors at large, together with the railway company, were parties to the agreement. By the terms of the agreement the holders of the first mortgage bonds were to accept the income bonds which were to be created at 80 cents of their face value, in payment of their unpaid interest; and agreed to reduce their interest for the ensuing six years to 4 per cent. per annum for the first three years, and to 5 per cent. for the last three years, and to accept the income bonds in payment of the difference between the original and reduced rate of interest. The agreement also provided that if at any time the surplus earnings of the railway company should be more than sufficient to pay the interest on the first mortgage bonds at the reduced rate for the six years, and in addition thereto the interest upon the income bonds, the excess of the net earnings should be applied to increase the payment of interest on the first mortgage bonds up to the full amount originally payable thereon.

Unquestionably the bondholders are entitled to an account of the earnings, and the sums charged against the earnings, for each six months from the date of the mortgage, if the proofs justify the conclusion that surplus income has been earned after deducting all payments or liabilities which were legitimately charged against the income 127 during the period of the earnings. The inquiry is whether there is any remainder of earnings after the payment of operating expenses, repairs, prior interest, taxes, etc. It is not essential that the company shall have actually paid the disbursements which arise from these sources during the period of the earnings; it suffices if the company has become liable to pay them, although the time of payment may have been deferred. The expenses and liabilities incurred for the maintenance and operation of the road, and for interest on prior liens during each interest period, are to be charged against the income for that period. The term "net earnings" is defined in the opinion of the court in the case of *Union Pac. R. Co.* v. *U. S.*, 99 U. S. 420, as follows: "As a general proposition, net earnings are the excess of the gross earnings over the expenditures defrayed in producing them, aside from, and exclusive of, the expenditure of capital laid out in constructing and equipping the works themselves." The expenses defrayed or incurred in producing the earnings for a given interest period are the only charges which can enter into the income account for that period, except the payment of interest on prior incumbrances, as stipulated by the terms of the mortgage. Applying this rule, it is preposterous to assert that the company could properly charge against income for any period during the life of the mortgage a payment or a liability incurred on account of old indebtedness existing before the mortgage was created, or arising from a loss incurred by the sale of bonds issued to pay off old indebtedness. It might, with equal propriety, seek to offset its whole funded debt against its income.

It is difficult to understand upon what theory the company assumes the right to charge against income items for interest, some of which has not been paid, and all of which has been discharged to the company by the agreement of the holders of the incumbrances. The company has assumed to charge against the income account the difference between the rate of interest which the first mortgage bondholders agreed to accept for six years and the original rate to which they would have been entitled if the agreement had not been made. The terms of the agreement are so plain that it does not seem possible to misconceive its effect, which was, as was intended, to substitute a reduced rate for the original rate for six years, unless a surplus should arise after the payment of the interest on the income bonds. When the holders of the first mortgage bonds received the income bonds the agreement was fully executed. In the face of this agreement the company undertakes to charge against income, not only the difference between the original and the reduced rate which it has paid to the bondholders for the last two of the six years, but also the difference for the first four years, which has not been paid, but has been funded, and is now represented by the income bonds.

It has been suggested for the company in the argument of its counsel that sanction is found for the position of the company in an adjudication in the suit between the company and the Union Trust Company, in the circuit court of the United States for the district of Kansas; but it is not apparent from the record in that case that any such question as is now presented was directly or indirectly in issue, or was considered by the court.

128 It is also insisted for the railway company that it can properly charge against earnings the sums required to be set apart annually for a sinking fund under the provisions of the first mortgage; that the company is in arrears nearly $2,500,000 in its appropriation for this sinking fund; and that, deducting this amount from its gross earnings, there is no net income applicable to interest on the bonds. This mortgage has not been put in evidence, but, assuming its provisions to be as stated in the brief of counsel, the sufficient answer to the contention is that the obligation of the company to the income bondholders is in explicit terms to appropriate all its earnings to the payment of interest upon the income bonds except such as are to be devoted to the expenses of operating and keeping in repair its railway and mortgaged property, and to the payment of the interest on the prior incumbrances. Disallowing the items which have thus been improperly charged against the income account, there is apparently a considerable sum arising from net earnings which should be applied to the payment of the interest on the income bonds....

By reason of the obligation of the company, as expressed in the bond and mortgage, to devote the net income semi-annually to the payment of interest, a duty arises by implication, and rests upon the company, to keep such an account of its earnings and its expenditures as will show the net income of each semi-annual interest period applicable to the payment of the interest. The company has not attempted to fulfill this duty, and the trustee for the income bondholders has apparently supinely relinquished to the officers of the railway company the supervision of the accounts which the trustee should have exercised itself. The railway company now produces an account of its income and expenditures, not divided into income periods, but covering a series of years in which there are charges against earnings so palpably unwarranted as to suggest the inference that its officers have strained their ingenuity to conceal a fund which it was their duty to pay over to the bondholders of the bonds. If upon such an accounting as the railway company will be directed to make it should appear that so large a sum has been withheld as there is now reason to suppose, it may become the duty of the court to appoint a receiver to protect the interests of the bondholders which seem to have been so inadequately protected by the trustee. It is not necessary, however, to decree at present any further relief than such an accounting as will afford the proper basis of a final decree appropriating any sum found due according to the rights of the holders of coupons and certificates.

A decree is ordered directing an accounting by the railway company before a master respecting its earnings and income for six months from the date of the mortgage, and its expenses during the same period for operating and keeping in repair its railway and property, as well as of the sums paid, or which it is liable to pay, for the interest upon the incumbrances prior to the income mortgage specified in the instrument, and for taxes and assessments. Upon such accounting the railway company is to be disallowed any sums paid or charged on account of debts which it had contracted prior to the creation of the income mortgage; is to be disallowed any charge against income arising from the sale of its income bonds at a price less than their face amount; and is to be disallowed any interest upon the first 129
mortgage bonds which it has not actually paid, or become liable to pay, and all which has been funded and is now represented by the income bonds accepted by holders of the first mortgage bonds in lieu of interest. The master will ascertain how much net or surplus earnings have been made by the company during each six-months period, to the time of the filing of the bill. The master will also ascertain the amount of coupons converted into scrip certificates, and the interest periods represented by the certificates, respectively, to the end that it may be finally decreed that the net income of each interest period shall be paid ratably to the holders of coupons or certificates representing interest for the same six months.

FITZPATRICK v. DISPATCH PUBLISHING CO.

83 Ala. 604 (1887)
Supreme Court of Alabama

APPEAL from the City Court of Montgomery, in equity. Heard before the Hon. THOS. M. ARRINGTON.

The bill in this case was filed on the 14th July, 1887, by Alva Fitzpatrick, a stockholder in the Dispatch Publishing Company, a private corporation organized under the general statutes, against the said corporation, to enjoin and restrain it, its officers and agents, from issuing additional stock or certificates of stock, as determined on by resolutions adopted at a meeting of the stockholders held on the 2d July, 1887. An injunction was granted on the filing of the bill; but, after answer filed, admitting the facts as stated, but denying that they authorized an injunction, the court dissolved the injunction on motion, for want of equity in the bill; and this decree is now assigned as error.

WATTS & SON, for appellant.

TROY, TOMPKINS & LONDON, *contra*.

STONE, C. J.—The Dispatch Publishing Company is an incorporated newspaper enterprise, with a paid-up capital stock of ten thousand dollars. This stock is divided into one hundred shares of one hundred dollars each, of which the complainant owns twenty shares, representing two thousand dollars. At a meeting of the stockholders, properly called for the purpose, at which all the stockholders were present, it was resolved, four-fifths of the stock being voted therefor, that the stock be increased to twenty thousand dollars, or two hundred shares of one hundred dollars each. A minute of the stockholders' meeting was kept, and it is made an exhibit to the bill filed in this cause. We copy from it as follows: "The chairman further stated, that the original capital of ten thousand dollars, for which stock had been issued, had been invested in property which had more than doubled in value, and was now worth, over and above all liabilities of the corporation, twenty thousand dollars. Thereupon the following resolution was offered: *Resolved*, that the capital stock of this company be increased ten thousand dollars, viz., one hundred shares of the par value of one hundred dollars per share, and that the same be distributed as a stock dividend of one hundred *per cent.* to the present stockholders of the company. On taking the vote on the foregoing resolution, the holders of 80 shares voted *aye*, and the holder of 20 shares voted *no*; and the resolution was adopted."

Fitzpatrick, the stockholder who was opposed to the increase, filed this bill, and obtained an interlocutory injunction, restraining the corporation from carrying the resolution into effect. On motion of the corporation the injunction was dissolved, and the present appeal is prosecuted to obtain a reversal of the decretal order of dissolution.

The ground relied on as giving equity to the bill is, that if the resolution be carried into effect, it will be violative alike of the State constitution, Art. 14, § 6, and the statute enacted upon the subject, Code of 1876, § 2035. The language of the constitution is: "No corporation shall issue stock or bonds except for money, labor done, or money or property actually received; and all fictitious increase of stock or indebtedness shall be void." The legislature, by act approved January 20th, 1876—Sess. Acts, 261—prescribed the manner in which private corporations may increase their capital
stock or bonded indebtedness, but added a *proviso*, "That 131
neither stock nor bonds shall be issued by any private corporation, except for money, labor done, or money or property actually received; and all fictitious increase of stock or indebtedness shall be void."—Code of 1876, §§ 2031 to 2035, inclusive. The *proviso* copied above is but a reiteration of the language of the constitution.

It will be observed that the only ground on which the right to issue increased stock was based, was the report made to the stockholders' meeting by the chairman, "that the original capital (ten thousand dollars) for which stock had been issued, had been invested in property which had more than doubled in value, and was now worth, over and above all liabilities of the corporation, twenty thousand dollars." It is not stated in what the original capital had been invested, nor in what its assets now consist. The corporation is a publishing company, and all men know that a press or presses, type, paper and many other things, are necessary appliances and material for making such enterprise successful. And patronage is none the less a condition of success. A newspaper is dependent for its gains on the extent of the subscription list, and the use of its columns as an advertising medium. The popularity, or good will of a newspaper enterprise, is sometimes claimed as property, and it enters into the commercial value of the adventure. All these elements of value are subject to fluctuation—to inflation and depression. In the present abnormal methods of commerce, nothing is perhaps of less stable value than property or stocks in incorporated companies. Another thought is, perhaps, not out of place. All men are inclined to over-estimate the value of their property.

We have indulged in these reflections, with no intention of taking issue with the averment of the bill, that the capital of the Dispatch Publishing Company has increased to double the value of the amount first paid in. We have no reason for suspecting anything improper in the proposed increase of stock. We are declaring a rule, however, which must govern alike this and all other propositions to issue additional stock, upon mere increased value of corporate property. The constitution, in terms, inhibits the issue of fictitious stock; that is, stock which has no valuable thing, or corporate assets, to rest on, and of which it is the representative. If it represents nothing, and has nothing to stand on, it is fictitious, it is fraudulent, it is unconstitutional.

Conceding, for the present, that if this corporation held accumulated, undistributed, tangible assets in excess of its capital stock, that excess or surplus would furnish a basis for the issue of additional stock, commensurate with the value of such excess, the case made by the report of the chairman of the stockholders' meeting falls very far short of what should be required, before an increased issue of capital stock

132 should be allowed. It should have been shown in what the original capital had been invested, in what its capital now consists, and what makes up the increased value, which the proposed additional stock is to represent. Less than this would open too wide a door for fraud, and would leave a credulous public exposed to the merciless greed of scheming rapacity. It behooves constituted authority to keep well abreast with the many inventions which modern cupidity has wrought out, and which, perhaps, more than any other agency, have called into exercise pernicious principles which threaten the overthrow of organized government. In this highly conservative, yet restraining spirit, the principle, constitutional and statutory, on which this case mainly hinges, had its origin, and finds its justification. Let us not, by timid interpretation, impair the strength of this bulwark, erected by our constitution-makers against the frauds which have become the reproach of the age we live in.

In the absence of constitutional restraint, it must be admitted that corporations may declare stock dividends, or, what must rest on the same principle, may issue increased stock, based on increased capital, or increased value of accumulated property, in excess of capital stock requirements. But, as said by Cook, Stock and Stockholders, § 51: "It seems to be generally conceded that, if the *capital stock and the* actual property of the corporation is not permanently increased to the extent of the par value of the stock distributed as a dividend, then that the issue of stock by such dividend is irregular, and, under certain circumstances, fraudulent." The italics above are our own, and the italicised phrase is so marked, because in our opinion the sense and meaning of the author would be precisely and with more accuracy expressed, if these words were omitted.

Farther than what is said above we need not go in this case. We have not decided, nor need we declare what would be our ruling, if it were shown that the Dispatch Publishing Company had an accumulated money surplus, or visible, tangible property in excess of its authorized stock, and proposed to make that the basis of additional stock to be issued. Upon that question we decide nothing. We simply declare that the report of the chairman to the stockholders' meeting did not authorize the issue of additional stock, based on the alleged increase in the value of the corporate property.

The decree of the chancellor is reversed, and a decree here rendered, reinstating the injunction.

PEOPLE v. SAN FRANCISCO SAVINGS UNION

72 Cal. 199 (1887)
Supreme Court of California

SEARLS, C. This cause was submitted to the court below upon an agreed statement. Defendant had judgment, from which plaintiff appeals. The defendant is a banking corporation, existing under and by virtue of the laws of this state, and was incorporated as such on the eighteenth day of June, 1862, under and in accordance with the provisions of an act of the legislature entitled "An act to provide for the formation of corporations for the accumulation and investment of funds and savings," approved April 11, 1862, (St. 1862, p. 199.) The act provides for the formation of corporations "for the purpose of aggregating the funds and savings of the members thereof and others, and preserving and safely investing the same for their common benefit." Corporations thereunder are authorized to loan and invest their funds, receive deposits of money, loan and invest the same, collect the same, with
134 interest, "repay such deposits without interest, or with so much of the earnings and interest as the by-laws of the corporation may provide." They may make by-laws prescribing the conditions upon which deposits shall be received, and the time and manner of dividing the profits. Section 10 of the same act provides that "it shall not be lawful for the corporation or the directors to make any dividends, except from surplus profits arising from the business of the corporation; and the directors shall, at such times and in such manner as the by-laws shall prescribe, declare and pay dividends of so much of the profits of the company, and of the interest arising from the capital stock and deposits, as may be appropriated for that purpose by the provisions of the by-laws."

It is provided and declared by the by-laws of the defendant that "at the expiration of every six months, ending thirtieth June and thirty-first December each year, the board of directors shall ascertain the net profits of the corporation, and shall determine the amount to be appropriated for a general dividend." During the six months commencing June 30, 1883, the surplus profits arising from the business of the corporation, including the interest arising from its capital stock and deposits, amounted to the sum of $280,092. In this amount of surplus profits, and as a part thereof, is included—*First*, the sum of $5,825 for interest which has accrued for the months of November and December, in the year 1883, upon the coupons of bonds of the United States held by the defendant, but which, by the terms of said coupons, is not payable until February 1, 1884; *second*, the sum of $23,917 for interest that has matured since thirtieth of June, 1883, but which has not been collected, upon a portion of the loans made by the defendant upon real-estate security. The value of the real estate held by the defendant as security for the said loans, and for each thereof, is more than double the amount of the respective loans and the matured interest thereon.

By the conditions of each of said loans, it is provided that, in case the interest thereon is not paid as it matures, it shall be added to the principal sum, and be secured by the real estate which is given as security for said principal sum, and thereafter bear interest at the same rate as said principal sum. The defendant being about to declare a dividend from the profits arising from its business during the six months ending December 31, 1883, expressed its intention to include in the amount which it should appropriate for that purpose its surplus profits aforesaid, amounting to the sum of $280,092, including therein the aforesaid sum of $5,825, for interest which had accrued upon the aforesaid coupons of bonds of the United States, but which would not be payable until February 1, 1884, and also the aforesaid sum of $23,917, for interest which had matured since the thirteenth day of June, 1883, (but which had not been collected,) upon the loans made as aforesaid, and secured as aforesaid. The "bank commissioners" objected to the action of the bank in including these sums, and this action is the result.

The question in difference and point of controversy upon which the decision and judgment of the court is sought, is the following: "Is the defendant authorized by law to appropriate and pay, as a dividend to its stockholders and depositors on the profits arising from its business, any portion of the interest upon its loans or investments that may have matured or accrued, but which have not been actually collected and received in money?" What are the *surplus profits* arising from the business of the corporation? The word "profits" signifies an excess of the value of returns over the value of advances. The excess of receipts over expenditures; that is, net earnings. *Connolly* v. *Davidson*, 15 Minn. 519, (Gil. 428.) The receipts of a business deducting current expenses; it is equivalent to net receipts. *Eyster* v. *Centennial Board of Finance*, 94 U. S. 500. In commerce it means the advance in the price of the goods sold beyond the cost of purchase. In distinction from the wages of labor, it is well understood to imply the net return to the capital or stock employed, after deducting all the expenses, including not only the wages of those employed by the capitalist, but the wages of the capitalist himself for superintending the employment of his capital stock. Adam Smith, Wealth of Nations, book 1, *c.* 6; Mill, Pol. Econ. *c.* 15. The "rents and profits" of an estate; the "income" or "net income" of it,—are all equivalent expressions. 135
Andrews v. *Boyd*, 5 Me. 202; *Earl* v. *Rowe*, 35 Me. 420. Profits are divided by writers on political economy into gross and net, the former being the entire difference between the value of advances and the value of returns, and the latter so much of this difference as arises exclusively from the capital employed.

In *People* v. *Board Sup'rs Niagara Co.*, 4 Hill, 20, BRONSON, J., said: "It is undoubtedly true that 'profits' and 'income' are sometimes used as synonymous terms; but, strictly speaking, 'income' means that which comes in or is received from any business or investment of capital, without reference to the outgoing expenditures; while 'profits' generally means the gain which is made upon any business or investment, when both receipts and payments are taken into the account. 'Income,' when applied to the affairs of individuals, expresses the same idea that 'revenue' does when applied to the affairs of a state or nation."

In *St. John* v. *Erie R. Co.*, 10 Blatchf. 271, it was said: "Net earnings are properly the gross receipts, less the expense of operating the road, or other business of the corporation. Interest on debts is paid out of what thus remains; that is, out of the net earnings. Many other liabilities are paid out of the net earnings. When all liabilities are paid either out of the gross receipts or out of the net earnings, the remainder is the profit of the shareholders."

Under these definitions, it is not easy to comprehend how *profits, or surplus profits*, can consist of earnings never yet received. The term imports an excess of *receipts* over *expenditures*, and without *receipts* there cannot properly be said to be profits. Money earned as interest, however well secured, or certain to be eventually paid, cannot in fact be distributed as dividends to stockholders, and does not constitute *surplus profits* within the meaning of the statute. To hold the contrary would, we think, tend to open the door to a practice under which the assets of corporations would be liable to distribution as dividends upon no surer basis than the judgment of their directors as to the value of their bills receivable. Such is not and should not be the policy of the law.

The capital, and all the assets except surplus profits, are to be retained intact, and form a fund to which creditors of the corporation have a prior right over stockholders. If some portion of this fund may be distributed in lieu of interest earned, but not collected, then cases may arise in which all of it may be so distributed,—a practice which we deem subversive of the essential principles upon which corporations of this character are organized, and under which practically the rights of creditors *might* be greatly impaired. The fact that defendant has security for the interest due does not make the unpaid interest a profit. Until paid in, it is not money in hand. Contingencies may arise to prevent its being realized. It is time to distribute this interest when it is actually received by the bank.

It follows that the judgment of the court below nonsuiting plaintiff should be reversed, and the cause remanded, with directions to the court below to enter judgment in favor of plaintiff as provided in the agreed statement contained in the record.

We concur: BELCHER, C. C.; FOOTE, C.

BY THE COURT. For the reasons given in the foregoing opinion, the judgment is reversed, and cause remanded, with directions to enter judgment in favor of plaintiff as provided in the agreed statement contained in the record.

MACKINTOSH v. FLINT & PERE MARQUETTE RAILROAD CO.

34 Fed. 582 (1888)
United States Circuit Court
Eastern District of Michigan

JACKSON, J. The above-entitled causes were heard together. The
first is filed by complainants on behalf of themselves and other holders
of provisional certificates, as hereinafter explained, to compel the Flint
& Pere Marquette *Railroad* Company and its directory to recognise them
in full as stockholders in said company, and to issue to them regular 137
certificates of stock therein, such as will give them the rights of actual
stockholders in said corporation, entitle them to vote and exercise a voice
in the management of its affairs, from which they claim to be at present
unjustly and improperly excluded. . . .

The fourth article of the certificate of reorganization, forming a part of the defendant company's charter, was intended to define the legal relations and relative rights of the two classes of stockholders therein described, and to designate, as between them, the funds of the corporation out of which dividends on preferred stock were to be paid. By that provision of the charter, which is obligatory upon the corporation and its directory, the funds applicable to the payment of dividends on the preferred stock was the net income of the company, "after paying interest on prior bonds, repairs, expenses of equipment and renewals." Any surplus of net income, after the payment of said dividend of 7 per cent. upon the preferred stock, was to stand undivided until the next dividend day, and so on, from year to year, until such time as holders of said preferred stock should receive five consecutive annual dividends of 7 per cent., or semi-annual or quarterly dividends equivalent thereto. There was to be no accumulation of dividends on preferred stock. When five consecutive annual dividends, or, in lieu thereof, semi-annual or quarterly dividends equivalent thereto, shall have been paid upon the preferred stock, then the common stock, with the right to vote, was to be issued and delivered to parties who held the certificates issued upon the surrender of the common stock of the old Flint & Pere Marquette Railway Company, or other certificates, which the new company may have issued in lieu thereof. Any surplus of the common stock was to remain the property of the new corporation. At the first meeting of the board of directors under the new organization, a resolution was formally adopted, September 8, 1880, defining the policy of the company, as follows:

"Resolved that the board of directors define their policy to be in conformity to the articles of association; that, under the head of operating expenses, only such improvements and additions shall be included as are necessary, in the judgment of the directors, to keep the property up to the proper standard of efficiency, and that such portion of additions and extensions beyond this, as the board decides, shall be provided for out of funds other than net earnings; that the stockholders are entitled to the benefit of all net earnings after paying expenses and coupons.". . .

No question is made as to the correctness of the company's expenditures; but the claim on behalf of the complainants is that their rights have been ignored and disregarded in improperly charging portions of such expenditures to operating, rather than to construction, whereby the net income applicable to dividends under the charter defining their relations to the company and the preferred stockholders, have been reduced to their prejudice. They further claim that receipts and revenues received have not been credited, as they should have been, to income account. It distinctly appears from the testimony of its officers, that the accounts of the defendant company have not been kept with any reference to the rights of the common stockholders; that no regard has been paid to the provisions of the fourth article of the charter in the keeping of the accounts; that the road was not operated with reference to the unpreferred stockholders at all. The general manager states that the books and accounts were kept, "as we
138 thought the proper way of doing and administering, with reference to its [the road's] permanence and safety. We have not operated it [the road] with reference to them [the common stockholders] at all. We have operated it in accordance with the public benefit and the maintenance of the property." His manner of dealing with the expenditures of the road is fairly illustrated in the following question and answer, (Record, p. 260:) "*Question.* And therefore you think that the question as to whether a reduction of grade should be charged to construction or to operating expenses, is simply a matter for the general manager to decide according to the state of the finances? *Answer.* No, sir; according to his judgment." Not only were the rights of the common stockholders not recognized, or considered in the keeping of the company's accounts, but, as stated by the auditor, Mr. Ledlie, no account was kept to show the surplus of net income yearly after the payment of the 7 per cent. dividend on preferred stock, as provided for in said fourth article of the charter. The policy thus adopted and pursued by the actual management assumed that the contingent rights and interests of the provisional certificate holders were entirely subject to the discretion of the directors, or those in control of the road, in deciding, not only what expenditures should be made, but how they should be charged, as between operating and construction. ...

It is not a sound proposition, as applied to this case, that the directors, selected by and from the preferred class, have and may exercise the same discretion as against the provisional certificate holders in dealing with, disposing of, or applying the net income of the company, which they might be entitled to exercise as against the preferred stockholders. They were entitled, as between the two sets of stockholders, to employ the net income in paying interest on prior bonds, old or new; in making repairs upon the road, buildings, and other property of the company, so as to maintain their efficiency; and in meeting the expenses of equipment and renewals, which evidently refers to repairs upon and keeping up of the rolling stock of the company, but does not include the purchase of new equipment. The company from the start adopted this construction as to the expenditures chargeable against income, as shown by the resolution already referred to, passsed at the first meeting of the board of directors.

With this limitation upon the company and its directors in the way of expending earnings as between the two classes of shareholders, we may

next consider what net income applicable to dividends were earned or received during the years 1881 to 1885, inclusive, and the manner in which the management of the company has dealt with or disposed of the same, or, generally, whether the company could reasonably and properly have declared and paid full 7 per cent. dividends during each of said years. As to the surplus lands and proceeds of land sales in the hands of Crapo and Prescott, these were undoubtedly equitable assets of the defendant company corporation, acquired under the trust conveyance of August 23, 1879, and the foreclosure sale, purchase, and reorganization in 1880. Subject to the prior mortgage lien, or liens on said lands, and land proceeds, the company was the beneficial owner thereof, and held the equitable title to the same. In respect to these surplus assets it had something more than the simple right to call the trustees to an accounting. It was the real equitable owner of the property; and the surplus thereof after satisfying prior incumbrances, belonged to the corporation, just as it held its other property subject to mortgage. As the obsolute owner of this equitable title and right in said surplus lands and proceeds arising from the same, whatever the company received from that source was 139
as much a part of its income or revenues as if it had been derived from any other source, such as receipts from operating its road, or rents collected for the use of its cars or other property. Income is not limited to the gain which results from business and labor, but it includes as well the proceeds derived from the use or sale of property. Now, what is the situation of these land assets, and what revenues have been actually derived therefrom during the years in question, or could have been received from that source, without impairing or interfering with the rights of creditors? When the new company acquired its right to these lands and assets, the prior charges thereon amounted to about $2,000,000. Of those prior bonds remaining on January 1, 1881, (Report of company for 1880, p. 21,) there were $1,704,000 of 8 per cent. land-grant bonds, and $300,000 of Flint & Holly 10 per cent. bonds. During 1881 the former were discharged, partly by funds in the hands of the trustees and partly by exchange of new 6 per cent. bonds of the company; so that, at the close of 1881, the $300,000 of Flint & Holly bonds constituted the only incumbrance on these land assets. They were also secured by a mortgage on the Flint & Holly branch of the company's lines of road. Now, on December 31, 1881, as shown by the company's annual report, the trustees had in their hands a balance of $575,978.77, arising from land sales, while the land commissioner who made the sale held bills receivable, amounting, principal and interest, to the sum of $902,058.73, and the unsold lands held by the trustees amounted to 138,454.28 acres, worth about $10 per acre. Here, then, were $2,863,577.88 of good assets in the hands of said trustees to secure $300,000 of 10 per cent. bonds, which were also secured by mortgage on one of the company's main branches. The cash balance in the hands of the trustees exceeded this bonded debt by $275,978.77. The dividend declared and paid for 1881 was 5½ per cent.,—less than 7 per cent. by 1½ per cent.,—which, on the whole $6,500,000 of preferred stock, amounted to $97,500. If this amount had been drawn by the company from the hands of the trustees, the full 7 per cent. could have been readily declared and paid without in the least impairing the security held by them for the payment of the $300,000 Flint & Holly bonds. On December 31, 1882, said trustees held a balance of $598,117.28. The bills receivable from sales of lands in the hands of the land commissioner, amounted to $747,532.78, and

there were unsold lands to the extent of 109,815½ acres, worth upon on average, say $9 per acre, or $988,340, making an aggregate of $2,133,-989.78, controlled and held by the trustees to secure said $300,000 of bonds. In 1882 the dividend declared and paid was 6½ per cent. The deficiency of ½ per cent., or $32,500, was actually in the hands of the company, as shown on page 6 of its annual report for that year. For that year it had a surplus of $35,613.52, after paying the 6½ per cent. dividend, which was carried over to 1883. It could have paid the 7 per cent. for the year 1882, without drawing on the land funds; but, if there had been an actual deficiency of income of $32,500 from other sources, it could have been withdrawn from the land assets, without in any wise impairing or endangering the security for the payment of the $300,000 bonds. In 1883 and 1884 full 7 per cent. dividends were declared and paid, leaving in the hands of said trustees large surplus assets, as follows, viz., on December 31, 1883, the balance in their hands was $681,259.29, the land commissioner held $627,021.55 in bills receivable, and their were 103,619.42 acres unsold, worth $932,574, aggre-
140 gating $2,240,854.84 of available assets charged with only $300,000 of liability; on December 31, 1884, the balance in the hands of the trustees was $693,681.33, the bills receivable from lands sold were $492,334.14 and there were 101,009.27½-100 acres unsold, worth $900,000, aggregating $2,086,015.47 of security, charged with $300,000 of bonds. On December 31, 1885, there remained of unsold lands 95,914.22 acres, worth upon an average, say $6 per acre, or $575,485, and the trustees held in their hands, as stated by Mr. Crapo, (pages 596,597 of the Record,) funds to the amount of $764,556; of that amount the sum of $579,-000, was invested in Flint & Pere Marquette Railroad new 6 per cent. bonds, while the balance, except perhaps a small cash deposit arising from daily receipts, was loaned out at interest,—partly to the defendant corporation, to whom this surplus fund belonged, and which paid interest thereon, which was charged to operating expenses. For the year 1885 the company only declared and paid a dividend of 4 per cent. on the preferred stock. The 3 per cent. shortage, amounting to $195,000, could readily, safely, and properly have been withdrawn from the large surplus in the hands of the trustees, without in the least impairing or endangering the security for the payment of the $300,000 of Flint & Holly bonds, which constituted the only charge against the funds and assets held by the trustees. The $579,000 of Flint & Pere Marquette 6 per cent bonds, which the trustees held, were worth in the market, and are still worth, a premium ranging from 15 to 20 per cent. If the deficiency of $195,000 had been withdrawn from the hands of the trustees, they would have still held $384,000 or more of the company's 6 per cents., worth a premium of 15 per cent., as security for the $300,000 of Flint & Holly bonds, beside unsold lands worth $575,485. On the 31st December, 1886, the balance in hands of the trustees had swelled to $826,-852.73. The $300,000 Flint & Holly bonds mature May 1, 1888. To say nothing of the branch road mortgaged for their payment, the trustees have for years held, and now hold, funds and assets for the security of these bonds, exceeding fourfold the amount needed, or necessary for their payment. This large surplus the company or its management have intentionally declined to draw upon for the purpose of making dividends, or of returning to income sums that were improperly charged to operating expenses, except in 1884, when the board of directors, after directing the general manager to transfer $78,472.59 from operating to construction account, called upon and received from said trustees $100,000,

which was used in making the dividend of that year. Why could not the $195,000 required to make up the 7 per cent dividend for 1885 have been called for from the same source? Why was it not called for and so applied? The board of directors, by resolution passed December 13, 1883, "resolved, that the trustees of the land funds be authorized to pay over to the treasurer of the company, from time to time, all land funds which shall come into their hands, in excess of what may be required to pay the securities outstanding, for which said land funds have been specially pledged, and all such payments heretofore paid by them to the treasurer be confirmed and approved." The land funds in the hands of the trustees at the close of 1885 in excess of what was required to pay the $300,000 of Flint & Holly bonds (the only securities outstanding and chargeable against said fund) was more than $400,000. Out of this excess, $195,000, for 1885, could have been drawn either to apply on dividends, or to restore to income or earnings what had been diverted from that fund, and applied to construction or new equipment. But, for some reason not explained, this was not done.

Now, aside from the $100,000 received from the trustees under the 141
resolution of December 19, 1884, how has the company or its management dealt with the moneys actually received from these land trustees? It appears that from October 1, 1880, to the close of 1885, said trustees paid over to the treasurer of the company at various times, as requested, sums of money aggregating $1,221,168.62, and which was used by the company as follows, viz., $646,000 in paying off 8 per cent. land-grant bonds, $100,000 for Bay City & East Saginaw bonds, $22,118.09 for improvement of Bayou Spur property in East Saginaw, $81,000 for coupons on Flint & Holly bonds, $4,500 and $22,550.53 for interest received, and $345,000 for the company's use, and which went into the general treasury, and was used "according to the necessities of the company for pressing needs of any kind," as stated by the general manager. But this $345,000 is not credited to income or earning. In the keeping of the company's accounts the provisional certificate holders are not allowed any benefit from this receipt. It is not permitted to go into earnings or income account. If that had been allowed, it would have more than covered the shortage in the 7 per cent. dividends for the five years in question. In other words, if that sum had been treated as applicable to dividends, or as an equitable restoration to earnings or income of what had been applied to construction, full 7 per cent. dividends could have been declared and paid during the five consecutive years under consideration. But how were these large receipts from the land assets disposed of in the company's account? By reference to the annual report for 1884 (pages 15 and 24) of the vice-president and general manager, it will be seen that the sum of $1,105,276.97, received from sales of lands and premiums on bonds, (the latter item amounting to $164,541.25,) was charged to depreciation, and deducted from the road-bed and equipment account of the company. This latter account was, at the same time, further reduced by a credit of $10,793.48, being the proceeds of narrow-gauge equipment, telegraph line, and portable engine sold. No depreciation account was kept by the company, as the general manager testified, (page 344, Record,) and, year by year, operating expenses, were charged with all repairs and expenses of equipment and renewals made or incurred in, about, or upon the road-bed, rolling stock, buildings, or other property of the company, as contemplated and provided by article 4 of the charter, and then, at the close of 1884, a lumping

charge of $1,116,070.45 is made to depreciation, and deducted from the road-bed and equipment account. While doing this the management of the company, without reason and in disregard of the rights of the provisional certificate holders, keep large surplus land funds in reserve, portions of which it borrows from the trustees from time to time, and pays interest upon its own funds, which is charged to operating expenses, to the prejudice of the unpreferred stockholders, who are excluded from any voice in the management of the corporate affairs. The court is unable to understand upon what principle the receipts or revenues derived from the surplus land assets are to be distinguished from other income or earnings of the company applicable to the payment of dividends under the facts of this case. These land assets were brought into the company by the consent of the old common stockholders, under the trust conveyance of August 23, 1879, made manifestly in furtherance of the reorganization scheme. But, whether that creates any equity or not in favor of the provisional certificate holders, they have the same interest in these land assets that they possess in other property of the company,
142 and the funds derived from that source are just as applicable to the payment of dividends on the preferred stock, so as to meet the contingency on which the unpreferred class are to be let in, as revenues derived from operating the road, or renting its cars and dining stations. The principle announced in *St. John* v. *Railway Co.*, 22 Wall. 149, where it is said: "We are aware of no legal principle which would authorize the stockholders in question to analyze the business, select out a portion of it, and to say that the net earnings specified must be a predicate of that part and none other," applies here. So in *Ryan* v. *Railway Co.*, 21 Kan. 365, the court says, in considering the rights of stockholders in reference to the sources from which profits are made "that it is immaterial at what time or from what sources these profits may have been derived. It is wholly immaterial whether they have accrued from rents, the profits of the construction of the road, or from the sale of lands equitably belonging to the company, they are all incidents to the shares." Without reference, therefore, to the diversion of income, or the improper application of earnings to construction, or the charging to operating expense what properly belonged to construction account, but taking the company's reports as made, and the dividends annually declared on the net earnings there shown, it is clear that there was at the disposal of the company ample surplus land funds in addition to such net earnings, to have made and paid full 7 per cent. dividends for each of the years 1881, 1882, 1883, 1884, and 1885, without in any way impairing the rights of its creditors, or neglecting its duty to the public. In the judgment of the court, fair dealing and a due regard to the contingent rights of the provisional certificate holders, required of the management that funds thus at their disposal should have been applied in making the full 7 per cent. dividends for the five years, so as to let the unpreferred stockholders into their inheritance. Is it to be said in a court of conscience that the preferred stockholders in charge of the corporate management and affairs, may have at their disposal ample funds to meet the contingency, and comply with the event on which the unpreferred class are to be let into their rights; that they may arbitrarily decline or wrongfully neglect to receive and apply such funds, so that the happening of the contingency is thereby postponed, and that they, or the corporation controlled by them, may thereafter set up and rely upon such contingency as an excuse or

defense against the admission of such unpreferred class into their corporate rights and privileges? To state this proposition is enough. A court of equity will not permit parties occupying towards each other either legal or trust relations, whether direct or through the instrumentality of an artificial body called a "corporation," thus to act, and thereby postpone or defeat the rights of the defendant class.

But, aside from the surplus land funds and assets, how stands the case in respect to income and earnings derived from other sources? Were they sufficient, if fairly and properly applied, according to the true meaning of the article 4 of the charter to have paid full 7 per cent. dividends on the preferred stock for the five consecutive years in question? This can only be determined by an analysis and examination of the company's accounts, showing receipts and disbursements during said period. It appears that the total issue of the company's new 6 per cent. bonds amounted to $3,924,000; that of these $1,058,000 were exchanged for 8 per cent. land-grant bonds; that the land trustees purchased over $500,000 of said bonds at par, and that the residue thereof were sold at a pre- 143
mium, ranging from 5 to 10 per cent. This premium on its bonds sold was received by the company as follows, viz.: $500 between October 1, 1880, and January, 1881; $107,257.25 during 1881; $34,702.50 in 1882; $12,136.50 in 1883; and $9,945 in 1884, aggregating $164,561.25. This premium was, at first, set upon the credit side of the company's ledger, or placed to the credit of construction, and afterwards, as shown by the annual report for 1884, (page 15) it was included in the amount of $1,105,276.97, charged to depreciation, and deducted from road-bed and equipment account. This premium was received by reason of the rate of interest which the bonds bore, and the ample security provided for their payment. Earnings were charged with the payment of that interest on account of which said premium was earned or received; and it would therefore seem to be proper to credit earnings or income with the amount of such premium. If income is burdened with a rate of interest which secures a profit on the bonds, then income is entitled to the benefit of that profit, just as it would be entitled to the profits made on any contract by the company. In crediting such premium to earnings and profits, there is no increase of the bonded debt, nor improper enlargement of the company's construction account. It is apparent that 5 per cent. bonds, secured as these were, could have been negotiated at par. In carrying 6 per cent., earnings are charged with the extra burden of $39,240 annually. It is, therefore, reasonable and proper that income should have the benefit of the profit which has been derived from the extra charge placed upon such income. The experts differ in opinion as to the proper disposal to be made of such premiums on bonds, and there is no uniformity in the practice of railroads in respect to such profits. In the judgment of this court, such premiums, in the present case, as between the two classes of stockholders, should have been credited to income during the respective years in which the same was received.

Next, as to the steel-rail account. At the close of 1880 the mileage on the main line of the road was 317.17 and 90.40 miles of sidings. Of the main line 200 miles were laid with steel rails. At the close of 1881 there were 345.16 miles in the main line and 111.29 in sidings and spurs, 283 miles of which were laid with steel rails (being an increase of 83 miles) during 1881, (page 5, annual report for 1881.) At the close of 1882 the main line and sidings amounted to 485.62 miles

laid with steel rails, being an increase in steel rails over 1881 of 19.72 miles. At the close of 1883 the main line was 361.31 miles; sidings and spurs 175.17; total 536.38 miles, with 341.31 miles on main line and 18 miles on branches laid with steel rails, being an increase in steel mileage over 1882 of 56.59 miles. At the close of 1884 there were 369.91 miles laid with steel rails, an increase over 1883 of about 10 miles. At the close of 1885 the main line, sidings, branches, and spurs amounted to 543.12 miles, of which 373.88 miles were laid in steel, an increase over 1884 of 3.97 miles of steel rails. Now, with the exception of some comparatively small amounts expended in 1884–85 on the yards at East Saginaw, Flint, and Evart, not a single dollar was charged to construction, or for betterments on the main line of the company's road for the years 1881 to 1885 inclusive. During that period about 15,772 tons of steel rails were purchased and paid for out of earnings. While the accounts of the company are in much confusion on that subject of these steel rails, it appears from defendant's Exhibit G that the cost of these rails, with freight and fittings, after deducting what
144 was on hand at close of 1885, amounted to about $900,346.10, while the total amount charged to construction as against this expenditure for the same period was only $540,616.81, and this was on the construction account for branches, sidings, spurs, and yards. Earnings were burdened with the difference, exceeding $350,000. Brown, the road-master, places the cost of steel rails during said period at $737,063.82. If from this is deducted the $540,516.81, charged to construction there will be left $196,547.01, which was borne by earnings for purchase cost of steel rails. The practice of the management was to remove the old iron rails from the main track, and use these in laying sidings, as required, and to put new steel rails in the main track in place of the old iron rails taken up. The difference between the cost of the new steel rail laid down on the main line, and as laid down, and the value of the old iron rail taken up, was charged to operating expenses, under the head of repairs to roadway, or "track repairs." Thus, in the report for 1881, it is stated that 4,000 tons of steel rails were laid down on the road. The cost of this, less the value of old rails removed, was fixed at $133,-779.09, which was charged to operating expenses, as "track repairs." The purchase cost of this 4,000 tons of steel rails, with fittings, to say nothing of the expense of making the change, was $240,000. In 1882 a similar charge was made to operating expenses for steel rails put down, to the amount of $31,224.56. During that year there were laid 1,697 tons of steel rails which cost $36,365. In 1883 the increase in steel-rail mileage on main track and sidings was 56.59 miles. Counting 38 tons to the mile, and the cost of steel rails at $37 per ton, this increased cost of steel rails alone was $184,257.04. For 1884 the cost of the steel rails used on the main line was about $32,560; and in 1885 about $12,926.32, aggregating $371,850 for steel-rail betterments, which was charged to operating expenses, and taken out of earnings. The complainants' expert, Jones, makes this expenditure for 1881, 1882, and 1883, as shown by defendant's Exhibit G, amount to $250,465. By taking the total cost of steel rails and deducting therefrom the amount charged to construction, old scrap rails sold, and what was on hand at the close of 1885, he makes this expenditure amount to $277,035.41, which, in the judgment of the court, is a most reasonable estimate; below, rather than above, the actual outlay for steel rails used in improving the track. The old iron rails, together with some light-weight steel rails taken from the main line, were used in sidings, spurs, and branches. A portion of

these were charged to construction account, the old rails being charged at their estimated value. But a considerable portion of such sidings, spurs, and branches, as shown by the road-master, Brown, were made at the expense of earnings. The extension of sidings and spurs from October 1, 1880, to December 31, 1881, thus charged to operating expenses, was something over 12 miles, of which the estimated cost, as made by the road-master, was $45,430. For 1882 there were 2.41 miles of net extension made at the expense of earnings, involving an estimated expenditure of $9,640. In 1884 there were 4.29 miles of net increase in such extensions, involving, as estimated by the road-master, an expenditure of $16,690. In 1884 the net increase of such sidings was 3.82 miles, involving an expense of $11,460; and in 1885 there was a net increase of sidings to the extent of 2.59 miles costing $5,400, aggregating, during the five years, $88,890. If the whole cost of the steel-rail betterments placed upon the road had been charged to construction account, as it should properly have been, as between the two sets of stockholders, then the items making up this aggregate of $88,890 might properly have been borne by earnings as operating expense; 145 but, instead of doing this, the road-bed, or track, is improved by substiuting new steel rails for old iron rails; the difference in their value is charged to operating expense, and taken out of earnings; and then, when the old rail is used for sidings and spurs, it is charged sometimes, when the management think proper and so direct, to construction, and at other times no charge is made to construction, and the whole expense of the change, and the entire cost of the siding or spur is made to fall upon the earnings. The "repairs," which article 4 of the charter provided should be paid out of net income, did not, as between the preferred and unpreferred, or provisional stockholders, warrant this method of dealing with the earnings of the company. It was neither just nor fair towards the latter class. Its effect was, not to keep the track in repair,—in the same state of efficiency as it existed in on October 1, 1880,—but to improve and enhance its value at the expense of earnings, which are thus reduced, and the provisional stockholders correspondingly postponed in coming into the company. If necessary to the assertion of complainants' rights, this court would order the whole steel-rail account to be charged to construction, and earnings credited back with all that has been expended therefrom for or on account of steel rails and steel improvements. But, without changing the account to that extent, the conclusion of the court is that at least $250,000 should be charged to construction on account of steel rails laid in the main tracks, and for outlays connected therewith, such as cost of work train, transportation of materials, etc., and that this sum should be credited back to earnings; and further, that earnings should be credited, and construction charged, with the $88,890 expended on sidings, as above stated. The expert testimony in the case warrants these changes, which are, moreover, within the true meaning and reasonable intent of the charter provisions of the company, on which the rights of both classes of stockholders depend.

Again, in 1883 two steamers owned by the company were enlarged and made more efficient, at a cost of $40,286.44, which was paid out of and charged to earnings. This change was made in the steamers to meet the demands of a new class or character of business, which sprang up shortly before, across Lake Michigan to Milwaukee. It was an addition of substantial and permanent character, which increased the value of the steamers to that extent, and the cost of the change should, in the opinion of the court, be charged to construction. It was actually charged to operating expenses, and taken out of earnings. This should be corrected by crediting that amount back to earnings for the year 1883. In 1884 there was a charge against expenses for depreciation on these steamers amounting to $6,000. In 1885 there was a like charge for depreciation, and also a charge of $2,500, as depreciation on dining-halls, the three charges making $14,500. These sums were not actually expended out of earnings, but were estimated and charged against operating expenses. This was not proper. No depreciation account was either kept or warranted by the charter as between the two classes of stockholders, and, no expenditure having actually been made to meet such depreciation, the estimated amount thereof could not properly be deducted from earnings, or net income. *U. S.* v. *Railway Co.*, 99 U. S. 459. The sum of $6,000 should therefore be credited back to earnings for 1884, and $8,500 for 1885.

In the spring of 1884, $142,000 was expended, under the orders of
146 the board of directors, for 8 new freight engines and 200 coal cars. The funds for this purchase were raised by loan, which was paid off by the company at the rate of $3,000 per month, and the sum so paid, in addition to interest on the loan, was charged to operating expenses, and withdrawn from earnings. See Reports for 1884, pp. 8, 23, for 1885, p. 8. This was clearly an improper charge against operating expenses. The outlay was not for the repair or renewal of old, but for the purchase of new, equipment, and should have been charged to construction. Fifteen thousand dollars were thus wrongfully charged in 1884, and $36,000 in 1885. These amounts should be credited to earnings for said years, respectively, and be charged to construction account.

During the years 1882, 1883, and 1884, earnings were charged with interest on temporary loans to the extent of $24,958.90. Whether these constitute a proper charge against net income or earnings, under the provisions of article 4 of the charter, admits of considerable question; but in the view which the court takes of other items of the company's accounts, as between construction and operating expenses, it is not necessary to pass upon the point. So, too. in reference to the sum of $4,225.28, charged to profit and loss on an old claim brought over from assets of the receiver. There are various other items which complainants insist, and which the experts testify, should not be charged to operating expenses, or which should go to construction, or be credited to earnings, but they need not be specially noticed, except as to dividend on the company's securities. A word of explanation is necessary as to this source of income. The whole $6,500,000 of preferred stock was not actually issued. Only $6,342,000 was issued, leaving in the hands of the company $158,000 of said preferred stock, the dividend on which the management credited to net income or earnings, as dividends on the entire $6,500,000 were charged against such earnings. If 7 per cent. annual dividends are to be charged on the whole preferred stock of $6,500,000, then the company should credit earnings annually with $11,060, being 7 per cent. on the $158,000 of stock still held by the company; or, in stating the account of earnings over operating expenses, said dividend should be charged only on the preferred stock actually issued, amounting to $6,342,000, making the annual dividend charge $443,940, instead of $455,000, as shown by the reports. The result will be the same under either method. It appears that the company's net earnings for the period from October 1, 1880, to December 31, 1880, was $132,-

584.69. If there is added to this the sum of $500,—the premium on bonds sold during that period,—we have the sum of $133,084.69 of income to be carried forward as applicable to dividends for 1881. Then, taking the net earnings and adding thereto the corrections, or credits due to earnings, as above indicated, the account for the several years will stand as follows:

Amount over from 1880 and applicable to dividends, -		$133,084 69
Net earnings, as reported by company, for 1881,	$244,037 94	
Add: Premium on bonds sold that year, -	107,257 25	
Relaying track with steel rails, - -	133,779 09	
Spurs and main line sidings, - -	45,430 00	
Balance on Co. securities not cred., -	2,357 50	
		532,861 78
Total applicable to dividends, - - - - -		$665,946 47
Less 7 per cent. dividend on $6,500,000 of preferred stock,		455,000 00
Surplus carried to January 1, 1882, - - -		$210,946 47

147

1882.

Surplus for 1881 brought over to 1882, - - -		$210,946 47
Net earnings reported for 1882, - - -	$438,989 89	
Add: Premium on bonds sold 1882, -	34,702 50	
Relaying track with steel rails, - -	31,224 56	
Spurs and sidings made out of earnings,	9,640 00	
Bal. of dividend on Co. stock, - -	647 00	
		515,203 95
Total applicable to dividends in 1882, - - -		$726,150 42
Less 7 per cent. dividend on $6,500,000 preferred stock, -		455,000 00
Surplus carried to 1883, - - - - -		$271,150 42

1883.

Surplus from 1882, - - - - - - -		$271,150 42
Net earnings reported for 1883, - - -	$488,799 13	
Add: Premium on bonds sold in 1883, -	12,136 50	
Relaying track with steel rails, - -	65,000 00	
Spurs and sidings made out of earnings,	16,960 00	
Enlargement of steamers, - -	40,286 44	
		623,182 07
Total applicable to dividends in 1883, - - -		$894,332 49
Less dividend of 7 per cent. on $6,500,000, - - -		455,000 00
Surplus carried to January, 1884, - - - -		$439,332 49

1884.

Surplus from 1883, - - - - - - -		$439,332 49
Net earnings reported for 1884, - - -	$400,303 40	
Add: Premium on bonds sold 1884 - -	9,945 00	
Relaying track with steel rails, - -	10,000 00	
Spurs and sidings made with earnings,	11,460 00	
Equipment renewals, - - -	15,000 00	
Depreciation on steamers, charged to expenses,	6,000 00	
		452,708 40
Total applicable to dividends in 1884, - - -		$892,040 89
Less 7 per cent. dividends on $6,500,000, - - -		455,000 00
Surplus carried to January 1, 1885, - - -		$437,040 89

1885.

Surplus from 1884,		$437,040 89
Net earnings reported for 1885,	$272,451 77	
Add: Relaying track with steel rails,	9,996 35	
Spurs and sidings made with earnings,	5,400 00	
Equipment and renewals charged to expenses,	36,000 00	
Depreciation of steamers and dining-hall,	8,500 00	
Dividend on Co. securities,	4,740 00	
		337,088 12
Total applicable to dividends in 1885		$774,129 01
Less 7 per cent. dividend on $6,500,000,		455,000 00
Surplus January 1, 1886,		$319,129 01

If, as the experts testify, the expenses of work trains engaged in construction, and freight on material used for construction, should be charged to construction account, and corrections were made in that re-
148 spect, the annual balance, after deducting the 7 per cent. dividend, would be still larger than as above given. It thus appears that, independently of the surplus land funds, the earnings or net income of the road, if the accounts between construction and operating expenses had been properly kept, in conformity with the provisions of the charter, and according to the rights of the two classes of stockholders, as therein defined, were amply sufficient, after paying interest on the company's entire bonded debt, repairs, and expenses of equipment and renewals, to pay the annual dividends of 7 per cent. on $6,500,000 of preferred stock for the five years in question. But, when the large surplus land fund is taken into consideration, it is difficult to see any reason for not declaring and paying that dividend for five consecutive years, except a deliberate purpose to keep the provisional certificates holders out of any voice or vote in management of the company, or to indefinitely postpone their admission. The 5 per cent. deficiency in dividends for the five consecutive years under consideration on the $6,500,000 of preferred stock actually issued amounts to $317,100. This could have been readily withdrawn from the surplus land funds if earnings had been inadvertently diverted to construction, and the management had desired to replace the amount, so as to make it applicable to dividends; or, if improper charges to earnings had not been made from year to year, as already shown, the deficiency would not have existed. While the earnings have been thus misapplied or diverted, the policy of the management has been steadily in the line of permanent improvements, and large enhancement in the value of the company's property. Its equipment has been greatly enlarged, its main tracks, sidings, spurs, and branches have been extended, and its general efficiency not merely maintained, but largely increased. When the company took possession in October, 1880, the road-bed and equipment were valued at $9,671,958.90. On the 31st December, 1880, that valuation had increased to $10,311,193.38. At the close of 1881 the valuation of road-bed and equipment had increased, as reported by the general manager, to $12,281,853.02. At the close of 1882 it had grown to $12,966,601.64. At the close of 1883 it was reported at $13,-506,231.94. At the close of 1884, after deducting $1,116,070.45, charged off to depreciation, the valuation stood at $12,657,430.55, and on December 31, 1885, it was placed at $12,512,928.81. If the arbitrary deduction had not been made in 1884, the valuation at the close

of 1885 would have stood at $13,628,999.26, making an increase since October 1, 1880, of $3,957,040.36; an amount exceeding the provisional certificates now seeking admission as unpreferred stock in the company. These valuations are independent of the large surplus lands and land funds. Look at the condition of the company from another stand-point. Its total funded debt is $5,299,000, while the preferred stock actually issued is $6,342,000, making its total capitalization $11,641,000. It has 361.64 miles of main line, and 115.72 miles of business producing tracks in addition; making 477.38 miles of roadway, on which there is of capital and funded debt only $11,641,000, or less than $25,000 per mile. The capitalization and funded debt of other railroads in the state of Michigan, it is said, will average about $45,000 to the mile. Under these circumstances, neither the company nor the preferred stockholders who control its management, which has been conducted more with a view to the permanency and security of their own interests than with regard to the rights and interests of the common or unpreferred stockholders, can rightfully longer exclude the latter from their charter share
in the corporate enterprise. This suit is practically a contest between 149
the two classes of stockholders. The preference class is in control, and is interested in keeping the other out. This result has been so far effected by expending the company's earnings and income in permanently improving the property, or for other purposes than those contemplated by article 4 of the charter, whereby net income applicable to dividends has been reduced, while the valuation of the company's road-bed and equipment has steadily increased....

The court, having been compelled carefully to examine the evidence, which is quite voluminous, and analyze the company's accounts, so as to determine the rights of the parties, and being fully satisfied from this investigation of the accounts that the aforegoing statement in respect to the yearly income applicable to dividends is substantially correct, it is not deemed necessary to refer these matters to a special master for a report, and thereby further delay the final disposition of the case. The conclusions of the court on this branch of the case are that complainants are entitled to the relief sought; that they are entitled to be admitted into the defendant company as regular stockholders of the common or unpreferred class; that this right accrued to them and to others similarly situated on January 1, 1886; that a sufficiency of surplus land funds is in the hands of the land trustees, and subject to the control of the company to pay, or make good, the deficiency of 1½ per cent., or $95,110, on dividends for 1881; ½ per cent., or $31,710, on dividends for 1882; and 3 per cent., or $190,260, on dividends for 1885, upon the preferred capital stock actually issued, amounting to $6,342,000; and the defendant company should be required to pay over to the preferred stockholders, *pro rata*, out of said surplus land funds or other funds at its disposal, said annual deficiencies, so as to make up to said preferred stockholders their full 7 per cent. dividends for five consecutive years, and thus comply with the conditions, as the company and its management should have done, on which the provisional certificate holders were entitled to be admitted; and, further, that the defendant company, its officers and agents, should be enjoined from depriving complainants, or those in like state with them, of their rights as common stockholders, in voting or otherwise, and from applying the income and earnings of the company, without the consent of said common stockholders, to improvements of a permanent character; all of which is accordingly ordered and decreed, with the further direction that the defendant corporation, its officers and directors, be ordered to issue regular certificates for common or unpreferred stock in the company to complainants and other holders of provisional certificates, severally, according to their respective holdings of the latter certificates, and upon the production and surrender of the same.

MARKS v. MONROE COUNTY PERMANENT SAVINGS & LOAN ASSOC.

52 N.Y. State Rep. 451 (1889)
Supreme Court of New York

RUMSEY, J. The defendant is a corporation organized under the authority of chapter 122 of the Laws of 1851. The plaintiff is a stockholder in the corporation, and at the time when the matters accrued which are alleged as the cause of action herein he had 50 shares in the stock of the defendant upon which he had paid $1,845.25, upon which sum he was entitled to dividends. The quarterly meetings of the corporation are held on the third Saturdays of November, February, May, and August, respectively. Article 15 of the constitution of the defendant requires that a dividend of the net profits shall be declared at each quarterly meeting, to be credited to each shareholder in a way and upon an amount to be ascertained as provided in that article, but which need not be referred to here. The statute (2 Rev. St. [7th Ed.] p. 1763, § 7) makes it the duty of the directors to declare the dividends. At the quarterly meeting in August, 1888, the directors resolved to and did declare a dividend of 4 per cent. upon the amount which each shareholder then had to his credit in the association. The amount of the dividend upon the plaintiff's credits was $73.81, and the total dividend upon all the shares was $1,146. It was reckoned on the earnings, or what was claimed to be the earnings or net profits, of the second quarter, and did not include the earnings or profits of the third quarter, although declared the end of that quarter....

The next claim of the plaintiff is that the dividend should be of the whole of the net earnings or profits of the corporation, and be at a greater rate than 4 per cent. on the deposits entitled to it. In regard to this claim it may be said, first, that although there may be profits properly applicable to a dividend, yet usually when it shall be made, and, if made, how much it shall be, rests in the fair and honest discretion of the directors, uncontrollable by the courts. Williams v. Telegraph Co., 93 N. Y. 162, 192, and cases cited. In this case the directors are bound by the by-laws or articles of association to declare a dividend of the profits, but I do not think that requires them to use all the profits earned at any time. There may be debts of the association not due, but to become due, or the business of the association may require the retention of money for some other purpose. In such case it is clearly within the power of the directors to retain such money as may be necessary, and the court will not interfere with that discretion. It does not appear here what is the state of affairs in that regard, and for that reason the court cannot say that the directors erred in refusing to declare a dividend greater than 4 per cent.

But, passing that, let us see whether there was on the 18th of August any fund out of which the directors might have declared a larger dividend. The statute says that they may declare dividends from the earnings, and from the earnings only. 2 Rev. St. (7th Ed.) p. 1763, § 7. This cannot mean, of course, that the directors are at liberty to devote all the earnings to dividends, without providing for the debts of the company or the expenses of its maintenance. It must be construed to mean that the dividends may be declared out

of the profits, which means out of the surplus of the earnings which may be left after paying the expenses of carrying on the business and all other current expenses. St. John v. Railway Co., 10 Blatchf. 271, 22 Wall. 136, 99 Amer. Dec. note p. 762. That is the general statutory rule of this state with regard to corporations, and the one which I think should be applied here. 2 Rev. St. (7th Ed.) p. 1533, § 2; Van Dyck v. McQuade, 86 N. Y. 38, 46, 47. The plaintiff claims that in computing the amount of this surplus the sum bid for premiums on each loan during the quarter should be estimated as earnings. This the defendant denies, and the question thus raised is the serious one on this branch of the case. To decide it, we must examine the way in which loans are made. It is this: When the money to loan is in the treasury, if more than one member applies for it, the loan is put up at auction, and the member offering the highest premium for it is entitled to have it awarded to him. Each member is entitled to borrow not more than the par value of the stock for which he has subscribed, if he gives satisfactory security.
152 When a loan to the amount of his stock is awarded to him, he gives to the association his bond and mortgage for the par value of the stock, and he receives for it, not the face of the bond, but that amount less the premium. For instance, if a member has five shares, the par value of which is $525, and bids $6 per share premium for a loan of that amount, he gives to the association his bond and mortgage for $525 and interest, and he receives from it the face of his bond, less the premium, which is $30; the transaction netting him $495. This he pays in weekly installments of 10 cents principal and 10 cents interest on each share represented by the loan, or, in the case used for illustration, $1 a week, until the payments and his dividends equal the amount of the bond and interest. It will thus be seen that the premium on each loan is not paid in cash, but goes into the bond and mortgage, and becomes a debt due to the association, payable at the rate of 10 cents a week for each share represented by it. The precise time when it will all be paid is not certain. It depends upon the amount chargeable to the member for insurance and taxes on the mortgaged property, and for fines and penalties imposed on him, as well as upon the dividend he shall become entitled to. Indeed, it may not be paid at all, but the member may default in his payments, leaving the association to repay itself by a foreclosure of the mortgage.

The transaction above set forth adds to the property of the association; that is, the association has for $495 become the owner of a bond and mortgage worth $525, upon which it will eventually realize that sum, with interest. But, while its assets are increased by the sum of $30, it has not received that amount of money. It is probable that the amount will be received, but it may not. This mortgage for $525 has become an asset of the company, and when it is paid the company will have made a profit by the transaction of $30 and interest. But I do not think that the profit can be said to be earned until the transaction is closed and the money is in the treasury. Until that is done, there may be no profit. The failure to pay may make the asset worthless. This distinction between the gain by the appreciation in value of an asset, and the final gain of money in hand by its sale at the enhanced value, is taken and made the rule of the decision in Jennery v. Olmstead, 36 Hun, 536. In that case it appeared that the defendant, Olmstead, had been president of a savings bank under an agreement that he should have a

salary out of the net profits. He credited himself with certain sums,
and an action was begun to recover them back. It appeared that
in 1869 the bank bought certain bonds, which appreciated in value
to the amount of $648.43, but which had not been sold. Olmstead
claimed that this enhanced value was a profit, which entitled him to
receive that sum as a salary. The court held not, saying that to es-
timate the value of bonds yet unsold, and, on finding the estimated
value to exceed the purchase price, to call the difference profits, was
not the way to ascertain the fact of profits, and that such apprecia-
tion was not profits in any sense of the term. I think the holding of
the court in that case, that profits are not realized because the value
of the assets is enhanced, is controlling here against the plaintiff.
It is to be noticed that while the by-law of the corporation uses the
word "profits," the statute says that dividends can be declared only
from the earnings. The profits out of which the trustees may de-
clare their dividend must be the profits out of the earnings. The
earnings are the receipts, the sum which the association received,
or became entitled to receive, during the quarter; not those 153
which it might receive at some future time, but which it has now no
right to demand. The conclusion here reached is sustained by many
cases, in which the terms "profits" and "earnings" have been defined,
some of which are cited above. Boone, Corp. § 125; Mor. Priv. Corp.
§ 437; Connolly v. Davidson, 15 Minn. 519, (Gil. 428.) That conclu-
sion requires that in estimating the net profits of any quarter the
amount of premiums which have been bid for loans during the quar-
ter, and included in mortgages, but not yet paid in cash, is not to be
estimated.

That conclusion puts an end to this case, for it is evident that, without estimating these premiums, the earnings of the association were not more than the dividend declared by them....

RICHARDSON v. BUHL

77 Mich. 632 (1889)
Supreme Court of Michigan

Bill to enjoin defendants from selling stock in a manufacturing corporation, held by them as security. Defendants appeal from decree directing retransfer of stock to complainant, and that defendants pay a balance of $35,219.25 found due complainant. Decree reversed and bill dismissed. The facts are stated in the opinion. . . .

SHERWOOD, C. J. . . .

The Diamond Match Company was organized December 3, 1880, under the laws of the state of Connecticut,
154 for the purpose of uniting in one corporation all the match manufactories in the United States. Its object was to monopolize and control the business of making all the friction matches in the country, and establish the price thereof; and it became necessary to buy many plants which had become established in the business, or were preparing therefor, and all the property used in connection therewith, and to obtain promises from the owners and manufacturers that they would not engage in the business themselves, or indirectly, through others, for ten or more years thereafter; and, for the purpose of obtaining the control and good-will of such factories and their properties, large powers were given by the legislature to the Diamond Match Company when organized, and under the by-laws by which it was controlled. . . .

The Diamond Match Company, in carrying out its purposes, found it necessary, in many instances, to buy a large quantity of useless material, and to pay large and exorbitant prices for the property purchased, which they could not make available; and in many cases in no other way was it possible to purchase the inactivity of manufacturers, and those who intended to enter into the business, and who would otherwise become competitors of the company in the trade. For the purpose of showing upon the books of the company the amount it was obliged to pay for unnecessary and useless property, and the excess in prices for the property they could use, to silence and prevent all competition, the company opened two accounts, —one headed "Real Estate and Machinery," and the other "Purchase Account." The capital stock of the company consisted of $2,250,000, divided into $1,400,000 of common stock, and $850,000 of preferred stock. For five years the preferred stock was entitled to an annual dividend of 10 per cent. before any dividend was to be paid on the common stock....

Each proprietor subscribed for a certain amount of preferred stock, which he paid for by transferring to the company such matches and match materials as he or it had on hand when they entered the company, at an appraised value, and, if this was insufficient to pay for such stock, the balance was paid in cash; but common stock was paid for all real estate, machinery, patents, good-will, bonds to stay out of the business, and all other property transferred to the company at the valuation agreed upon when the proprietor or proprietors came into the company, except matches and match materials, for which preferred stock was issued.... 155

Schedule A of the testimony shows that among the match factories that passed into the control of the Diamond Match Company at the time of its organization was that of the Richardson Match Company of Detroit, ...

It was, however, necessary, in consequence of the uncanceled liabilities of the defendants, and the desire of Mr. Richardson to raise more money to take the position he wished to in the new company, that a different agreement should be made...

between the complainant and defendants, and ...

the contract, as finally concluded, reads as follows:

"Memorandum of agreement between David M. Richardson, of the first part, and Christian H. Buhl and Russel A. Alger, of the second part, all of Detroit, Michigan, witnesseth as follows:

....And as it will be necessary for said Richardson to borrow the principal part of said ninety-five thousand dollars, for which he is to receive ninety-five thousand dollars of the preferred stock of said Diamond Match Company at its par value, the said second parties agree to indorse the said Richardson's notes for such sum as is required to make up said ninety-five thousand dollars ($95,000), after deducting the amount of the net earnings due said Richardson from the proceeds of the Richardson Match Company since July 1, 1879, and to raise the money on said notes. . . .

All the remaining stock, both preferred and common, is to be taken in the name of the first party, and, with the exception of ten shares of said common stock, is to be immediately transferred by him to said C. H. Buhl, to be held by said Buhl as security for the indorsements as above stated, and any and all other indebtedness of said first party or said Richardson Match Company to said parties, or either of them, ...

"The dividends on the stock of the Diamond Match Company, both common and preferred,...

and the 10 shares retained by said Richardson, for one year and six months from January 1, 1881, shall be applied—...

to the payment of interest on the notes so indorsed by said second parties; and
156 ... to the payment of interest to each of the parties hereto on the money advanced by them respectively in making up said sum of $95,000. Of what there remains, one-quarter shall be paid to each of the said second parties, and the other half applied to the payment of the principal of the notes so indorsed by said second parties, and of any advances that may be made by them....

"*It is expressly understood that said second parties are to receive one-half (each one-quarter), after deducting the payments for interest as above stated, of the net earnings of said stock, and not merely one-half the dividends; and in settlement with said first party, he is to pay them, in addition to one-half the dividends declared, the one-half of any surplus or reserved fund which, if divided, would pertain to said stock; and on such settlement no loss that may be charged on account of the purchase and sale by said Diamond Match Company of other match factories shall be taken into account; and, if such settlement is made at the end of a half-year, the earnings of the whole year shall be averaged so that the said second parties shall receive the full half of the earnings of said stock for the whole year. Provided, that on such settlement the second parties shall estimate such earnings from the trial balance or books of said Diamond Match Company, and shall make such allowances as to them shall seem just and equitable for loss and shrinkage in values of said Diamond Match Company, and shall take into consideration improvements that have been made out of the earnings thereof.*

"David M. Richardson.
"R. A. Alger.
"C. H. Buhl.

"*Detroit, Dec.* 28 1880."

. . . The defendants, . . . allege that the net earnings of the Richardson stock in the Diamond Match Company for 1881 were $81,099.31, and for 1882 are $139,757.92; and that there is still due them on their share thereof $52,061.38, less the dividend of $24,400, received by them since the bill was filed. Thus it will be discovered that the issue in the case is made upon the proper construction of the contract of December 28, 1880, assuming that said contract is in all respects a valid instrument.

When the Diamond Match Company opened the books containing the account of its transactions, as has been hereinbefore alluded to, all of its purchases were kept in 157
two accounts. Under the head of "Purchase Account," were matches and match material, appraised at cash value; and it would appear that under the head of "Real Estate and Machinery Account," everything else purchased by the company as taken and appraised was included. This account was represented by the common stock of the company, with which it was purchased; the other by preferred stock, which was given for it. There seems to be a general understanding that the property contained in the purchase account, or very much of it, was taken by the company at a large overvaluation, in some instances many times its worth was given; and it is claimed in like manner was there an overvaluation made and listed under the head of "Real Estate and Machinery Account;" that this became necessary in order to make the desired purchases, and secure the complete monopoly intended, that is to say, to increase the value of the company's stock and its gains by destroying all competition, whether the result of individual enterprise or corporate action, and to secure the non-action of the proprietors of the factories taken in or purchased. The parties to this suit were all benefited by such action in proportion to the amount of stock held by each, as all were stockholders. It is true the complainant's stock, or a large portion of it, was at the time held by defendants as security, but that does not change the rules or the results which govern and follow the action taken by the company.

There appear in the record, as returned to this Court, from the books of the Diamond Match Company, commencing with August 1, 1881, 19 trial balances, ending with August 1, 1883. That of December 31, 1881, shows a credit to the profit and loss account of $647,433.43, and a debit of $7,175.67, leaving a balance to the credit of that account of $640,257.76. The trial balance of December 30, 1882, shows a credit to the profit and loss account of $1,118,848.42, and a debit of $15,496.29, leaving a balance to the credit of that account of $1,103,352.13. The board of directors, on February 9, 1882, adopted the following preamble and resolutions:

"*Whereas,* the several ledgers and general balance sheets of the company, at date of December 31, 1881, show the aggregate net earnings of all the factories earn-
158 ing a profit to be the sum of $647,433.43, and the aggregate losses of the factories making losses to be $7,175.67, making total net earnings, $640,257.76; and—

"*Whereas,* there are standing on the several ledgers of the company various purchase accounts, which are debited with an aggregate sum of $173,733.89, which represent the cost of same up to December 31, 1881; and whereas, the actual value of said purchase accounts is $5,500; therefore—

"*Resolved,* that the difference of $168,233.89 between the actual value and the book value of these purchase accounts be charged to Dr. of net earnings of the company for 1881, and that the president be instructed to furnish the managers with the proper forms of entries to carry this resolution into effect.

"*Whereas,* many of the real-estate and machinery accounts of this company have a book value, or are charged with a cost sum in excess of their actual value; therefore, *resolved,* that $247,023.87 of the sum described as net earnings be applied to the reductions of the book values of such real-estate and machinery accounts, and in such proportions as the executive committee may approve, and that the president be requested to furnish the managers with the proper entries to carry this resolution into effect on the several books of account and ledgers of the company."

At the same meeting of the board of directors, a 10 per cent. dividend was declared. Three 10 per cent. dividends were declared for 1882; the last one at a meeting of the board February 14, 1883. At the same meeting it was resolved—

"That the balance remaining as credit of profit and loss account, after providing for the dividend declared at this meeting, be applied to the reduction of the book values of the company's real-estate and machinery accounts, such reduction to be apportioned among the several properties by the executive committee; the amount so to be applied being $310,922.26."

Subsequently a reduction was made in the purchase account of $117,429.87. This fact is admitted by a stipulation of the parties, and by said stipulation the following is given as a tabulated statement of the action of the company's board of directors in disposing of the profit and loss account for the two years in question:

1881.			
To the credit of profit and loss account		$640,257 26	
Dividends	$225,000 00		
Charged off purchase acct	168,233 89		
Charged off real estate and machinery acct	247,023 87		
		$640,257 76	
1882.			
To the credit of profit and loss acct		$1,103,352 13	159
Dividends	$675,000 00		
Charged off purchase acct	117,429 87		
Charged off real estate and machinery account	310,922 26		
		$1,103,352 13	

The defendants claim that they are entitled under their agreement to their share of the amounts charged off, the same as though these amounts had not been so disposed of upon the books. Complainant claims that defendants are entitled to one-half of the dividends paid, and no more; that dividends and net earnings mean the same thing, as used in the contract between the parties in this case; and that they have received the amount to which they are entitled.

It is undoubtedly true that—

"The function of a profit and loss account is to show earnings, or the lack of them; and that everything being credited which ought to be credited, and everything being charged which ought to be charged, the profit and loss account will show what the net earnings or net losses are;"—

And I am satisfied that the learned counsel for the complainant is correct when he says—

"That the first thing to be done by any manufacturer who would ascertain his net earnings during the preceding year, is to take a careful inventory of what he has left, including his plant and machinery, and then make just and full allowances for all losses and shrinkages of every kind that he has suffered in his property during the year, and for all expenses of every kind, ordinary or extraordinary, that have occurred during the year, and, having made such inventory, and deducted such losses and shrinkage of every kind, his net earnings will be the difference between all his investments in his business and all his expenses of every kind on the one hand, and this new inventory, with the reductions properly made, and all that he has received of every kind on the other hand; and if his books are properly kept, and proper deductions made, these net earnings will finally appear on the balance sheet to the credit of the profit and loss account."

There is no dispute as to what the items "charged off" in the account represented, and that they stood upon the books of the company, under the direction of its managers, in the account as debited to the company. It represented the agreed valuation of the property purchased by the company, or taken into it at its organiza-
160 tion, and for which common stock of the company was issued or given to the owner or owners, and included therein is the bond, required in each instance where a purchase was made, that the vendor would not prosecute the business for a series of years thereafter

The stock was taken at par, the amount of the valuation and the amount of the stock being equal, and the value of the stock was never less than when taken, and remained at par except when sold for more; and it is a little difficult to see why it should be said, so long as this was the case, that there was a loss to the company or a shrinkage in value. It is true the value of the chattel property and real estate conveyed to the company may have greatly depreciated; but at the same time the rights surrendered to the company by the owner under his bond might, in the mean time, have greatly appreciated. It seems quite certain that no means are shown, if any exist, by which such loss or depreciation could be made to appear to a board of directors or to any one else with any degree of certainty....

I think, that in the settlement to be made between these parties it was expressly provided that in ascertaining the half of the net earnings of the stock, to which the defendants were entitled, no such "charging off" from such earnings was to be allowed; and I do not think, as is urged by complainant's counsel,—

"That, in the absence of bad faith or mistake, the action of the board of directors in reducing the amounts to the credit of the profit and loss accounts is conclusive upon the parties to this suit as to the amount of the earnings or profits to be divided between them;"—

And it is of no consequence whether their action in this regard can be impeached or not, if the defendants are not bound by the action of the board of directors. There is no doubt but that the Diamond Match Company in doing a legitimate business would have had the right to have the par value of its shares of stock maintained out of the profits or earnings of the company, and it was maintained; and for that purpose it was entirely unnecessary for its board of directors to direct any "charging off," as was done in this case. Its stock was not only at all times at par, but, as we have before said, largely above par, and has always been at a premium; and from its earnings the year after the agreement ended the complainant himself received a stock dividend amounting to 161
$70,000.

If it were necessary, but little difficulty would be found, I think, in showing that the sums "charged off" were not properly expenses or losses in running the business of the company. I think the learned counsel for defendants was right in saying—

> "It was an acquisition of the very property the company at the outset had determined to acquire, and was of more permanent value than if it had been invested in new factories. The object of the company was to crush others, that it might be valuable. It did that, and expended out of its earnings for 1881 and 1882 $285,663.76, not as an expense of running the business, but for the purpose, and with the inevitable effect, of increasing its property. What was acquired with this money was none the less property because intangible. Every dollar thus expended added itself to the value of the business, and became a permanent part of it. Richardson owns $285,000 of the stock of this company (exclusive of $70,000 acquired by stock dividend from earnings of 1883), every dollar of which was permanently enhanched in value by these expenditures. * * * It was a permanent investment. The company had determined to monopolize the business, and therefore the more perfect the monopoly became the more valuable its property became. Every factory it bought and closed, every patent it acquired, every good-will it purchased, every man it bought up, added to the value of its stock not only the amount paid, but from the very necessity of the case, very much more." . . .

I think no one can read the contract in question, and fail to discover that considerations of public policy are largely involved. . . .

All combinations among persons or corporations for the purpose of raising or controlling the prices of merchandise, or any of the necessaries of life, are monopolies, and intolerable; and ought to receive the condemnation of all courts.

In my judgment, not only is the enterprise in which the Diamond Match Company is engaged an unlawful one, but the contract in question in this case, being made to further its objects and purposes, is void upon the ground that it is against public policy.

The decree at the circuit should be reversed, and the complainant's bill dismissed, with costs. . . .

HUBBARD v. WEARE

79 Iowa 678 (1890)
Supreme Court of Iowa

THE Williams Harvester Company was organized as a corporation under articles dated May 13, 1878, fixing the capital stock at eighteen thousand dollars in shares of one hundred dollars, each, with the defendant as president, which position he continued to hold during all the time the company carried on business....

The representations set out by all the plaintiffs as being made by the defendant, and by which they were induced to subscribe and pay for stock, may be summed up as follows: (1) That said corporation was well organized and well conducted, upon a good business basis; (2) that it had made large gains and profits, and had actually earned the dividends declared; (3) that a greater dividend than ten per cent. might have been declared in 1880, but that it was thought best by defendant to hold a surplus; and (4) that there were sufficient profits and earnings to have declared a dividend of ten per cent. in 1882, but that the money could be used to great advantage in the business....

GIVEN, J.— ...

2. —: by officers of corporation as to its condition: presumption.

Officers of corporations, who hold out to individuals, or to the public, advantages which will accrue to persons who take shares in their corporation, and invite them to take shares on the faith of their representations, are bound to state everything with strict and scrupulous accuracy, and not only to abstain from stating as facts that which is not so, but to omit no fact within their knowledge, the existence of which might affect the advantages held out as inducements to take shares. Such officers will be presumed to have known that which it was their duty to know. Before making representations as to the condition of the company as inducements to take stock therein or extend credit thereto, it is their duty to use reasonable diligence to know that the representations are true, and they will be presumed to have used such diligence, and to possess the knowledge which its exercise would bring to them.

Special emphasis should be given to these wholesome rules of the law, in view of the large investments that are being made in corporate enterprises, where the investors must necessarily trust largely to the honesty and fidelity of the officers of the corporation for the management of their investments. Outside investors can know but little of the affairs of the corporation, while its officers may and should know them fully. One who makes a false representation as being true to his personal knowledge, without knowing whether it is true or false, for the purpose of inducing another to act, and upon which he does act to his injury, should certainly
164 be held liable for the deceit; and yet it is argued that he is not liable because he did not know the representation to be false. A person making a false representation as true to his personal knowledge will not be heard to say that he did not have knowledge as to its truth or falsity....

4. ——: statements made upon alleged personal knowledge: estoppel.

Some difference is expressed as to what are profits, and how they are to be arrived at. This is fully answered in *Miller v. Bradish*, 69 Iowa, 278, where it is said: "The assets, resources and funds of the corporation must consist of cash on hand and other property, and, if such assets exceed the liabilities, a dividend can be lawfully declared;" in other words, a profit exists. Money paid out is not on hand, and should not be reckoned as assets. If paid for property that is on hand, the property is assets. If expended in a way that has enhanced the value of the general assets, it is included in their valuation. If so expended as to have brought no property, or no enhancement of that on hand, then it is a loss, and should not be counted as assets....

5. Corporations: assets: dividends.

Appellants contend that certain items were improperly included as assets, and others omitted from the statements of liabilities upon which the dividends were declared, and hence that it was not true that the corporation had made large gains and profits, and had actually earned the dividends declared, nor that a greater dividend than ten per cent. might have been declared in 1880. The profits upon which dividends were declared were arrived at by deducting what was stated as the liabilities of the company from what was stated as its assets. In the statement of assets to September 1, 1879, $498.32 was

6. ——: ——: what are and what are not: special cases.

included as profit of season 1878. No such profit had been declared, or in any way was separated or withdrawn from the general assets. The profit, if any, remained as a part of the assets, and was included in the application thereof. To state it as a separate item was to include it twice.

There was included in this statement of assets, "Moving account, $67.58;" and, in the statement for 1880, "Moving account, $1,608.41." It does not appear with certainty what these items represent. Appellants contend that it is money paid out for removing the works from the old to the new location. Appellee suggests that they represent the cost of bringing property the company had purchased and made a part of the plant from Chicago or elsewhere. We see no other reasonable explanation than that it was money paid out for moving machinery or materials, or both, that went into the buildings, and is, therefore, proper to be included in the assets; but not as a separate item, if the aggregate value of the buildings into which it entered is given. In 1879 the buildings were not valued as a whole, but in 1880 they were. The $67.58 was, therefore, properly included as a separate item, and the $1,608.41, in 1881, was not.

"Fair machines account, $144.97," was included as assets. Here, again, we are without definite explanation. Appellants contend that it was money paid out as expenses in exhibiting machines at the fairs, while appellee suggests that it represents machines on hand made for exhibition. Judging from the other items of the inventory and the amount, we conclude that it does not represent machinery on hand, but expenses of exhibiting machines. Whatever benefit comes to the corporation for such expenditure must be in the way of the enhancement of the value of its property and business, and not as in the case of the purchase of property which remained on hand. Entering, as it did, into the value of the general assets, it was covered by the estimate placed thereon, and should not have been included as a separate item.

"Outstandings, $22,821.39," was stated as assets in 1879. This is understood to include accounts mostly with agents and their customers for machines, some of which were in the hands of agents; others of which had been sold. No deduction was made for shrinkage or loss in collections. That a loss would occur is inevitable, and, though that loss could not be determined with exactness, experience would indicate about what it would be. Without such an approximation, the result would not show with any reasonable certainty the state of the company's affairs.

The statement for 1880 included as assets, "Accrued interest on bills receivable, $756.22." There is nothing included in liabilities for interest on the thirty-five thousand, five hundred dollars bills payable. It is argued that bills payable were largely to banks and for merchandise; that bankers require interest in advance; that the company, being prosperous, paid at maturity, so that no interest was accruing against it. Common
166 experience, and the subsequent history of the company, hardly warrant such a conclusion. We think that an approximation should have been made of the accrued interest for which the company was liable.

"Material and labor expense on self-binder, $1,708.78," was also included as assets in the statement of 1880. This represents what had been expended in the effort to perfect the new self-binder. Valuations in 1880 were to be made according to what was then known. The value of this machine, other than as old iron, depended entirely upon whether it could be made to work successfully. It was not possible at that time to determine what its real value was, and hence it was put in at what it had cost. Those having confidence in the success of the invention no doubt valued it very highly, while those not having such confidence might not give it any value. The object of valuing the assets was to see whether any profit had been actually earned up to that time that might be divided among the shareholders. It required future developments to determine whether the binder was of any value or not, and until it had an actual value it should not have been included as assets. The amount expended upon it was not assets, but a loss, that would come back or not, as the machine would or would not prove successful. Surely, as yet, there was nothing in the machine to divide; and in estimating the profits for the purpose of division, and as an inducement to persons to take stock, no such an uncertain element should have been included.

We have already considered the $1,608.40 moving account included in the estimate of 1880. There was also included, "Expenses, $391.99." We are unable to see how money that had been paid out as expenses can be considered as assets on hand for distribution, except as it has entered into the property on hand in the enhancement of its value. The property being estimated at its value, this item should not have been included.

"Bindery account, $2,919.59," is included in the statement of assets for 1881 as profits. Appellants claim that it was a total loss, and should have gone to the other side of the account, thus making a difference in the result of $5,839. The *status* of the new binder was about the same in 1881 that it was in 1880; that is, it was incomplete, and it had not yet been demonstrated whether it would be successful or not. While we are not prepared to say that this sum should have been included as a loss, we are satisfied, for the reasons 167
already stated, that it should not have been included as profits or assets. No dividends were declared for 1882.

The results arrived at by the committee, in its review of the statements up to and including 1881, are not entitled to much consideration, as their estimates were based upon facts disclosed following the several dates at which dividends had been declared. In determining whether the dividends were earned, we must take the facts as they existed at the time they were declared. From what we have stated, it will be seen that our conclusions are that it was not true that the company had made large gains and profits, and had actually earned the dividends declared, nor that a greater dividend might have been declared in 1880 or 1882....

We think it fairly appears that Hubbard relied upon the representations of the defendant as to the earnings of the company, and was induced thereby to take and pay for the stock that he did, except as to the five hundred dollars taken and paid for July 1, 1878....

While it appears that Hubbard took but little more part in the business after his election, in 1883, than before, yet, in view of his official relation to the company, and the ascertainment of these large losses by committee and otherwise, we may fairly presume that he knew of the loss and report before making either of the indorsements, and, knowing it, no longer relied upon the defendant's representations as to profits. We think that he, with others, joined in the indorsements, hoping to save the company from bankruptcy, and themselves from further loss, and that he is therefore not entitled to the relief asked, as against these indorsements. . . .

Our conclusion, upon the whole case, is that the plaintiff Hubbard is entitled to recover of the defendant Weare all amounts paid in cash for stock, except the five hundred dollars paid in July, 1878, with six per cent. interest from the time of payment; and that he is not entitled to any part of the relief asked as to the loan of one thousand dollars, or the indorsements made by him for the company. . . .

EXCELSIOR WATER AND MINING CO. v. PIERCE

90 Cal. 131 (1891)
Supreme Court of California

BEATTY, C. J.—This is an action by a California corporation against one of its former directors to recover the amount of certain dividends declared and paid to its stockholders with the concurrence of the defendant while a director. It is alleged by the plaintiff that such dividends were not paid out of the surplus profits of its business, and the action is based upon the provisions of section 309 of the Civil Code, which reads as follows:— ...

"Sec. 309. The directors of corporations must not make dividends, except from the surplus profits arising from the business thereof; nor must they divide, withdraw, or pay to the stockholders, or any of them, any part of the capital stock; nor must they create debts beyond their subscribed capital stock, or reduce or increase the capital stock, except as hereinafter specially provided. 169

...

It appears therefrom that the plaintiff was incorporated in March, 1877, with a nominal or share capital of five million dollars, divided into fifty thousand shares of one hundred dollars each. The object of the incorporation was to carry on hydraulic mining, etc., and the defendant was, from the beginning down to September, 1879, a stockholder and director in the company. In April, 1877, plaintiff acquired all the property of the Excelsior Water Company, consisting of mining-ground, farm, ditches, flumes, store and merchandise, stock in other mining companies, bills, notes, bullion in flumes, etc., giving in exchange 36,732 shares of stock, and shortly afterwards it obtained a like conveyance and transfer of all the property of the Pactolus Mining Company in exchange for 3,000 shares of its stock. These, with a few others, amounting in all to 39,809 shares, were the only shares ever issued by plaintiff.

The Excelsior Water Company and Pactolus Mining Company were largely indebted at the time they transferred their property to plaintiff, and this indebtedness was assumed by plaintiff as a part of the purchase price of the property. Its net amount, over and above the solvent credits transferred by the two companies, was $173,710.80, which was paid during the directorship of the defendant. During the same time the sum of $233,-723.60 was expended by plaintiff in the purchase of other mining property, the construction of ditches, tunnels, permanent improvements on farm, machinery on mine, procuring United States patents for mining-ground, and in assessments on stock in other companies.

During the same time the plaintiff was carrying on its mining and other multifarious business, and it received from sale of bullion and water, and as profits of its store and farm and other investments, the gross sum of $1,095,719, while its outlay for operating its mines, salaries, taxes, interest, and other strictly current expenses was $638,303, leaving a balance of earnings of $457,416. The amount of the eighteen dividends declared and paid during this time was only $241,629, or $215,724 less than the net earnings.

But the plaintiff contends that the surplus profits were only about ninety-eight thousand dollars, and that about one hundred and forty-three thousand dollars over and above the surplus profits were divided, while the defend-
170 ant claims that much less than the surplus profits was divided.

This difference between counsel for plaintiff on the one side, and the superior court and counsel for the defendant on the other, arises out of a difference of theory as to what constitutes surplus profits of a mining corporation.

Counsel for plaintiff contends that the payment of the debts which plaintiff assumed as part of the price of the property acquired from the Excelsior Water Company and the Pactolus Mining Company, as well as most of the items of expenditure for construction of tunnels, levees, ditches, etc., should be rated as current expenses and charged against its gross earnings, in order to ascertain the actual surplus profits of its business; while counsel for defendant contends, on the contrary, that the payments of the principal of its indebtedness, and its investments in what are called betterments of its property, should not be charged to current expenses of the business. As to the payment of the debt assumed by the plaintiff when it commenced business, or that incurred in making improvements, we do not understand its counsel to contend that it was necessary to pay them off before any dividends could be declared, but merely that whenever any part of its gross earnings was applied to the payment of a debt it was unlawful thereafter to replace such sum with the proceeds of a loan, and thereupon declare a dividend. . . .

The term "capital stock" has a double meaning, as applied to corporations. In one sense it is the sum mentioned in the articles of incorporation as the amount of the capital stock; in other words, it is the share capital, or nominal capital, and does not necessarily represent a corresponding amount of actual capital. In case of mining corporations, it is always arbitrary and generally extravagant in amount.

The capital stock referred to in the statute, however, (Civ. Code, sec. 309) is the actual property of the corporation contributed by the share-holders of the nominal capital. In this case the nominal or share capital of the plaintiff was five million dollars. Its actual capital was its mining and other property (less the debt with which it was encumbered) received in exchange for the shares which it issued, and this actual capital was what it was forbidden to divide.

This inhibition, however, did not extend to the net proceeds of its mining operations; for a mining corporation, like any other corporation organized for the purpose of utilizing a wasting property,—a property that can be used only by consuming it,—as a mine, a lease, or a patent, is not deemed to have divided its capital merely because it has distributed the net proceeds of its mining operations, although the necessary result is that 171
so much has been subtracted from the substance of its estate. (Morawetz on Corporations, sec. 442; *Lee* v. *Neuchatel Asphalte Co.*, L. R. 41 Ch. Div. 24.) It may distribute its net earnings, although the value of its mine is thereby diminished. But it may not sell the mine, or any part of it, and distribute the proceeds. In this sense, and in this sense only, provisions of law similar to those of section 309 of our Civil Code have been held to apply to mining corporations.

If the mine belonging to a mining corporation when it commences operations is free from debt, and provided with all the necessary openings and appliances for its convenient working, the problem of ascertaining the amount of its surplus profits from time to time would be very simple, and would consist in merely deducting the gross outlay from the gross receipts, and the balance, less a reasonable reserve to meet contingencies, would be the legitimate subject of a dividend. But when the mining property has been taken subject to a debt, or when as a preliminary operation it becomes necessary to incur a debt in running an expensive tunnel or sinking an expensive shaft, the problem becomes complicated. Must the whole of such debts be paid out of the first earnings, before making a dividend? or must only a part be paid? and if so, what part?

We do not think it would be necessary to pay, in the first place, the whole of such debts, but it would be necessary to pay accruing interest, and to provide a sinking fund sufficient to extinguish the principal before the mine was exhausted. There can be no doubt, we think, that this is a correct theory; but in case of a property of such uncertain, fluctuating, and precarious value as a mine, it would undoubtedly be extremely difficult in most cases to practically apply it. Fortunately, however, the right of the creditors to insist upon payment

of their demands as they fell due, and the prudence of capitalists to whom the company would be compelled to resort for loans with which to extend the payment of its maturing indebtedness, would always furnish a sure corrective for any disposition of the directors of a corporation to provide an inadequate fund for the extinguishment of its indebtedness, and it may be safely assumed that in the case supposed, unless the debts of the corporation were paid at a rate satisfactory to its creditors, they would put a stop to the payment of dividends by the means within their power. At all events, we are clear that the directors of a mining corporation, which has become indebted either by acquiring its property encumbered with debt, or by making permanent improvements for the thorough and systematic working of its mines and other property, are not guilty of an infraction of section 309 of
172 the Civil Code merely because they declare and pay dividends out of the net proceeds of their mine without first paying the whole of such debts.

On the contrary, if they have fairly and honestly applied towards the payment and extinguishment of the debts of the company a share of the net earnings satisfactory to its creditors and reasonably proportioned to the amount of its indebtedness, the extent and permanence of its mine, or the rate at which it is being exhausted, they may properly and safely pay out the remainder in dividends, because such remainder may in such cases be justly regarded and treated as surplus profits of the business. . . .

Plaintiff was a stock-holder in the Deer Creek Company, and paid its assessments for the construction of its tunnel run for the purpose of working its mines. Clearly, this was an investment of capital, and not a current expense. The other item mentioned stands on similar grounds, and so do a number of others, aggregating a large amount which we have not mentioned.

It is argued by plaintiff that a number of these investments turned out to be unprofitable in the end, and reference is made to the fact, disclosed by the evidence in this case, and otherwise notorious, that all these hydraulic mines have been shut up by injunction sued out by the riparian proprietors on the streams into which they were washing their earth. This is undoubtedly a serious misfortune to the present stockholders in the various companies, including the plaintiff, but the defendant is not responsible for the losses they may have suffered in consequence of the injunctions, nor is the wisdom or the prudence of his investments to be measured by a result which at the time few persons anticipated. When the expenditures were made they were, no doubt, considered judicious, and if the event has proved the contrary, the result must be treated as a loss of capital, and the expenditures must not be converted *ex post facto* into a current working expense. . . .

Judgment and order affirmed.

UNITED STATES v. CENTRAL PACIFIC RAILROAD COMPANY

138 U.S. 84 (1891)
Supreme Court of the United States

Mr. Justice Bradley delivered the opinion of the court.

This is an appeal from the Court of Claims. The claimant, the Central Pacific Railroad Company, filed a petition October 31, 1887, to recover from the United States the sum of $804,-094.31, alleged to be due for services rendered to the War, Post Office, and other departments, and the sum of $321,-157.72, alleged to have been exacted by the Treasury Depart-
174 ment, and paid by the claimant, in excess of the amount actually due from the claimant to the government for the 25 per cent net earnings required to be paid by the fourth section of the act known as the Thurman act, passed May 7, 1878. The Court of Claims rendered a decree in favor of the claimant for the first of the above-mentioned sums, and for a portion of the second claim, amounting to $198,422.83, the other part of the sum demanded having been barred by the statute of limitations. Both parties appealed from the decree, but the claimants have dismissed their appeal and the government has consented that the decree shall be affirmed as to the said sum of $804,094.31 due to the claimants for services rendered to the departments, so that the only matter of controversy remaining on the record is the decree for the said sum of $198,422.83 the alleged amount of over-payments exacted for 25 per cent of net earnings during the years 1881, 1882, 1883 and 1884. The ground of appeal on the part of the government as to this sum is that in arriving at the net earnings of the railroad company for the years before mentioned, the company claimed and the court allowed certain expenses which, as contended by the government, were not for current expenses and repairs, but were for betterments and improvements on the road, its buildings and equipments, whereby the capital of the company invested in its works was increased in permanent value. These expenses, the government contends, ought not to have been allowed under the provisions of the Thurman act. They are of the same class, as appears by a supplemental return made by the Court of Claims, which were allowed by this court as fairly chargeable under the head of expenses under the act of 1862, in the case of *Union Pacific Railroad Co. v. United States*, 99 U. S. 402. But the accounts in question

in that case arose before the Thurman act was passed, and the phraselogy of this act was probably adopted in view of the construction of the act of 1862 claimed by the railroad companies in that case. As the law stood prior to 1878, under which 5 per cent of the net earnings of the companies was to be paid into the Treasury towards the liquidation of the bonds loaned to them by the government, we held that in arriving at such net earnings it was admissible for the companies to charge, as they had done, a reasonable amount for betterments and improvements, rendered necessary by the gradual increase of traffic, the better discharge of business, and the public accommodation; not including, however, the cost of any important improvement, such as additional track, or any other matter 175
involving a large outlay of money. This view was based upon the practice and usage of conservative and well managed railroad companies, which tended to the suppression of extravagant dividends that might be the result of a showing of large net earnings. But Congress, in the Thurman act, *ex industria* used language with regard to the character of the expenses to be allowed in ascertaining the amount of net earnings, which seems to preclude any charges for improvements or betterments, or increase of permanent value of the works in any manner whatever. The language referred to is as follows: "That the net earnings mentioned in said act of eighteen hundred and sixty-two, of said railroad companies respectively, shall be ascertained by deducting from the gross amount of their earnings respectively the necessary expenses actually paid within the year in operating the same and keeping the same in a state of repair, and also the sum paid by them respectively within the year in discharge of interest on their first mortgage bonds, whose lien has priority over the lien of the United States, and excluding from consideration all sums owing or paid by said companies respectively for interest upon any other portion of their indebtedness; and the foregoing provision shall be deemed and taken as an amendment of said act of eighteen hundred and sixty-four, as well as of said act of eighteen hundred and sixty-two." 20 Stat. c. 96, § 1, p. 58.

Considering the time and the circumstances under which this act was passed, and the express declaration that the clause in question was to be deemed and taken as an amendment of the acts of 1864 and 1862, we think its meaning cannot be mistaken as intending to exclude from the category of expenses to be taken from gross receipts in order to ascertain the "net earnings," all such expenditures as have the effect of permanently improving the value of the company's property and works; and, taken prospectively, it is to be regarded as valid under the decision in *The Sinking Fund Cases*, 99 U. S. 700. As the expenses in question are of the category referred to, and the allowance of them by the Court of Claims reduced the 25 per cent of net earnings by the said amount of $198,-422.83, it follows that the judgment, as to that sum, must be reversed, and be affirmed as to the said sum of $804,094.31; and the cause

Remanded with instructions to enter judgment in conformity with this opinion.

CONVILLE v. SHOOK

24 N.Y. Supp. 547 (1893)
Superior Court of New York City

Appeal from judgment on report of referee.

Action by Thomas Conville against Sheridan Shook and another. From a judgment for defendants, plaintiff appeals. Affirmed.

The opinion filed by the referee is as follows:

The plaintiff claims he is entitled to recover from the defendants the sum of $6,779.40 for his share of the profits of the business during the year ending February 28, 1886. The defendants claim that the plaintiff's share of the profits of the business during that year was greatly less than the sum claimed by the plaintiff; that they have discovered numerous errors in the amounts and calculations, according to which the plaintiff had received from them sundry sums of money for his share of the profits of the business during previous years; that the sums so paid during those years exceed the true and correct amount to which the plaintiff was entitled, and that such overpayments, being set off against the plaintiff's share of the profits of the last year, entirely wipe out any indebtedness on their part for that year, and leave the plaintiff still indebted to them in large amount for such overpayments. The plaintiff has rested his case, and a motion is made in behalf of the defendants for a dismissal of the complaint on the ground that, upon the evidence as it stands, the defendants are not indebted to the plaintiff, but that, on the contrary, the plaintiff is indebted to the defendants. The chief witness for the plaintiff is Mr. James D. Lyon, who was the bookkeeper for the defendants during the whole period of the plaintiff's employment by the defendants. He states that the amount to which the plaintiff is entitled for his share of the profits of the last year's business is $6,779.40, and he testifies that he arrived at the amount so stated from an examination of the books of the defendants' firm. The process by which the witness arrives at this conclusion that the sum above mentioned is a correct statement of the plaintiff's share of the last year's profits is as follows: The defendants' books show that in closing the books for the year ending February 28, 1886, the amount of profits was ascertained to be the sum of $11,563.31, of which 90 per cent. belonged to Mr. Shook and Mr. Everard in equal shares, being $5,203.49 to each, and the remaining 10 per cent., $1,156.33, to Mr. Conville, the plaintiff. After the closing of the books the plaintiff was credited with the further sum of $1,393.06 for his share of the estimated profits upon sales of goods which had been manufactured under the management of the plaintiff, and which were still unsold on February 28, 1886, when the plaintiff's employment as brewer terminated. The witness Mr. Lyon makes the defendants' books the basis of his testimony to support the plaintiff's claim. He enumerates eight separate entries which appear in the journal in the account by which the profits of the last year were ascertained, and which he claims were improperly placed in the account. If those eight entries should be taken out from the account the plaintiff's share of the profits would be (I calculate the additions and subtractions) $6,796.36, which is slightly in excess of the amount as stated by the witness. The inquiry, therefore, arises concerning those eight entries or items in the defendants' journal. If it appears by the evidence in the case that the entire aggregate of those items is properly chargeable against the plaintiff, then the defendants' final figures are correct, and the plaintiff is entitled to the amount shown in his favor by the books, viz. $2,539.49, and no more. If some of those eight items are properly chargeable and others not, the said sum of $2,539.49 should be increased accordingly. The defendants claim, however, not only that the plaintiff is properly chargeable with all of those items, but also that it appears by the testimony that the witness Mr. Lyon omitted in the keeping of these books to charge off other sums which should have been charged off, and that, if 10 per cent. of those sums should be charged against the plaintiff, the amount of such 10 per cent. will not only wipe out the said sum of $2,539.48, but will bring the plaintiff in debt to the defendants. It becomes necessary, therefore, to examine minutely into the items in dispute, in order to ascertain upon which side the indebtedness exists, and to what amount.

First. Charge of $5,330.68, Taxes, Interest, etc. The defendants have charged off the sum of $5,330.68 as follows: "Expense account, debtor to stock account, taxes, interest on mortgages, etc., on property, that have been charged to a stock account. $5,330.68." The witness Mr. Lyon admits that of that amount the sum of $4,950.52, which had been paid from time to time for taxes upon the brewery property, had been improperly charged to stock account. The plaintiff's witness Mr. Waddell, an expert accountant, also states that such items should properly have been charged to expense account. The witness Mr. Lyon also states that it had been his intention to charge back that amount if he had had the making up of the books at the end of the last year. The defendants were therefore right in charging back this item, but upon the evidence as it stands the amount should have been $4,950.52, instead of $5,330.68. It may be that the larger amount is correct, but for the purposes of the present motion the amount must be stated at $4,950.52.

Second. Cask Account. The testimony shows without contradiction that during the whole 10 years covered by the account Mr. Lyon had been in the habit of charging to cask account the money expended for repairing the casks and barrels used in the business, except the sums expended for such repairs as were done in the brewery by the men employed there. The last-mentioned amount being charged to expense account, the larger part by far of the amounts expended for such repairs was charged to cask account, and
178 went into the general summary of the accounts in the journal, not as an expenditure, but as an asset, excepting that at the end of each year cask account was credited with 10 per cent. of the balance of that account at that time. The defendants have now charged to expense account the amounts which, at the end of each year, were so journalized as assets, being for the expenditure during that year, for repairs to casks and barrels, less the 10 per cent. above mentioned. The plaintiff claims that the original entry was correct, and that the defendants improperly charged back the items in question, amounting in the aggregate to the sum of $14,262.48. The expenditures for the purchase of new casks were concededly a proper charge to cask or stock account, but I cannot see that upon any fair principle the sums expended from time to time in the repairs of old casks could properly be so charged as to create an asset, instead of indicating an expense. Both Mr. Lyon and Mr. Waddell seek to justify the charge, but their views seem to me illogical. Without enlarging upon this point, it is sufficient to say that, in my opinion, the defendants properly charged back the balance of the sums which had been charged, as I hold, improperly to cask account, amounting, as above stated, to the sum of $14,263.48.

Third. Rebates and Allowances. The testimony shows that the defendants' firm were in the habit of allowing to their customers percentages upon the scheduled prices of their goods, varying in the cases of different customers, and also to make special allowances to the customers of varying amounts, according to special circumstances. The defendant Everard had exclusive charge of the matter of fixing such percentages and allowances, which were necessarily arbitrary in amount, according to his judgment in each particular case. In making up the last account some of such percentages known as "rebates," which Mr. Lyon had omitted to journalize, were charged off, and Mr. Lyon himself admits the correctness of such charges. He claims, however, that the percentages and allowances charged in the last account were excessive, but what his claim in that regard simply amounts to is this: that he thinks that if he, instead of Mr. Everard, had been arbiter, the amounts would have been less by about $4,000, and he therefore asks a credit for the plaintiff of $4,000. A mere statement of the plaintiff's contention in this regard is sufficient to show that it cannot be sustained, and that the credit of $4,000 claimed by him cannot be allowed.

Fourth. Bad Debts. The plaintiff claims that his account is improperly charged with "bad debts" to the amount of $4,593.89, but the evidence fails to show that any of the claims so charged have been paid, or are collectible. The amount, therefore,—$4,593.89,—is properly charged in that respect.

Fifth. Charges for Rent. It appears that the firm owned a part of the land and buildings used in the business and hired the other part, paying for the latter a rental of $400 per month. For the use of the part that was owned by the defendants no charge was made on the books, so that the plaintiff, to the extent of his proportionate interest in the profits, had the benefit of that property without expense. The defendants claim that a sum equal to 10 per cent. of the cost of the property should have been charged off each year as an equivalent for rental, and they have accordingly, in making up the account, charged off the sum of $7,709.74 for that purpose. I am of the opinion that they were clearly entitled to make a charge of that character, but while it may be that the amount specified is the proper sum to be so charged, there is no evidence in the case upon that point, either as to the propriety of charging that particular sum or as to what would be a proper sum or percentage to be charged off for the purpose mentioned. On the evidence as it stands, the charge in question for the purposes of the motion under consideration must therefore be disallowed.

Sixth. Depreciation of Original Plant. It seems that while a sum equal to 10 per cent. of the balance at the end of each year of cask account, stock account, and improvement account was charged off each year for wear and tear, no such deduction was ever made for the plant originally purchased by the defendants from Mr. Whitney. The bill of sale, and Mr. Lyon's testimony, show that the amount paid for the property was $45,000, and the testimony also shows that if 10 per cent. of that sum had been charged off each year the total amount so charged off would have been $29,309.45. There is certainly no reason why the original plant should have been carried on the books for 10 years at its original cost. The charge is sustained, not only by a consideration of the subject as a matter of business propriety and fairness, but also by a fair reading of the testimony of Mr. Lyon and Mr. Waddell. They substantially admit the propriety of such a charge, but claim that $25,000 of the original cost was for "good will" or "royalty," of which there is no evidence. The charge, therefore, claimed by the defendants of $29,309.45, for wear and tear of the original plant, should be allowed. 179

Seventh. Items of Schwarzwaelder & Clark. These items are charged off by the defendants,—one amounting to $1,394.44, and the other to $1,594.01. As the case stands, there is no evidence to sustain them, and for the purposes of the present motion they must be disregarded.

Eighth. Inventory. The plaintiff claims that in making the inventory at the end of the last year the defendants undervalued the stock on hand by the sum of $20,502.56. The contract between the parties provided that the stock should be taken at the end of last year in the same manner as in previous years. In previous years the stock had been valued at the estimated selling price. The defendants made it up for the close of the last year at cost price, and the plaintiff claims that, if taken as it had been in previous years, it would have exceeded the sum at which it was taken by the amount above stated, making a difference to the plaintiff of $2,050.25. The supplemental statement in the defendants' books, in which they credit the plaintiff with the estimated profit on the sale of stock on hand, gives the plaintiff credit for all which he can fairly claim. He would be fairly chargeable with the cost of manufacture and of sale and delivery, as stated in the supplemental statement. There is nothing to show that the inventory was not fairly taken, or that the plaintiff is entitled to any credit for the stock on hand which the defendants have not allowed to him, so that the plaintiff's claim of $2,050.25 in that regard must be disallowed. The amounts with which the plaintiff has sought to surcharge the defendants' account, and which I have decided were properly charged in defendants' books, are as follows: For taxes, etc., $4,950.52; repairs to casks, etc., $14,263.48; rebates, etc., $4,000; bad debts, $4,593.84; inventory of last year, $20,502.56: aggregating $48,310.40. I have also decided that the account is chargeable for wear and tear of the original plant with $29,309.45, making a total of $77,619.85, of which 10 per cent., or $7,761.98, is chargeable to the plaintiff, an amount exceeding by about $1,000 the sum claimed by the plaintiff. It follows that the defendants' motion should be granted, and the complaint is therefore dismissed, with costs. Wm. C. Traphagen, Referee.

New York, March 20, 1891.

Argued before FREEDMAN and GILDERSLEEVE, JJ.

J. McMahon, for plaintiff.

A. J. Dittenhoefer, for defendant Shook.

Gratz Nathan, for defendant James Everard.

PER CURIAM. The judgment should be affirmed, with costs, upon the opinion filed by the referee.

WHITTAKER v. AMWELL NATIONAL BANK

29 Atl. 203 (1894)
New Jersey

BIRD, V. C.

The Star Rubber Company, one of the defendants in this suit, became insolvent and a receiver was appointed to wind up its affairs. Subsequently, Jonathan Steward, who was one of the directors of the Star Rubber Company, made an assignment for the benefit of his creditors. Mr. Steward, at the time of making
180 his assignment, held large claims against the Star Rubber Company, and in order to ascertain their character and value, his assignee filed a bill against the receiver of the Star Rubber Company and numerous other creditors of the Star Rubber Company, including twenty-five national banks. This bill also aimed at a complete administration of the claims of the creditors against Mr. Steward, and to a large extent necessarily involving the rights of the creditors of the Star Rubber Company.

The receiver of the Star Rubber Company filed an answer and an answer by way of cross-bill against the claim of the assignee of Mr. Steward as one of the directors of the Star Rubber Company, as well as against the other directors of said company, alleging that Mr. Steward and the other directors were personally liable, under the seventh section of the act respecting corporations, for the declaring and payment of dividends contrary to the provisions of the seventh section of said act. This section provides that—

> "It shall not be lawful for the directors of such corporation to make dividends except from the surplus of net profits arising from the business of the corporation, nor to divide, withdraw or in any way pay to the stockholders, or any of them, any part of the capital stock of the said corporation, or to reduce the said capital stock, except according to this act, without the consent of the legislature, and in case of any violation of the provisions of this section, the directors under whose administration the same may happen, shall, in their individual and private capacities, jointly and severally be liable at any time within the period of six years after paying any such dividend to the said corporation and to the directors thereof, in the event of its dissolution or insolvency, to the full amount of the dividend made or capital stock so divided."

Semi-annual dividends were declared during the years 1887, 1888 and 1889, and one in 1890, amounting in all to over $68,000. The allegation is, that all of these were in violation of the statute referred to....

I shall first consider whether or not the dividends so declared and paid were paid out of the surplus or net earnings of the company.

This proposition is to be determined by ascertaining the actual value of all the live assets of the company at the termination of six months, during which the supposed surplus or net earnings are said to have accrued. This can only truly be done by taking into the account the cost of repairs and also a reasonable allowance for depreciation for wear and tear or constant use, giving credit for all actual permanent improvements. The statute not only warrants but compels this course. The capital invested by corporations is all that creditors have for their protection. The legislature, which creates them and gives them favors which individuals do not have, imposes upon them the necessity of main- 181
taining their capital to its maximum value before they can reap any benefit from the venture. In view of these statements, but against the protest of counsel for the assignee of Mr. Steward, testimony was admitted showing that, as above stated, in 1881 and 1882 the real estate and machinery accounts were valued at $62,000 and $67,000 respectively, and that at the end of the period of six months, during which the first dividend of $6,000 was declared, the real estate and machinery accounts had been advanced to $101,000 and $110,000 respectively. From this large increase in value, according to the books of the company, it was urged that a fraud had been perpetrated upon the creditors. It was thought at the time that such testimony was relevant; however, as will be seen, by no means controlling. I still think it was properly received, and in the view I find myself compelled to take of the case, of the highest importance.

To aid in a proper understanding of the case, besides the books of the company in which its accounts were kept, there is the testimony of expert witnesses. One of these witnesses, Mr. Ridgway, who had been with the company for fifteen years, and for several years prior to 1882, as a mechanical engineer, says that during that year the entire plant was reconstructed, and that all of the old machinery except the grinders and calenders was cast aside and new machinery put in its place. The account-books of the company make no mention of this significant and far-reaching fact. This statement suffices to show that it is impossible for me to rely entirely upon the books of account of the company as a guide and do justice to the parties interested.

. . .

I shall therefore determine the validity of the dividends by the testimony of the experts rather than by the books.

The inquiry therefore will be, What was the fair value of the machinery on the 31st day of December, 1886, when the surplus or net profits were supposed to be $33,667, upon which the first dividend of $6,000 was declared? Mr Ridgway was called by the receiver to assist him in making an inventory and valuation upon the machinery. He rendered such assistance. When called as a witness, with this inventory in his hands, he was interrogated as to the value of the machinery, and fixed such value, being, as he said, the cost thereof to the company, at $49,723.13. After fixing the cost price, he said that the machinery, as there located ready for use, was worth very nearly $100,000. This includes the cost of the foundations and all other costs and expenses in placing or locating the machinery for
182 actual use. The cost of the foundations he and one other of the experts fixed at $15,000, while the third makes it $20,700. This item of cost of foundations, however, should not be reckoned in the machinery account, because, as I believe from an examination, it has been placed in the real estate account.

Again, it must be remembered that the present object is to ascertain the value of the machinery on the 31st day of December, 1886, but Mr. Ridgway, in his estimate, values all of the machinery that was in the plant at the period of the appointment of the receiver, being an increase, according to the books, of over $19,000. Therefore, to ascertain the fair value on the 31st day of December, 1886, when the first dividend was declared, all that was added after that date must be deducted from the total value as given by the experts.

Hence, what is to be understood by the statement of Mr. Ridgway when he says the value of that machinery so located for use was very nearly $100,000? I am obliged to deal with that statement. In doing so I must have regard for the rights of creditors as well as of the directors. I can find nothing in the case to justify me in placing the valuation of all the machinery beyond $90,000. This is a liberal view, taking both the books and the testimony of Mr. Ridgway as a guide, deducting from the book value the value of the machinery which Mr. Ridgway says was cast aside at the period of the reconstruction.

Besides, if there is any uncertainty about it, neither the creditors nor the receiver are or is responsible.

Placing the whole value, therefore, at $90,000, there must be deducted therefrom the value of the foundations, $15,000, and the value of the machinery purchased after the 31st day of December, 1886, which was over $19,000, according to the books. These items aggregate $34,000; deducting them from the $90,000 and we have $56,000 as the value of the machinery at the time when the first dividend complained of was declared.

But the book value of the machinery at that time was, as above stated, $110,324 38, being $54,324.38 in excess of the true value, according to the testimony of Mr. Ridgway. This book value was of course carried into the trial balance and employed in making the surplus or net profits upon which the first dividend of $6,000 was declared. This supposed surplus or net profits appears upon the trial balance to be $33,667. This statement reduces the book assets more than $20,000 beyond the supposed surplus or net profits. So that in pronouncing judgment on this first dividend, I must conclude that it was declared in violation of the provisions of the statute. . . .

It will be seen that all of the dividends except the last were declared at the expiration of every six months, or semi-annually, 183
and the last at the expiration of a little over a year from the one immediately preceding. This last dividend was not declared until after the real estate had been advanced $50,000 by resolution of the board, as above described.

From the foregoing statements it must appear that all of the dividends declared were in violation of the statute. And since it has been shown that the directors were all present and participated in the meetings when such dividends were declared, and entered no protest, they are jointly and severally liable to the extent of the dividends so declared and paid.

But recurring again to the statement of Mr. Ridgway, to the effect that when the plant was reconstructed in 1882 all of the old machinery was set aside except the grinders and the calenders, and proceeding with that in view, and being guided solely by the books, after making the deductions which his statements justify, the result will not greatly differ from that above reached. . . . The book value of the machinery, therefore, on the 31st of December, 1881, was $67,704, only $20,600 of which was retained in actual use in reconstruction. This $20,600, and what was actually added after the 31st of December, 1881, and before the 31st of December, 1886, will give the full book value of the machinery at the last-named period. The value of the machinery added between those dates, according to the books, is $42,616, and the old machinery retained is the $20,600, making a total of $63,416. . . .

Taking this statement as true, there was then a net surplus of $7,780. In my judgment this should not stand, because it is fully overcome in the wear and tear of machinery and in the depreciation of real estate, and in the items of articles sold which have not been entered in the accounts, to which should be added the $5,500, the increase of the machinery and real estate account in the year 1882, which, so far as I can discover, was purely arbitrary.

It cannot be successfully contended that all such machinery is not subject to depreciation from wear and tear or actual use. That all machinery does not suffer alike is equally plain. Those who deal in or use the different kinds are best informed as to the extent of depreciation in the different articles. The testimony in this case leads me to the conclusion that the depreciation was at least two per cent. a year. Detail is unnecessary, but calculation will show that if $5,000 be charged to this item it will be moderate. No testimony was offered showing the probable depreciatien in real estate of this character. Fourteen hundred dollars at least should have been credited in the machinery account for an article which was sold for $800, but which
184 cost $2,200, and so appears in the account.

If I had made the first calculation on the basis of $100,000 valuation instead of $90,000, the result would not have differed very materially from the last calculation.

On this branch of the case it is eminently proper that I should say that the books of account of the company have not been established in the ordinary sense in which books of account are required to be established before they are received as evidence of what they contain. No person acquainted with the books during the period of time which they cover, and who had any general or special knowledge of the entries made in them, has been called to speak concerning their truthfulness. No clerk or secretary or other person authorized to make entries therein, or who actually made entries therein, or from time to time witnessed the making of entries therein, has been produced. Experts in bookkeeping have been called. One of these, with no little reason, insists that in making up the trial-balance which exhibits the supposed net surplus or earnings, entries have been falsely made; by means of which, such surplus or net profits have been unjustifiably increased. The other states, generally, that the books have been kept upon correct principles in all respects. Neither of these experts knew anything about the correctness of the different items which were entered in these books.

TRADESMAN PUB. CO. v. KNOXVILLE CAR WHEEL CO.

32 S.W. 1097 (1895)
Supreme Court of Tennessee

McALISTER, J. This is a creditors' bill, filed—First, to have the Knoxville Car-Wheel Company declared an insolvent corporation, and its assets equally distributed among all its creditors; and, second, to hold the directors of said company, who are made defendants, individually liable for all debts created in excess of the capital stock paid in. The complainant also seeks to have annulled certain mortgages, for the reasons: First, that they were executed by said corporation after its ascertained insolvency; and, second, because preferences are thereby created in favor of certain debts for which the directors are sureties. The directors are also sought to be held liable upon the ground that they had declared and received certain dividends from said corporation at a time when it was insolvent. . . .

The defendant car-wheel company answered the bill, and, among other defenses, denied its insolvency, and averred its assets were worth more than double its debts, and that its business had been uniformly profitable until the recent panic which swept over the country, causing the railroads to cut off their purchases, and to default in the payments of goods already purchased: that this fact so depleted its revenues that it was deemed best to temporarily suspend operations until business should resume its normal conditions; that it had always done a good business, and paid the interest on its bonded debt, and promptly met all of its obligations; that it was in no sense insolvent, and its suspension of business was only temporary, and was not intended to be permanent. . . .

The claim of the company that it was solvent is, in our opinion, based largely upon extravagant valuations of its assets, and especially upon an overestimate of the value of certain lands owned by the company in Carter county. The valuation put upon this land by the stockholders was entirely arbitrary, and without any sufficient reason to justify such an exaggerated figure. The evidence shows that there was no market for such real estate in 1892, that on account of the general depression in business it was impossible to sell real estate, and that such an asset was entirely unavailable. When this was filed the company's matured and unsettled floating indebtedness exceeded $70,000, its bonded indebtedness of $100,000 would mature in two months, the entire assets of the company were covered with deed of trust, and the company was entirely without resources to liquidate this heavy indebtedness. The question, then, is whether a creditor, on May 10, 1892, after the trust deeds had been executed, and the assignees had taken possession of the entire property of the company, could file and maintain a bill to wind up the affairs of the company as an insolvent corporation. We think the right to maintain the bill is clear and unquestionable. . . .

The next assignment is that the chancellor erred in decreeing that all the debts of the company contracted after April 30, 1885, were created with the assent of the directors. It may be conceded that this assignment presents a question of some difficulty, and probably the determining issue in the case. The language of the statute is, viz.: "If the indebtedness of said company shall at any time exceed the capital stock paid in, the directors assenting thereto shall be individually liable to the creditors for said excess." It may be remarked that this clause is peculiar to charters of mining and manufacturing companies, and is a discrimination, to some extent, against this class of domestic corporations. It has been uniformly held that such statutes, being in derogation of the common law, must be strictly construed. . . .

The liability of a director is contingent, and is made to depend upon four conditions, namely: First, assent by him to the creation of the particular debt upon which he is sued; second, that the debt has not been paid; third, that the assets of the corporation have been exhausted; fourth, that the particular debt is in excess of the capital stock. . . .

So we think, when it is sought to hold a director to individual liability under the provisions of this highly penal statute, it must be shown that his assent was given in his capacity as director, acting concurrently with a majority of the official board. We do not hold that the only evidence of this official assent must be found in the minutes of the board, but we do hold there must have been an official meeting when assent was given, whether it appears on the minutes or otherwise. In other words, we hold the official minutes do not constitute the only evidence of official assent, provided it is made otherwise to appear that at a meeting of the official body the directors sought to be charged assented to the creation of the particular debt. Tested by this rule, we find, upon an examination of the record, that only one of the debts with which the directors are sought to be individually charged was officially assented to, namely, that in favor of Peter Staub for lease of foundry.

It is not assigned as error that the chancellor refused any relief against the directors on account of the payment of dividends
186 amounting to $28,000. It is contended by counsel that said dividends were paid at a time and under circumstances that rendered the payment unlawful, and was a diversion of the assets of the corporation. The charter of this company provides, viz.: "If the directors declare and pay any dividend when the company is insolvent, or which declaration of a dividend would diminish the amount of the capital stock, they shall be jointly and severally liable to creditors for the amount of dividends thus declared. Any director may avoid liability by voting against the dividend or by filing his objections in writing as soon as he ascertained a dividend has been made." The dividends in question were paid, viz.: April 30, 1884, 4 per cent., $4,280; April 30, 1886, 4 per cent., $4,280; April 30, 1887, 4 per cent., $4,280; April 30, 1888, 4 per cent., $4,280; April 30, 1889, 5 per cent., $5,350; April 30, 1890, 6 per cent., $6,420. It is insisted that the first dividend, paid April 30, 1883, was paid out of the proceeds of the bonds which had been sold by the company at a discount of 22 per cent., and that the remaining dividends were paid at a time when the corporation was insolvent, and when its indebtedness exceeded the amount of its paid-up capital stock. The chancellor, upon the hearing, was of opinion that the directors were warranted in the payment of these dividends, and that the defendants were not liable to the creditors of the corporation. It is true, as argued by counsel, that when these dividends were declared the indebtedness of the corporation did exceed the amount of capital stock paid in; but under the statute last cited this fact does not determine the liability of directors. The inhibition of the statute is against declaring dividends when the company is insolvent, or when such dividend will diminish the amount of the capital stock. If the assets were reasonably worth, or are honestly believed to be worth, largely more than the company's indebtedness, and upon this basis profits are estimated, the company is not insolvent, although its indebtedness may exceed its capital stock paid in. The record discloses that when these dividends were declared this company was engaged in a very extensive business, and was realizing large receipts from the sale of the products of its manufacture. Its assets were estimated by its directors to be largely in excess of the company's liabilities, and the proof shows that said assets, which consisted largely of mineral lands, were largely more valuable then than at a later period. The proof indicates that during the years covering the declaration of dividends the company was realizing a net profit in its business, and there was no reason why those profits should not have been distributed among its stockholders. The conduct of the directors is to be viewed in the light of the financial status of the company at that period, and is not to be determined by its ultimate insolvency, precipitated, doubtless, by the universal paralysis of business then prevailing throughout this country. When the large volume of business transacted by this company is considered, it is not perceived how its insolvency could have been superinduced by the small dividends declared. We are of opinion there was no error in the action of the chancellor upon this branch of the case. . . .

WITHEROW v. SLAYBACK

11 Misc. (N.Y.) 526 (1895)
Superior Court of New York City

McAdam, J. The action is to recover $11,072.68, with interest, from the defendants as officers of the Port Henry Steel & Iron Company, Limited, upon a note alleged to have been indorsed by that corporation for the accommodation of one Thomas F. Witherbee. The corporation was formed under the Business Corporation Act of 1875 as a limited liability company, and the defendants, together with Thomas F. Witherbee and Andrew Dickey, were its officers.

The plaintiff alleges five grounds of liability, making each a separate cause of action. These grounds are as follows:

I. Failure to file a report within twenty days after January 1, 1886.

II. Failure to file a report within twenty days after January 1, 1887....

The liability sought to be enforced was based on a note made by T. F. Witherbee in October, 1886, and indorsed "Andrew Dickey, Treasurer," which by its terms became due April 6, 1887. Assuming, for present purposes, that the act of Dickey bound the corporation, its obligation was that if Witherbee did not, on April 6, 1887, pay the note upon presentation at the place where it was payable, and if it was duly notified of the presentation of the note and the failure of Witherbee to pay, then the corporation would pay. This was not an absolute engagement to pay, but a conditional one, and would have been avoided if the maker had paid the note at maturity; or if the plaintiff had failed to present it at the time and place fixed for its payment, and neglected to follow the default by notice to the corporation, as indorser, of such presentation and nonpayment. The report filed in February, 1887, was, therefore, filed two months before any claim against the company accrued to the plaintiff, and consequently no liability of the defendants was established on either of those grounds. Laws 1875, chap. 611, § 18; *Torbett* v. *Godwin*, 62 Hun, 407; 17 N. Y. Supp. 48; *Garrison* v. *Howe*, 17 N. Y. 458; *Oviatt* v. *Hughes*, 41 Barb. 541; *Victory Webb Co.* v. *Beecher*, 26 Hun, 48; 97 N. Y. 651; *Gold* v. *Clyne*, 134 id. 262. The sufficiency of the defense arising upon these facts to the first and second causes of action is not affected by the alleged falsity of the report, even if such falsity had been established. *Bonnell* v. *Griswold*, 80 N. Y. 128; *Whitney Co.* v. *Barlow*, 68 id. 34. . . .

Another reason which seems to justify the conclusion reached is that the fifth alleged cause of action relates to the falsity of the report filed February 16, 1887, and, while the liability of the corporation as indorser on the note did not become complete until April 6, 1887, the debt represented by it, and presumably owing by Witherbee, the maker, was contracted in October, 1886. The statute being highly penal, and, therefore, one which must receive a strict construction, no liability attaches against officers of a corporation for a false
188 report, unless it appears that the report was filed before the credit was given. *Torbett* v. *Godwin*, *supra*. For the purpose of the report is that the public may be correctly informed of the financial condition of the corporation, in order that it may judge whether credit should be given it or not. As to debts contracted or liabilities incurred before the filing of the report, clearly no one could be misled to his prejudice; and the plaintiff, being in no manner injured, cannot complain.

The judgment appealed from must be affirmed, with costs.

SEDGWICK, Ch. J., and BEEKMAN, J., concur.

Judgment affirmed, with costs.

WING & EVANS v. SLATER

19 R.I. 597 (1896)
Rhode Island

July 24, 1896. TILLINGHAST, J. This is an action brought by the plaintiffs, who are judgment creditors of the American Wood Paper Co., to enforce an alleged liability of the defendant as a stockholder in said company, under Pub. Stat. R. I. cap. 155, §§ 11, 12, which provide as follows:

"SEC. 11. Every manufacturing company included within the provisions of this chapter shall file in the office of the town clerk of the town where the manufactory is established annually on or before the fifteenth day of February a certificate signed by a majority of the directors, truly stating the amount of its capital stock actually paid in, the value as last assessed for a town tax of its real estate, the value of its personal assets, and the amount of its debts or liabilities on the thirty-first day of December of the next year preceding.

"SEC. 12. If any of such companies shall fail so to do, all the stockholders of such company shall be jointly and severally liable for all the debts of the company then existing and for all that shall be contracted before such notice shall be given, except as hereinafter provided, unless such company shall have become insolvent and assigned its property in trust for the benefit of its creditors, in which case the obligation to give such notice by the filing of such certificate shall cease." . . .

Whether the statute upon which the action is based is a penal statute, strictly so called, it is not necessary to decide, although there is good authority for holding that it is. *Sayles* v. *Brown*, 40 Fed. Rep. 8. But that said statute is of a penal character, so far at least as the defendant is concerned, and also that it is in derogation of the common law, and hence to be construed strictly, there can be no doubt.

. . . The language of the statute, in case of the failure to file the certificate required thereby, is that "all the stockholders . . . . shall be jointly and severally liable for all the *debts* of the company *then existing*, and for all that shall be contracted before such notice shall be given," &c. "The time of the existence of

the debt is therefore a material inquiry." *Congdon* v. *Winsor*, 17 R. I. 236. We think it is clear that there was no debt existing at the time of the making of said contract; nor was any debt contracted by the making thereof, prior to the delivery of the merchandise contracted for. A debt is a liquidated demand, or a sum of money due by certain and express agreement. 3 Bl. Com. 154; *McElfresh* v. *Kirkendall*, 36 Iowa, 224. Or a debt may be defined to be a fixed and certain obligation to pay money or some other valuable thing in the present or in the future. *City of Erie's Appeal*, 91 Pa. St. 398, 402. In *People* v. *Arguello*, 37 Cal. 525, the court say: "Whether a claim or demand is a debt or not, is in no respect determined by a reference to the time of pay-
190 ment. A sum of money which is certainly and at all events payable is a debt, without regard to the fact whether it be payable now or at some future time. A sum of money payable upon a contingency, however, is not a debt, or does not become a debt until the contingency has happened. . . . . So of a covenant to pay rent quarterly. It creates no debt until it becomes due, for before that time the lessee may quit with the consent of the lessor, or he may assign his term with his consent, or he may be evicted by a title paramount to that of the lessor, in either of which cases he will be discharged from his covenant." *Wood* v. *Partridge*, 11 Mass. 488. In *Haynes* v. *Brown*, 36 N. H. 545, the court held that the statute could not be restricted to debts or liquidated claims. But the statute of that State is much broader than ours, making the stockholders and officers of corporations liable for the debts and *contracts* of the corporation. For a collection of the authorities on the question what constitutes a debt, see 5 Amer. & Eng. Encyc. of Law, 143–162. Applying the foregoing definitions to the statute under consideration, it cannot be properly said that there was any existing debt growing out of said contract until after a delivery was made thereunder. In *Garrison* v. *Howe*, 17 N. Y. 458, which was an action brought against a stockholder on the ground that the whole capital stock had not been paid in, and also because the corporation had not made the report required by law, the court said: "We do not think a debt for lumber furnished under the contract, subsequent to its execution, can be said to have been contracted when the agreement was signed. That instrument contains mutual stipulations, by the plaintiff to furnish and by the defendant to pay for the lumber; and there is no debt in existence until lumber has

been delivered." In *Jones* v. *Barlow*, 62 N. Y. 202, which was an action to enforce the liability of the trustees of a corporation for a failure to file the annual report thereof required by law, the court held that they were only liable for debts actually due and for which a present right of action existed against the corporation. See also *Chase* v. *Curtis*, 113 U. S. 452, 462–463.

In support of the plaintiffs' contention that the defendant's liability attached at the time of the making of said contract, he relies specially on *Byers* v. *Franklin Coal Co.*, 106 Mass. 131. That was a bill in equity against said coal company and certain persons alleged to be officers thereof, for neglecting to file the annual certificate required by the statute, the language of which is substantially like our own. The debt 191
in that case arose as follows: On April 3, 1886, the plaintiff accepted two drafts for the accommodation of the corporation, drawn by its treasurer, one payable in five months and the other in six months from their date. These drafts were negotiated at or about the time they were accepted, and at or about their maturity were paid by the plaintiff. And the question which arose was whether the debt thus created was a debt contracted at the time when the plaintiff paid the drafts or at the time when he accepted them. The court held that the plaintiff was an accommodation acceptor, and the relation between the corporation and him was that of principal and surety; and that, under the decision in *Rice* v. *Southgate*, 16 Gray, 142, the liability of a principal to indemnify his surety, for any payment the latter may be compelled to make to the former, takes effect from the time when the surety becomes responible for the debt of his principal; and that, upon payment by the surety, his debt is *a debt contracted* at the time be became responsible, and not at the time of such payment. We do not think the case controls the one before us. There a liability had been incurred by the plaintiff to pay a certain and definite amount of money at a definite time for the accommodation of the defendant, and the plaintiff was obliged to pay and did actually pay the draft when it fell due. And upon well settled principles of law it is clear, as held in *Rice* v. *Southgate*, *supra*, "that the contract of a principal with his surety to indemnify him for any payment which the latter may make to the creditor in consequence of the liability assumed, takes effect from the time when the surety becomes responsible for the debt of the principal. . . . . No new contract is made when

the money is paid by the surety, but the payment relates back to the time when the contract was entered into by which the liability to pay was incurred." No such liability, however, was incurred by the American Wood Paper Co. by the making of the contract aforesaid. No debt was created, in the strict sense of the term at any rate; nor did any exist until a delivery was made under said contract. "Suppose," as said by the defendant's counsel, "the plaintiffs had never made any deliveries. Could they have sued for anything in February, 1892, eight months before they made any deliveries?" We think it is clear that they could not. It follows, therefore, that, there being no debt either due or owing, and no debt contracted by said corporation in favor
192 of the plaintiffs at the time of the filing of the certificate aforesaid, they have no cause of action against him. We are therefore of the opinion that the demurrers to the defendant's special plea in bar should be overruled and the pleas sustained.

Judgment for the defendant for costs.

SAN DIEGO WATER COMPANY v. CITY OF SAN DIEGO

118 Cal. 556 (1897)

VAN FLEET, J.—The plaintiff is a corporation engaged in the business of supplying water to the city of San Diego and its inhabitants. In February, 1890, the common council of the city passed an ordinance fixing the water rates for the year beginning July 1, 1890. In May, 1890, the plaintiff brought this action against the city, the common council, the mayor, and the individual members of the council, to annul this ordinance and enjoin its enforcement. The complaint alleged in substance that the entire revenue which plaintiff could receive during the year in question, under the rates so fixed, would be insufficient to pay its operating expenses and fixed charges for that year, and would, therefore, afford no reward whatever to plaintiff for furnishing the water, and that the ordinance would deprive plaintiff of its property without process of law and without compensation. . . .

We shall not attempt in this opinion to review the many cases on this subject. It is sufficient to say that the supreme court of the United States (whose decisions on this matter are controlling) has repeatedly decided that the power of the state to fix and regulate the rates of compensation to be charged by persons and corporations in charge of certain public utilities is so limited by the constitution of the United States that it cannot be exercised to such an extent as to require any such person or corporation to furnish its property or services without reward; . . .

The question of what is just compensation in such a case is, we think, in all respects analogous to the question which arises in every case of appropriation under the power of eminent domain; and it may be reduced to the formula that the public must pay the actual value of that which it appropriates to the public use. In determining such value three, and we believe only three, methods are possible: 1. Either by ascertaining what the property could be sold for (its market value); or 2. By ascertaining what it would cost to replace it; or 3. By ascertaining the revenue it is capable of producing. In cases like the present, however, neither the first nor the second method can be resorted to. The judicial test of market value depends upon the fact that the property in question is marketable at a given price, which in turn depends upon the fact that sales of similar property have been and are being made at ascertainable prices. But such property as this is not so sold, at least, not often enough to furnish a fair criterion; and the very fact of governmental regulation would necessarily control the price. Until the rates are fixed no one can say how much the property would sell for, and therefore that price cannot be ascertained as a basis for fixing those rates.

The second method is entirely inapplicable to property of this kind. The construction of municipal waterworks is a matter of
194 growth. . . . It would, therefore, be highly unjust to permit the consumers to avail themselves of the plea that at the present time similar works could be constructed at a less cost, as a pretext for reducing the rates to be paid for the water. The reduced expense, if it be reduced, is due in part at least to the very fact that the city has been provided at the cost of the water company with increased facilities for doing business. . . .

Nor would it, on the other hand, be just to the consumers to require them to pay an enhanced price for the water, on the ground that it would now cost more to construct similar works. Such a contingency may well happen; but to allow an increase of rates for such reason would be to allow the water company to make a profit, not as a reward for its expenditures and services, but for the fortuitous occurrence of a rise in the price of materials or labor. The law does not intend that this business shall be a speculation in which the water company or the consumers shall respectively win or lose upon the casting of a die, or upon the equally unpredictable fluctuations of the markets. . . .

We must then have recourse to the third standard of value—the revenue which the property is capable of producing. . . . What revenue money is capable of producing is a question of fact, and, theoretically at least, susceptible of more or less exact ascertainment. Regard must be had to the nature of the investment, the risk attendant upon it, and the public demand for the product of the enterprise. It would not, of course, be reasonable to allow the company a profit equal to the greatest rate of interest realized upon any kind of investment, nor, on the other hand, to compel it to accept the lowest rate of remuneration which capital ever obtains. Comparison must be made between this business and other kinds of business involving a similar degree of risk, and all the surrounding circumstances must be considered. An important circumstance will always be the rate of interest at which money can be borrowed for investment in such a business; and, where the business appears to be honestly and prudently conducted, the rate which the company would be compelled to pay for borrowed money will furnish a safe, though not always conclusive criterion of the rate of profit which will be deemed reasonable. . . .

It is the money reasonably and properly expended in each year in collecting and distributing the water which constitutes the current expenses which may be allowed; and it is the money 195
reasonably and properly expended in the acquisition and construction of the works actually and properly in use for that purpose, which constitutes the investment on which the compensation is to be computed. The amounts stated in the findings in this case are found to be of that character.

But it is contended that the findings in several particulars are unsupported by the evidence.

It is claimed that the evidence does not justify the finding that $750,000 had been actually expended in the purchase and construction of the plant. On this subject the evidence is extremely unsatisfactory. . . . In fact, the case appears to have been tried largely on a wrong theory, the greater portion of the evidence consisting of the testimony of expert witnesses as to the value of the property. This is at the best an unsatisfactory way of determining the question of actual cost (for which purpose only could it be admissible), and should not be resorted to when better evidence can be obtained. As against the company, at least, its books furnish better evidence on this subject, and cannot be disregarded. These books certainly show the cost to have been less than $750,000, though we are unable to determine the precise amount properly shown by them; and the evidence clearly discloses that portions of the plant included in that cost are not now in use, if, indeed, they have not been totally abandoned. We think, therefore, that this finding is not justified by the evidence. . . .

The finding that the expenses of the company for the year in question were $40,000 is also attacked. The books of the company put the amount at $44,255.30. Of this amount appellants object to items of about $5,000 as unnecessary and improper, and object particularly to an item of $12,800, being an un-

paid bill which is disputed by plaintiff, and on which its liability is left doubtful. Counsel for respondents have not attempted to answer these points. As the evidence is presented to us in an unsatisfactory shape, we will say no more than that it does not support the finding. Whether all of the items complained of are proper or improper cannot be determined upon this record, but some of them are not shown to be proper. It will be the duty of the court on a retrial to allow no item of expenditure which is not satisfactorily shown to be an actual and proper charge in the actual conduct of the business of supplying water; and, when legal or other general expenses are claimed, they must be shown to have had a proper relation to that business. Of course, the items of expenses in the present action
196 should be disregarded. The trial being had after the expiration of the year for which the rates in question were fixed, the amounts of revenue and expenses are capable of exact proof.

With regard to the question of the depreciation of the plant by use, it is sufficient to say that ordinary repairs should be charged to current expense, that substantial reconstruction or replacement should be charged to the construction account, and that depreciation should not otherwise be considered. It is doubtless difficult in many cases to properly discriminate between current and ordinary repairs and such repairs as amount in effect to new construction. Such difficulties, when they arise, must be solved by the application of the principles on which ordinary business enterprises are conducted.

It may be added that when, as appears to have been the case in this instance, portions of the company's expenses are specifically repaid by the consumers, such expenses should be eliminated from the computation. This will apply at least to the "taps" put in for private consumers. . . .

For the reasons above set forth, the judgment and order appealed from are reversed, and the cause remanded for a new trial.

Henshaw, J., and McFarland, J., concurred.

GAROUTTE, J., concurring.—

In the fixing of water rates by a city, as contemplated by the constitution, it is evident that the valuation of the plant is the basic element upon which the whole investigation rests. The original cost of construction is simply an item to be considered in fixing the present valuation. It is a circumstance, strong or weak, entering into the final conclusion of the municipality upon the question. But as to the amount of the bonded indebtedness, or the amount of interest annually accruing thereon, we fail to see their materiality in determining the value of the plant, or the sum total of revenue to be raised from the sales of water. It is not a question in which rate payers are concerned, whether the water company has no outstanding indebtedness, or is floundering under a bonded debt which threatens to sink it at any moment. If the municipality is required to establish a scale of rates which will produce a revenue sufficient to pay interest upon outstanding bonds, this provision of the constitution would not only be a perpetual guaranty to the bondholders for the payment of their annual interest, but a constant incentive to additional issues of bonds. . . .

Taking the findings of fact as they stand, the schedule of rates fixed by the city should not be disturbed. The valuation of the plant is $750,000; the operating and current expenses are $40,000. The revenue from the sale of water under the schedule of rates would be and actually was $65,000. This leaves a profit of $25,000 upon the investment. To be sure it is small, when we consider the amount of money invested. . . .

This balance of $25,000 is profit, unless it is swallowed up by the finding of the court that plaintiff's plant suffered an annual depreciation of three and one-half per cent, and the conclusion of law therefrom that a percentage upon the investment to that amount should be added to the operating expenses before the point is reached where profit begins. We are satisfied that this finding has no support in the evidence, even conceding the conclusion of law drawn therefrom sound. In the first place, the evidence develops that there can be no general depreciation of this plant as a whole. There are tunnels, wells, reservoirs, water rights and real estate, amounting to more than one-half of the valuation of the plant. There is no depreciation of these things; there is no wear and tear, no permanent and gradual destruction by use and age. Most of them stand as everlasting as the hills.

The theory of plaintiff in this regard seems to be that the life of a plant of this character may be approximated at thirty years, and that a sinking fund of one-thirtieth of its value should be collected from the rate payers annually and laid aside to be handed to the stockholders upon the sad occasion of its demise, as an alleviating salve to their sorrow. But such a thing is all wrong, for it results in the consumers of water buying the plant and paying for it in annual installments. Consumers of water cannot be charged with cost of construction. They are only to pay a fair interest upon such cost; and as we look at this matter, if this three and one-half per cent is not stowed away in the vaults as a sinking fund to make glad the hearts of the stockholders upon the expiration of the thirty years, which theory cannot be tolerated for a moment, then it must go into the plant as cost of construction, and, therefore, not chargeable against the consumers. The result of such expenditure is only to increase the valuation of the plant, and to thereby draw from the consumers an income upon the amount of the investment. If improvements are made in the plant, the cost of these improvements should be charged against the construction account. If repairs are made upon the plant as it stands, as, for example, a new pipe substituted for an old piece of the same size and quality, such charge should be considered operating expenses.

198 Upon an examination of the record we find these views fully corroborated in the evidence of the water company, given by one of its most important witnesses. He testified: "Where we took up one pipe line or a portion of it on the street, and put down another, if it was the same size pipe, to renew it we would charge it to expenses. If it was a different size we would charge the difference between them, the increased size, to construction. Where we sell pipe that we take up, we credit that to construction. If we have to renew any portion of the same size pipe, we charge it to expenses."

This question has arisen incidentally in *Union Pac. R. R. Co. v. United States*, 99 U. S. 402, and also in *Reagan v. Farmers' Loan etc. Co., supra*, but neither case looks the other way from the views we have expressed. When the question arises between the corporation upon the one side and its bondholders or stockholders upon the other, or when it arises upon a construction of a contract with the government, as in one of the cases just cited, operating expenses, cost of construction, and net earnings may stand upon a different footing. Those cases are not this case. This is neither a question of bookkeeping nor net earnings. The particular system pursued by corporations in segregating and applying their gross receipts is likewise immaterial. The whole matter is a pure question of what is just and right between all parties interested. The consumers of water have rights, and possess equities which must be considered equally with those of the company. They are to be taxed to pay the amount called for by the schedule of rates, and these rates, in justice to them, should be fixed at the smallest possible amount, taking into consideration what is just and equitable to the owners of the property. In cases of the present character under the head of operating expenses the company is entitled to charge for keeping the plant in its normal condition; and the sinking of new wells, the building of new reservoirs, the erection of additional buildings, and the substitution of larger and better pipe (to the extent of the difference), do not come under the head of operating expenses, but should be charged to construction account. If this were not so, a water plant inferior in all things in a few years could be transformed into a water plant superior in everything, at the expense of the consumer. This would be an advantage to the owner and a burden to the rate payer neither contemplated nor justified by the law.

For the foregoing reasons I think the judgment and order should be reversed and the cause remanded.

TEMPLE, J., concurring.—I agree generally in the views expressed by Mr. Justice Garoutte. . . . 199

HARRISON, J., concurring. . . .

BEATTY, C. J., dissenting.—I think the judgment and order appealed from should be affirmed. In fixing water rates, it is the duty of the city council to provide for a just and reasonable compensation to the water company. Anything short of that is simple confiscation, and is not only a violation of constitutional rights but is an extremely short-sighted policy. Rates ought to be adjusted to the value of the service rendered, and this means that the water companies should be allowed to collect annually a gross income sufficient to pay current expenses, maintain the necessary plant in a state of efficiency, and declare a dividend to stockholders equal to at least the lowest current rates of interest, not on the par or market value of the stock, but on the actual value of the property necessarily used in providing and distributing the water to consumers.

To arrive at the actual value of the plant, water rights, real estate, etc., cost is an element to be considered, but is not conclusive. The plant may have cost too much, it may have been planned upon too liberal a scale, its construction may have been extravagantly managed, the real estate and water rights may have cost less or more than their present value, and, therefore, cost will seldom represent the actual capital at present invested in the works, but such present value is the true basis upon which compensation, in the shape of dividends, is to be allowed.

As to current expenses, all operating expenses reasonably and properly incurred should be allowed, taxes should be allowed, and the cost of current repairs.

In addition to this, if there is any part of the plant, such as main pipes, etc., which at the end of a term of years—twenty years, for instance—will be so decayed and worn out as to require restoration, an annual allowance should be made for a sinking fund sufficient to replace such part of the plant when it is worn out.

In its findings and conclusions the superior court seems to have conformed to these views, and, making every allowance for any minor errors that may appear in the record, the evidence is amply sufficient to sustain every material finding, and the findings clearly sustain the conclusion that in this case the rates fixed were grossly and palpably unjust to the water company.

The judgment and order should be affirmed.

DYKMAN v. KEENEY

45 N.Y.S. 127 (1897)
New York Supreme Court, Appellate Division
[affirmed on opinion below]

Appeal from trial term. Kings county.

Action by William N. Dykman, as receiver of the Commercial Bank, against Seth L. Keeney and others, to recover from defendants, as directors of said bank, the amount of a dividend declared by them at a directors' meeting on June 28, 1892, and paid on July 5, 1892, amounting to $4,293. From a judgment in favor of defendants, entered on a verdict rendered by direction of the court, plaintiff appeals. Affirmed.

Argued before GOODRICH, P. J., and CULLEN, BARTLETT, HATCH, and BRADLEY, JJ. . . .

HATCH, J. . . .

The transaction by which the Knowlton notes were surrendered and the Hassel notes taken by the bank, it is claimed, did not operate as payment of the Knowlton indebtedness within the meaning of the statute. . . . we must dispose of the case upon the assumption that the bank received the Hassel notes as payment of Knowlton's pre-existing obligations. As between these parties, therefore, Knowlton's obligations were paid.

This brings us to the question whether, for the purposes of the statute, they may be regarded as paid in the sense that the Hassel notes might be treated by the directors of the bank as an asset upon which a dividend might be based. The language of the statute is that the bank shall charge in the account of profit and loss, and deduct from the actual profits, all losses sustained by it, and they shall include as losses all debts owing to it, which shall have remained due without prosecution, and upon which no interest shall have been paid, for more than one year. Banking Laws (Laws 1892, c. 689, § 26). It does not appear that the Knowlton notes had remained due without prosecution for more than a year, and only in the sense that no money was actually paid had interest remained due. In fact, the notes had been renewed, for principal and interest, as they fell due from time to time. We think that the intent and meaning of this statute is that it embraces debts due for which no provision has been made by those liable thereon for a year, and upon which interest has not been paid. We do not think that it was intended to relate to, or that it embraces, notes which have been received from time to time in the ordinary course of business, and which by the terms of the renewal obligation are not then due, even though the renewal obligation embraced interest as well as principal, and the debt had been continued beyond a year. This was a bank of discount, in which the assets of the bank consisted largely of notes discounted and in renewals thereof, and in the usual prosecution of the business it might frequently happen that extensions and accommodation to its customers would result in its possession of perfectly good notes, where no payments either for principal or interest have been made within a year in money, and yet where the bank held a live and enforceable obligation not yet due by its terms. To hold that such an obligation must be charged up as a loss, and deducted from the assets of the bank, for the purpose of the declaration of a dividend by the directors, would, we think, impose an obligation not contemplated or intended by the statute. Such construction would certainly render the declaration of a dividend by the directors at any time extremely hazardous. The statute is abundantly satisfied by limiting its application to those debts which have become due, and remain unprosecuted, and upon which no interest has been paid for a year. Such are its terms, and such we conceive to have been its spirit and intent. Of course, if the contract was renewed for the purpose of evasion of the statute, the directors might be held liable; and there may be other circumstances which would reach a like result. But there is nothing in the present case which has a tendency to show that the acceptance of the Hassel notes in the discharge of Knowlton's debt was not done in good faith and in the usual course of business. We see no reason, therefore, for departing from the construction which we have heretofore placed upon this transaction. . . .

WASHBURN v. NATIONAL WALL-PAPER CO.

81 Fed. 17 (1897)
United States Circuit Court of Appeals
Second Circuit

This is an appeal from a decree of the circuit court, Southern district of New York, dismissing the bill.

The suit was brought by complainants, who are large owners of the stock of the defendants, the National Wall-Paper Company, to restrain the payment of interest upon certain obligations of the company called "debenture stock." The complainants insisted that such payment was not justified by the terms of the debenture stock itself, but was in violation of the agreement between the company and the complainants, and of the provisions of the articles of association and by-laws of the company. The company's president and treasurer were joined as defendants.

The defendant company was organized June 2, 1892, under the New York business corporation law, to carry on the business of manufacturing and dealing in wall paper, with a capital stock originally of $14,000,000, but which was soon increased to $30,000,000, all of which, however, has not been issued. The certificate of incorporation provided for the creation of obligations in the nature of certificates of indebtedness to the extent of $8,000,000, to be known as "debenture stock," and sold for cash or for property or assets purchased by the corporation at the fair market value thereof. It further provided that: "The debenture stock hereby authorized to be issued shall be and remain an obligation of the corporation, or payable at the expiration of the corporate existence, and entitled meantime to interest at a rate not exceeding eight per cent. per annum, payable quarter-yearly, as an expense of the business, from and out of the profits of the company, before any dividend can be declared or paid on the stock or share capital. No payment of interest can or shall be made on such debenture stock which will impair the capital, nor unless the amount paid shall have been actually earned by the company. The holders of debenture stock shall not be entitled to demand or sue for the interest payable upon the obligations held by them unless such interest was actually earned by the company, in which event the amount earned shall be distributed amongst and paid to the holders of debenture stock, to the proportion of their holdings, but the unpaid interest shall, notwithstanding, become and remain an obligation of the company, payable out of any future profits to the full extent of the amount represented by the outstanding certificates before any dividends can be declared or paid on the stock or share capital. In the event of the dissolution or winding up of the company, the holders of debenture stock or of certificates representing the ownership thereof shall rank pari passu with other unsecured creditors of the corporation, and shall be entitled to receive in full out of the assets of the company the amounts represented by the outstanding certificates of indebtedness or debenture stock in priority to the claims of the shareholders to be paid any amount in respect of such shares." The by-laws provided that the board of directors shall select accountants as official auditors to the company, who shall supervise its books of account, and all interest paid upon the debenture stock, and all dividends declared on the share capital, shall be based upon the net earnings of the company as certified by such auditors.

. . .

At the time of the organization of the company the appellants, constituting the firm of Cresswell & Washburn, were manufacturers and dealers in wall paper under the firm name of Cresswell & Washburn. Other firms and individuals were engaged in like business in various parts of the country. These various concerns commenced negotiations with the National Wall-Paper Company, which resulted in the acquisition by the latter of the property and assets of the several concerns, including complainants' firm of Cresswell & Washburn.

. . .

It will be perceived from the foregoing statement that the stock of the defendant company was issued for the "good will" of the different manufacturing plants (and some patents, trade-marks, etc.), the tangible assets of which plants, viz. machinery, fixtures, material, book accounts, etc., were paid for by the issue of the debenture stock. Practically the entire capital stock (i. e. the common stock) is represented by the good will of the establishments which the defendant company bought up. Complainants received for their old plant, book accounts, good will, etc., $326,000 in debenture stock, and $1,831,800 in common stock, of which, by reason of the uncollectibility of certain accounts, they subsequently returned $7,702.19 of debenture stock and $135,200 of common stock. When the suit was begun, the accountants, designated under the by-laws as auditors, had made no certificate of net earnings. Subsequently, and on April 22, 1896, they certified that they had examined the books and accounts from the date of inception to February 29, 1896, and found the net profits for the entire period to be $3,046,639.66. They further certify that "the surplus profits remaining on hand on said 29th day of February, 1896, representing the net earnings of the company available for the payment of interest on its debenture stock, over and above the sums already expended for interest, amount to $1,410,522.39." This sum so certified is $866,528.29 in excess of the debenture interest unpaid and claimed to be accrued on February 29, 1896;
204 i. e. for 11 months at 8 per cent. per annum, viz. $543,994.

E. M. Shepard, for complainants.

Louis Marshall, for defendants.

Before WALLACE, LACOMBE, and SHIPMAN, Circuit Judges.

LACOMBE, Circuit Judge (after stating the facts). The contention of the complainants is that, notwithstanding the certificate of the auditors, no debenture interest could be paid without impairing the capital of the company, and that in fact there were no profits. They contend that they have demonstrated the impairment of the capital stock to an extent more than sufficient to prevent the payment of debenture interest: First, on the theory that the capital stock was originally issued for far less than its par value, and has never been fully, if at all, paid; second, on the theory that, even if it were originally fully paid, there has been an enormous depreciation in the value of the capital stock since that time; third, by losses and depreciations in assets other than the good will for which the capital stock was originally issued.

The first of these propositions suggests the questions whether stock is issued for "property actually received," within the meaning of the statute, when it is issued for good will only; and whether, assuming that the entire stock could, under the New York act of 1892, be issued solely for good will, the good will taken in this case was taken at its actual value. These questions are discussed at great length in the briefs. It is contended that, although "good will" is property in the sense that it is a subject of bargain and sale, it is nevertheless but a so-called "parasitical species of property, which cannot exist apart from the substantial property of which it is an attribute"; that it is not a thing of value by itself; that the capital of a corporation must be invested in property capable of existence by itself; that in this case no effort was made to ascertain the actual value of the good will; that the value at which it was appraised and stock issued against it was purely arbitrary, and in no sense a proper valuation, and that in determining this arbitrary valuation elements of alleged profits were taken into consideration, which could not fairly be considered such. Upon this interesting, and possibly perplexing, discussion we do not find it necessary to embark. Good will has been defined as "all that good disposition which customers entertain towards the house of business identified by the particular name or firm, and which may induce them to continue giving their custom to it." There is nothing marvelous or mysterious about it. When an individual or a firm or a corporation has gone on for an unbroken series of years conducting a particular business, and has been so scrupulous in fulfilling every obligation, so careful in maintaining the standard of the goods dealt in, so absolutely honest and fair in all business dealings that customers of the concern have become convinced that their experience in the future will be as satisfactory as it has been in the past, while such customers' good report of their own experience tends continually to bring new customers to the same concern, there has been produced an element of value quite as important—in some cases, perhaps, far more important—than the plant or machinery with which the business is carried on. That it is property is abundantly settled by authority, and, indeed, is not disputed. That in some cases it may be very valuable property is manifest. The individual who has created it by years of hard work and fair business dealing usually experiences no difficulty in finding men willing to pay him for it, if he be willing to sell it to them. Legislation devised to restrict the accumulation of the fruits of industry may impair its value by denying to its producer the right to enter into a contract enforceable at law not to interfere with its enjoyment by the purchaser, but, so long as any belief in human honesty remains, there will be found some persons willing to buy such property, the very existence of which implies honest business dealing in the past. And so long as it remains salable it is valuable. Nor is it indissolubly connected with any particular locality, or any specific tangible property. Reference has been made on the briefs to the publishing house of "Harper & Bros." If its present establishment in Franklin Square were destroyed by fire to-morrow, and everything therein contained were swept out of existence, it is surely manifest that, so long as the firm itself survived, and continued to transact its old business, it would still hold its "good will," although the business should be thenceforward conducted in a new building erected on some uptown street, and supplied with entirely new machinery and equipments. If good will be a "parasite," it is a "parasite" of the business from which it sprung, not of the mere machinery by which that business was conducted.

Since good will is property, and since in some cases it is valuable property, it would follow that in some way or other it must be practically possible to determine what that value is. Whether the particular method employed in the case at bar to ascertain such value is or is not a proper one, and whether the appraisement made when these several wall-paper concerns were bought up by the defendant company was accurate, we are under no obligation to inquire upon the complainants' request. The method of valuation was one which they fully approved, and which was applied in fixing the value of their own property, as the result of which they received $1,831,800 in common stock of the defendant. They certainly, participating in the transaction, and reaping its benefits, are in no position now to claim that the good will bought by the defendant company with common stock was overvalued.

The second proposition which has been discussed at great length in the briefs of counsel is the one advanced on behalf of complainants, viz. that, "even if the capital stock were originally fully paid, there has been an enormous depreciation in the value of the capital

stock since that time." We do not find it necessary to review the discussion of this question as to what constitutes depreciation of capital, within the meaning of the statute and articles of incorporation. The defendants insist that "in determining whether a company is entitled to pay a dividend, the property acquired for permanent use in carrying on business may be valued at the price actually paid for it, although it could not be sold again except at a loss." Complainants' counsel controverts this proposition; but, even if complainants' contention be sound, the result here would be the same. There is an insuperable practical difficulty in the way of deciding whether or not there has been depreciation in the capital of defendant company, or in so much of the assets as represent good will. The case discloses no evidence advising us what the good will of these various concerns bought by the defendant company was worth on the day of purchase and what it was worth on February 29, 1896. With absolutely no information as to either minuend or subtrahend, we cannot make any determination as to what the difference may be between
206 them. This court is advised of no rule or method of appraisal which can be applied to such facts as are in proof in order to determine the value of this asset at either time. The evidence is not entirely persuasive that the rule adopted when the properties were purchased is the true one; and the mere circumstance that complainants, who profited by that valuation, cannot now be heard to question its accuracy, does not make it so. No estimate or appraisal as of either date is testified to, no experts have made calculations, and rehearsed the results thereof. The fact that some of the workshops bought by the defendant company have been closed and dismantled, the business of selling goods to the customers of the concerns who formerly owned such shops being still carried on, does not dispose of the question. Even if the good will of such concerns has ceased to exist (which is by no means certain), it does not follow that the entire value of the good will of all the properties has depreciated. It may be that the disappearance of these concerns from the field has increased the value of the business of such as are left. It is manifest that any conclusion as to this branch of the case would be but surmise based upon conjecture, and without definite information as to the actual value of this asset this court cannot undertake to say whether or not it is less than it was four years ago.

Complainants further contend that on February 29, 1896, there were not profits sufficient to warrant the payment of interest on the debenture stock, such interest concededly being payable only out of profits. This interest, it will be remembered, amounted to $543,994, and the auditors certified that the profits on that day aggregated $1,410,522.39. It is insisted that certain items of assets were taken by the auditors at an excessive valuation, that in some cases items not properly assets were included on the credit side of the account, and that sufficient sums were not deducted for depreciation, reserves, etc. These items are:

Birge good will	$2,100,000 00
Birge bonus	300,000 00
Addition to Block account	100,000 00
Selling expenses treated as an asset	166,050 17
Reserve for depreciation	300,000 00
Reserve for bad debts of business of 1892 to 1894	50,000 00
Reserve for bad debts of business of 1894 to 1896	150,000 00
Eight per cent. for valuation of manufactured goods	60,000 00
	$3,226,050 17

The first two items may be considered together. About the time when complainants sold their business to the defendant company, in 1892, some effort seems to have been made to buy up the establishment and business of the firm of M. H. Birge & Sons, of Buffalo, upon the same terms as all the others, but Birge & Sons refused to entertain the offer. Subsequently, in December, 1894, a fire destroyed part of the Birge plant at Buffalo. Thereupon defendant company, apparently with a view of ingratiating itself with the firm, offered to lease it one of the defendant's factories, which was temporarily shut down. Negotiations for the purchase of the entire Birge business and outfit were subsequently begun, and finally Birge made an offer to sell at a certain price, leaving his offer open for but a brief period. It was accepted, although not without disapproval by a minority of the board of directors, including complainant Washburn. The price agreed upon was $300,000 in cash on the day of signing the contract, $2,100,000 in common stock, $50,000 in debenture stock, and an additional sum in cash, to be paid when appraisement 207
of the tangible assets was completed, and which turned out to be $129,286.36. The auditors treated this transaction as a purchase of assets for permanent investment, and $2,400,000 of it as paid for good will and patents. This is a strictly accurate statement of the transaction, and the only possible objection to the auditors' figuring is the suggestion that the good will and patents were not worth $2,400,000, either when bought, in February, 1895, or when counted as an asset, in February, 1896. Here, again, the question is presented, what is the actual value of this property? But the record gives us no information upon which to answer. . . .

Evidently the majority of the board of directors supposed it was worth the price paid, or they would not have paid it. It would seem to require affirmative evidence to discredit their conclusions. . . .

Upon the testimony as it stands, we cannot find that the auditors erred in treating the Birge good will and patents as an asset worth what the company paid for it.

It will not be necessary to review the other items objected to in the auditors' balance sheet. As to some of them—e. g. the "addition to block account" and the "selling expenses"—the testimony seems to sustain the action of the auditors. But further discussion is unnecessary. Eliminating the two Birge items, it will be found that the others objected to aggregate $826,050.07, but the balance sheet gives a surplus over and above the debenture interest of $866,528.39; so that, whatever conclusion should be reached as to these other items, there would be sufficient profit to pay the interest, and complainants are not entitled to enjoin such payment. . . .

The decree appealed from is affirmed, with costs of this appeal.

MILWAUKEE ELECTRIC RAILWAY & LIGHT CO. v. CITY OF MILWAUKEE

87 Fed. 577 (1898)
United States Circuit Court
Eastern District of Wisconsin

SEAMAN, District Judge. The main controversy in each of these actions is whether the ordinance of June 11, 1896, unreasonably fixes rates of fare which would deprive the complainant of its property without due process of law, and thus violates the fourteenth amendment to the constitution of the United States....

208

Are the earnings of the property insufficient, in view of all the conditions, to justify this reduction in the rates of fare? Solution of this inquiry depends upon the showing (1) of earning capacity at existing rates, and (2) of the "amount really and necessarily invested in the enterprise," and upon the conclusion (3) whether the ratio of return upon the investment is excessive. In the statements which are referred to both parties have adopted a ratio, so far as necessary, to separate the electric lighting plant owned by the complainant, so that the statements which follow relate exclusively to the street railway plant, except where otherwise mentioned.

First. The question of earning capacity is confined by the testimony to the results of three years' operation, being after the system was fairly installed, and inclusive of the year in which the ordinance was adopted, namely, 1894, 1895, and 1896. It is suggested on behalf of the defendant that those years were exceptional, for one cause and another, and are not a fair criterion for future earnings under more favorable circumstances; but the suggestion is without force in this case, because the ordinance operates upon these very conditions, and must, of course, be predicated upon them,--upon existing facts, and not upon mere future possibilities,--and, so determined, the instant case cannot affect rights under new conditions.

The proofs on the part of the complainant furnish, in detail, from the books of account, the gross earnings, the various items of expense and of charges for which deduction is claimed, excluding any payments of, or allowance for, interest on the bonded indebtedness, and state the net earnings as follows: In 1894, $64,868.77; in 1895, $269,202.30; in 1896 $100,628.81. In this showing it appears that deduction of $247,324.88 is made in 1894 for "depreciation," being the amount apportioned in that year to meet the alleged annual loss by physical depreciation of the plant, to keep the capital intact. No such deduction is made in 1895 and 1896, because not shown in the books, although it is insisted that like credit is due in each year, for the purposes of this case.

The defendant concedes the correctness of the showing as to the gross earnings, but disputes certain large items for 209
which deductions are made in the above statement, corrects some items, and denies that any allowance should be made for depreciation. Aside from the fact that reports and statements of financial condition made from time to time by the company omit many of the deductions here asserted, these contentions on the part of the defendant rest solely upon the books of account kept by the company, and the testimony of Mr. De Grasse, stating his conclusions as an expert accountant from examination of such books, with the following result as to net earnings: In 1894, $387,074.70; in 1895, $479,621.11; in 1896, $66,520.99. But this total for 1896 erroneously includes an allowance of $160,550 paid for interest on bonds, which should be excluded on the basis assumed, and would make the net earnings for that year, on his computation, $227,070.99. In this statement the allowance for depreciation in 1894 is excluded by Mr. De Grasse, because that item was in fact charged off upon change in the system of bookkeeping. He also excludes large amounts of undoubted expenditures upon the hypothesis that they belong to "construction account," as covering permanent improvements, and not to "expense of maintenance," as stated; rejects certain payments as accruing on account of previous years, and certain sums apportioned and charged off to meet damage claims; and makes corrections as to taxes, for which the book entries were made in advance upon estimates by way of apportioning the expenses of the year, pending litigation and other causes. However valuable this testimony is for analysis of the bookkeeping methods and for correction of certain charges, it is clearly insufficient, without other support, to contradict the undisputed testimony, both posi-

tive and expert, on the part of complainant, which verifies substantially its contention upon the disputed subjects of deduction, namely, that the expenditures so charged were largely, if not wholly, of such nature as to justify deduction for "maintenance"; and that depreciation is a well-recognized fact in all such plants, for which allowance must be made to save the capital from impairment, without regard to any question of its entry upon the books.

Making allowances for maintenance alone, in accordance with the analysis presented by the expert witnesses Goodspeed, Coffin, McAdoo, and Beggs, taking in each instance the estimate most favorable to the defendant, I am
210 satisfied that the defendant's claim of net earnings must be materially reduced, and that the largest amounts which can be assumed upon its theory, excluding any allowance for depreciation (except that for 1894 the "maintenance" allowance is increased, to bring it--the general allowance--up to the minimum estimate by the experts), would approximate the following sums:

In 1894	$230,000
In 1895	340,000
In 1896	115,000
	$685,000

----Making the average earnings per year, say $228,333.

In reference to the element of depreciation, the witness Beggs gives the following explanation:

"I think experience has demonstrated that the utmost life that can be expected from the best roadbed that can be laid to-day would be, at the outside, ten to twelve years, when it would have to be almost entirely renewed. The Milwaukee Company is in that condition to-day, because of the different periods that their track went down, and due to the fact that it was not all put down at one time, and it must now of necessity commence to lay about 12 miles of track annually, being about one-twelfth of its total mileage; and will be required, whether they wish to or not, to lay that amount annually heareafter, and will thereby be keeping their tracks fairly up to the standard. The same applies, I might say, to the equipment. In my estimate I have calculated that the Milwaukee Company must do this year, which,

as a matter of fact, it is doing, what it did last year,--in other words, put on not less than 20 of the most modern, best-constructed equipments, thereby keeping its standard up to the minimum it has now, of 240 equipments; because I think it is fair to assume that the average life of the double equipment, taken as a whole, will not exceed 12 years, the life of the motor being somewhat less than that, and that of the car we hope may exceed it possibly several years,--I mean the car bodies; but that, in the main, we hope that we will get an average life of twelve years out of them. So, taking 20 equipments annually, you would keep to your standard of 240 equipments, which is absolutely necessary to maintain--to operate--the Milwaukee Street Railway. I mean cars complete, with motors and complete electrical 211
equipment."

For the causes thus stated, within general rules which are well known, it is manifest that this element must be taken into account before it can be determined that earnings derived from a plant are excessive; and in the same line there is much force in the argument of counsel that consideration should also be given to the factor of depreciation by amortization of franchises, as all the franchises in question terminate in the year 1924. The latter item, if allowed, would be a matter of simple computation; but a just measure of physical depreciation seems, to some extent, although only partially, involved in provisions for maintenance, and, while the testimony is very full and instructive upon this subject, it does not clear the case from serious difficulties in the way of stating a definite ratio or sum for such allowance. I am, however, clearly of opinion that neither of these elements is essential to the determination of the issues upon any aspect presented by the testimony, and that depreciation may be left to serve as an important factor of safety, in either view.

Second. As to valuation:...I am satisfied that the property of complainant represents a value, based solely upon the cost of reproduction, exceeding $5,000,000. And I am further satisfied that this amount is not the true measure of the value of the investment in the enterprise. It leaves out of consideration any allowance for necessary and reasonable investment in purchase of the old lines and equipments, which were indispensable to the contemplated im-

provement, but of which a large part was of such nature that it does not count in the final inventory. No allowance enters in for the large investment arising out of the then comparatively new state of the art of electric railways for a large system, having reference to electrical equipment, weight of rails, character of cars, and the like, of which striking instance appears in the fact that the electric motor which then cost about $2,500 can now be obtained for $800; so that work of this class was in the experimental stage in many respects, and the expenditures by the pioneer in the undertaking may not fairly be gauged by the present cost of reproduction. Of the $5,000,000 and over paid for the acquisition of the old lines, it would be difficult, if
212 not impossible, from the testimony, to arrive of any fair approximation of the share or amount of tangible property which enters into the valuation in this inventory. It does appear that the roadways required reconstruction with new rails and paving, and that the amount stated was actually paid by the investors, making their investment nearly $9,000,000. How much of this may be defined or apportioned as the amount which was both "really and necessarily invested in the enterprise" (vide Road Co. v. Sandford, supra) I have not attempted ascertain, except to this extent: that I am clearly of opinion that at least $2,000,000 of those preliminary expenditures are entitled to equitable consideration, as so invested, beyond the reproduction value, if the valuation of the investment is not otherwise found sufficient for all the purposes of this case, but no opinion is expressed in reference to the remaining $1,885,644.

Third, The final inquiry, whether the net earnings shown are in excess of or equal to a just return upon the investment, presents no serious difficulty, under the premises above stated. Assuming $5,000,000 as the basis of investment, the ratio of earnings would be as follows: (1) At the extreme computations of defendant, the yearly average would be $364,000, which would yield .072 per cent.; (2) at the complainant's figures, after adding the corrections for taxes, the return would be .033 per cent.; (3) at the amounts which are above stated as my deductions from this testimony, the yearly average, being $228,333, would make .045 per cent. Assuming $7,000,000 as the basis, the ratio of earnings would be, upon each of said versions, as follows: For the first, .052 per cent.; for the second,

.023 per cent.; for the third, .032 per cent.

The interest rate fixed in the bonds issued by the company is 5 per cent. The rate which prevails in this market, as shown by the uncontroverted testimony, is 6 per cent. for real-estate mortgages and like securities. If the $5,000,000 basis be adopted, surely a better rate must be afforded for the risks of investment than can be obtained on securities of this class, in which there is no risk. Upon the basis of $7,000,000, which is more logical and just, the 5 per cent. named in the bonds is clearly not excessive, and should be accepted by a court of equity as the minimum of allowance; and, even upon the defendant's partial showing, the return would be less than one-quarter per cent. above 213
that, with the large margin for depreciation left out of account.

I am of opinion that the testimony is not only convincing in support of the material allegations of the bill, but is uncontradicted and conclusive that the improved service received by the public, with the universal system of transfers, is well worth the five-cent rate charged therefor; that the company has not received earnings in excess of an equitable allowance to the investors for the means necessarily invested in furnishing such service; that enforcement of the ordinance would deprive complainant of property rights, by preventing reasonable compensation for its service; and that, therefore, the ordinance clearly violates the constitution of the United States, and is invalid. Decree must enter accordingly, and for an injunction as prayed in the bill.

PEOPLE ex. rel. THE UNITED VERDE COPPER COMPANY v. ROBERTS

156 N.Y. 585 (1898)
Court of Appeals of New York

APPEAL from an order of the Appellate Division of the Supreme Court in the third judicial department, entered January 24, 1898, affirming, on certiorari, a decision of the state comptroller imposing a franchise tax, including penalty and interest, upon the capital stock of the relator employed within this state.

214 The facts, so far as material, are stated in the opinion. . . .

BARTLETT, J. The relator is a domestic corporation, organized in 1883, in the language of its certificate, "for the purpose of carrying on some of its business in the city of New York, but the mining, milling and other operations of the company are to be carried on near the city of Prescott, county of Yavapai, Arizona Territory." . . .

The relator insisted before the comptroller that the only capital stock of the company employed within this state was represented by office furniture, valued at five hundred dollars, and its average bank balance.

The tax under review was imposed for the year ending November 1st, 1895.

The comptroller found that $480,000 of the capital stock of relator was employed within this state and made up as follows, viz.: Average bank account and chattels and the amount invested by the corporation in the bonds and stock of the United Verde and Pacific Railway Company, a corporation operating a railroad in the territory of Arizona, under the following circumstances:

The relator is the owner of copper mines located at Jerome, Arizona; its capital stock is $3,000,000, all of which was issued for the mines.

The company operated its property for some years, transporting its product by wagons to the nearest railway station, a distance of twenty-five miles. Owing to the almost impassable condition of the roads in the winter season it became necessary to construct a railroad over this route, and the United Verde and Pacific railway was built.

It is conceded that nearly the entire business of the railroad company consists in transporting goods to the mines and the copper product therefrom.

The relator took $329,000 worth of stock and bonds of the railroad, which amount was sufficient to build and equip it.

It appears that some little time after this money was advanced to the railway company, and in December, 1895, the bonds were issued to the relator in the city of New York, but very soon after were sent to the president of the company in Arizona.

It also appears that the company had prosperously operated its mine for some years, paying an annual dividend at times as high as ten per cent, and at others varying from six to ten per cent.

When the mining company determined to purchase the bonds and stock of the railroad company, it ceased paying dividends until that amount was accumulated. 215

It is undisputed that this amount was surplus, unless the theory adopted by the comptroller and to be presently referred to, is correct.

The vice-president of the company when on the stand was asked the following questions in regard to this amount:

"Q. It might have been profits and it might have been other moneys?

"A. Well, it must have been profits, because the same year we paid $75,000 in dividends and still had a bank balance left.

"Q. And paid the officers of the company their salaries and the wages of employees?

"A. Yes, sir."

In order to meet this direct evidence, that the money used in the purchase of the bonds and stock was accumulated by passing dividends and thus surplus, the learned attorney-general argues that as the mines had been worked ever since 1883, the ore extracted and sold and large dividends paid, they were necessarily to some extent depleted and exhausted and the capital stock of relator impaired, so that no surplus as matter of law could be accumulated.

The logic of this argument leads to the conclusion that the most prosperous mining corporation, doing the heaviest business and paying the largest dividends, is suffering from the greatest impairment of capital and has drifted furthest towards final and hopeless insolvency.

The learned Appellate Division, while affirming the decision of the comptroller, stated that the operation of a mine may decrease its value by exhaustion, or increase it by development. This is very true, and the future of most mining enterprises is matter of conjecture. It is common knowledge that there are copper mines which have yielded enormous returns for years and at present show no signs of exhaustion, but rather increased development.

We are of opinion that this speculative theory as to mining in general, does not overcome the positive proof that these bonds and stocks were purchased by the surplus moneys of the relator.

The English courts have held that a company working a wasting property like a mine or patent is not prohibited from making dividends, nor is it obliged to set apart a sinking fund to meet any anticipated depreciation. (*Lee* v. *Neuchatel Asphalte Co.*, English Law Rep. [41 Ch. Div.] p. 1.)

In the case cited the company was operating under a lease, which might be more of a "wasting property" than a copper
216 mine well located.

Mr. Morawetz, in his work on Private Corporations (Section 442), points out that the capital of a mining company is not designed to be used like that of a banking or manufacturing company, in carrying on business permanently; that the exhaustion of a mine cannot be repaired, and there would be no object in accumulating the money obtained by the company through working the mine, so as to keep up the original amount of capital.

He then adds: "It is implied from the character of the speculation of a mining company that the income derived from working the mine shall be distributed among the shareholders as dividends, after deducting the expenses and making reasonable provision for contingencies."

The Appellate Division affirmed the decision of the comptroller upon the ground that the burden rested upon the relator to show that the comptroller was wrong in his valuation of the capital stock employed within this state.

It is undoubtedly the established rule that the determination of the comptroller must stand upon the question of valuation, unless clearly shown to have been erroneous. (*People ex rel. A. C. & D. Co.* v. *Wemple*, 129 N. Y. 558; *People ex rel. Roebling's Sons' Co.* v. *Wemple*, 138 N. Y. 587; *People ex rel. Western Electric Co.* v. *Campbell*, 145 N. Y. 587.) This rule, however, has no application to the case at bar, as it appears by undisputed evidence that the purchase of the bonds and stock was made with the surplus money of relator, and as the theory adopted by the comptroller to show the contrary is unsupported by evidence or authority, it follows that the amount represented by this investment must be deducted from the total amount of capital stock found to be employed within this state.

This surplus of the relator, even if placed in the stock and bonds of the railroad company as an independent investment, cannot be regarded as a part of its capital stock employed within this state. (*People ex rel. Singer Mfg. Co.* v. *Wemple*, 150 N. Y. 46.)

This corporation tax under the Laws of 1880 (Ch. 542, as amended), is not imposed upon property, but in the case of a domestic corporation on its franchises and of a foreign corporation on its business. (*People ex rel. Penn. R. R. Co.* v. *Wemple*, 138 N. Y. 1.) 217

In the case of the relator, where its principal business was conducted outside of this state, it became the duty of the comptroller to ascertain the amount of capital stock employed within this state (Ch. 501, Laws of 1885, § 11) for the purpose of computing the franchise tax. . . .

The order appealed from should be reversed, with costs, and the comptroller directed to readjust the account against the relator by deducting from the amount assessed against it for capital stock employed within this state the sum used in purchasing the stock and bonds of the United Verde and Pacific Railway Company.

All concur, except VANN, J., not voting.

Order reversed.

DAVENPORT v. LINES

72 Conn. 118 (1899)

218 ACTION by the receiver of a corporation to recover certain sums claimed to have been illegally paid to a stockholder by way of dividends, brought to the Court of Common Pleas in Fairfield County and reserved by that court, *Curtis, J.*, upon a finding of facts, for the consideration and advice of this court. *Judgment advised for the plaintiff.* . . .

The court found the following facts: . . .

During the year ending July 1st, 1894, 370 pianos were sold, the material in which cost $25,689.82. 22. In determining said assets the real estate was taken at its cost, $11,332.77, and the cost of certain additions to the building was added thereto, making the above sum. 23. To the sum paid for the scales and patterns the sum of $2,229.24 was added, being money expended in an exhibit at the World's Fair at Chicago in 1893, for the purpose of advertising. Said sum represented no tangible asset. 24. In the item 'stock on hand,' the materials on hand were actually inventoried and found to be worth $9,650.94. The expenses to date not apportioned to the products sold but apportioned to the material on hand, were valued at $8,992.44. I find that said sum represents the balance of the expenses from the last inventory, after applying a portion thereof, to wit: $26,834.90, to the pianos since completed and sold. 25. In apportioning said expenses, I find that the expenditures for the preceding year, plus the expenditures found to have been previously incurred on material on hand at the beginning of the preceding year, were distributed by estimation between the pianos sold during the year and the stock on hand when the inventory was made, approximately in proportion to the value of the materials in the pianos sold and the value of the materials on hand. . . .

All the questions arising upon this record were reserved for the advice of this court. . . .

TORRANCE, J. . . .

One of the important questions in the case is whether, upon the facts found, the corporation was insolvent and its capital stock impaired when the money in question was paid; and its solution depends upon the further question whether certain items included among the assets of the corporation in its inventories of July 1st, 1894 and 1895, were rightfully so included at all, or were rightfully so included at the amount stated in the inventory.

The inventory of July 1st, 1894, showed a surplus of $1,610.56. This result was reached by including among the assets three items, one of which the plaintiff claims is largely overvalued, and two of which he claims should not be included at all. 219

The first is the pattern and scales account, inventoried at $15,155. This was the value placed upon the patterns and scales when bought by the corporation at its organization, as stated in the finding, in October, 1892. This valuation as then made included the "business" or good will of the copartnership from which the patterns and scales were bought. Assuming for the purposes of the argument that the "good will" of the copartnership might be purchased and included as part of the assets of the corporation when it was organized, and that the good will and the patterns and scales together were at that time worth the price paid for them, it does not follow that that valuation continued the same down to July 1st, 1894. The court finds that in July, 1894, the patterns and scales themselves were not worth one half of the sum at which they were then inventoried; and it cannot find and fails to find what the "good will" was worth, as no evidence appears to have been offered upon that subject. This, we think, for the purposes of this case, must be regarded as a finding that this item was overvalued in the inventory to the extent of at least one half of the amount there stated.

One of the other items charged as an asset was the sum of $2,229.24, which represented money expended in an exhibit at the World's Fair in Chicago in 1893 for advertising purposes. "Said sum represented no tangible asset." This expenditure may or may not have increased the business of the corporation, but the court has failed to find that as an asset it had any value, and this is equivalent to a finding that it had none at that time, and ought not to have been included among the assets.

In this view of the case the corporation, in July, 1894, was insolvent and its capital stock impaired, without reference to the other item to which the plaintiff objects, and which therefore need not be specially considered. Suffice it to say, that upon the facts found we think this last item, expenses on material on hand, amounting to $8,992.44, ought not to be included among the assets. The inventory of July 1st, 1895, was made up in substantially the same way as to these three items as that of 1894, and showed substantially the same condition of things as to insolvency and impairment of capital stock. . . .

The remaining question is whether the money paid to the defendant under the circumstances set forth in the record can be recovered back in this action. . . .

The general rule, even in the absence of any statute on the subject, is that dividends, in a going concern, can be properly declared and paid only out of profits, and not out of capital,
220 or assets required for the security and payment of creditors. . . .

In addition to this our statute expressly says that "no corporation shall declare any dividend while its capital stock is impaired," and makes the officers voting in favor of such dividend, "knowing or having the means of knowing that such capital is impaired," liable for all losses resulting from such declaration, and their action in so voting is made a misdemeanor. General Statutes, § 1932.

The dividends here in question were declared and paid when the corporation was insolvent and its capital stock impaired, and were thus declared and paid in direct violation of these legal principles and of this statutory enactment. The money paid to the defendant in the form of dividends was wrongfully paid to the prejudice of the creditors of the corporation, to one who was not only a stockholder of the corporation but was also a director therein from its organization until it went into the hands of the receiver. Its condition when the dividends in question were declared and paid was clearly shown upon its books, inventories and quarterly statements; and it is expressly found that the attention of the defendant was specifically called to its financial condition as it appeared upon its books, at the very time these dividends were declared and paid. It thus appears that the defendant, when he participated in the declaration and payment of these dividends, and when he accepted them in payment, knew or had the means of knowing that the money really and in fact belonged to the creditors of the corporation, because it was required for the payment of their claims, and could not legally be paid away under the form of a dividend, to one standing in his position. Under these circumstances the money paid to the defendant was part of a trust fund which belonged to the creditors of the corporation, to which he could acquire no title as against them, because he took it without consideration and with full knowledge of the trust which existed in their favor. The plaintiff in this case, as the representative of the creditors of the corporation, is entitled to sue for and recover back the money so paid. *Crandall* v. *Lincoln*, 52 Conn. 73; *Greene* v. *Sprague Mfg. Co.*, ibid. 330.

The court of Common Pleas is advised to render judgment for the plaintiff to recover the dividends paid to the defendant, with interest from the respective dates of payment.

In this opinion the other judges concurred.

Accounting Books Published by Garland

NEW BOOKS

- *Altman, Edward I., *The Prediction of Corporate Bankruptcy: A Discriminant Analysis.*
  New York, 1988.

- Ashton, Robert H., ed. *The Evolution of Accounting Behavior Research: An Overview.*
  New York, 1984.

- Ashton, Robert H., ed. *Some Early Contributions to the Study of Audit Judgement.*
  New York, 1984.

- *Bodenhorn, Diran. *Economic Accounting.*
  New York, 1988.

---

* Included in the Garland series Foundations of Accounting
† Included in the Academy of Accounting Historians, Classics Series, Gary John Previt, ed.

■ *Bougen, Philip D. *Accounting and Industrial Relations: Some Historical Evidence on Their Interaction.*
New York, 1988.

■ Brief, Richard P., ed. *Corporate Financial Reporting and Analysis in the Early 1900s.*
New York, 1986.

■ Brief, Richard P., ed. *Depreciation and Capital Maintenance.*
New York, 1984.

■ Brief, Richard P., ed. *Estimating the Economic Rate of Return from Accounting Data.*
New York, 1986.

■ Brief, Richard P., ed. *Four Classics on the Theory of Double-Entry Bookkeeping.*
New York, 1982.

■ Chambers, R. J., and G. W. Dean, eds. *Chambers on Accounting.*
New York, 1986.
Volume I: Accounting, Management and Finance.
Volume II: Accounting Practice and Education.
Volume III: Accounting Theory and Research.
Volume IV: Price Variation Accounting.
Volume V: Continuously Contemporary Accounting.

■ *Clark, John B. (with a new introduction by Donald Dewey). *Capital and Its Earnings.*
New York, 1988.

■ Clarke, F. L. *The Tangled Web of Price Variation Accounting: The Development of Ideas Underlying Professional Prescriptions in Six Countries.*
New York, 1982.

■ Coopers & Lybrand. *The Early History of Coopers & Lybrand.*
New York, 1984.

■ Craswell, Allen. *Audit Qualifications in Australia 1950 to 1979.*
New York, 1986.

■ Dean, G. W., and M. C. Wells, eds. *The Case for Continuously Contemporary Accounting.*
New York, 1984.

■ Dean, G. W. , and M. C. Wells, eds. *Forerunners of Realizable Values Accounting in Financial Reporting.*
New York, 1982.

■ Edey, Harold C. *Accounting Queries.*
New York, 1982.

■ Edwards, J. R., ed. *Legal Regulation of British Company Accounts 1836-1900.*
New York, 1986.

■ Edwards, J. R. ed. *Reporting Fixed Assets in Nineteenth-Century Company Accounts.*
New York, 1986.

■ Edwards, J. R., ed. *Studies of Company Records: 1830-1974.*
New York, 1984.

■ Fabricant, Solomon. *Studies in Social and Private Accounting.*
New York, 1982.

■ Gaffikin, Michael, and Michael Aitkin, eds. *The Development of Accounting Theory: Significant Contributors to Accounting Thought in the 20th Century.*
New York, 1982.

■ Hawawini, Gabriel A., ed. *Bond Duration and Immunization: Early Developments and Recent Contributions.*
New York, 1982.

■ Hawawini, Gabriel A., and Pierre A. Michel, eds. *European Equity Markets: Risk, Return, and Efficiency.*
New York, 1984.

■ Hawawini, Gabriel A., and Pierre Michel. *Mandatory Financial Information and Capital Market Equilibrium in Belgium.*
New York, 1986.

■ Hawkins, David F. *Corporate Financial Disclosure, 1900-1933: A Study of Management Inertia within a Rapidly Changing Environment.*
New York, 1986.

■ *Hopwood, Anthony G. *Accounting from the Outside: The Collected Papers of Anthony G. Hopwood.*
New York, 1988.

■ Johnson, H. Thomas. *A New Approach to Management Accounting History.*
New York, 1986.

■ Kinney, William R., ed. *Fifty Years of Statistical Auditing.*
New York, 1986.

■ Klemstine, Charles E., and Michael W. Maher. *Management Accounting Research: A Review and Annotated Bibliography.*
New York, 1984.

■ *Langenderfer, Harold Q., and Grover L. Porter, eds. *Rational Accounting Concepts: The Writings of Willard Graham.*
New York, 1988.

■ *Lee, T. A., ed. *The Evolution of Audit Thought and Practice.*
New York, 1988.

■ Lee, T. A., ed. *A Scottish Contribution to Accounting History.*
New York, 1986.

■ Lee, T. A. *Towards a Theory and Practice of Cash Flow Accounting.*
New York, 1986.

■ Lee, T. A., ed. *Transactions of the Chartered Accountants Students' Societies of Edinburgh and Glasgow: A Selection of Writings, 1886-1958.*
New York, 1984.

■ *Loft, Anne. *Understanding Accounting in Its Social and Historical Context: The Case of Cost Accounting in Britain, 1914-1925.*
New York, 1988.

■ McKinnon, Jill L.. *The Historical Development and Operational Form of Corporate Reporting Regulation in Japan.*
New York, 1986.

■ *McMickle, Peter L., and Paul H. Jensen, eds. *The Auditor's Guide of 1869: A Review and Computer Enhancement of Recently Discovered Old Microfilm of America's First Book on Auditing by H. J. Mettenheimer.*
New York, 1988.

■ *McMickle, Peter L., and Paul H. Jensen, eds. *The Birth of American Accountancy: A Bibliographic Analysis of Works on Accounting Published in America through 1820.*
New York, 1988.

■ *Mepham, M.-J. *Accounting in Eighteenth-Century Scotland.*
New York, 1988.

■ *Mills, Patti A., trans. *The Legal Literature of Accounting: On Accounts by Diego del Castillo.*
New York, 1988.

■ *Murphy, George J. *The Evolution of Canadian Corporate Reporting Practices: 1900-1970.*
New York, 1988.

■ *Mumford, Michael J., ed. *Edward Stamp—Later Papers.*
New York, 1988.

■ Nobes, Christopher, ed. *The Development of Double Entry: Selected Essays.*
New York, 1984.

■ Nobes, Christopher. *Issues in International Accounting.*
New York, 1986.

■ Parker, Lee D. *Developing Control Concepts in the 20th Century.*
New York, 1986.

■ *Parker, Lee D., ed. *Financial Reporting to Employees: From Past to Present.*
New York, 1988.

■ *Parker, Lee D., and O. Finley Graves, eds. *Methodology and Method in History: A Bibliography.*
New York, 1988.

■ Parker, R. H. *Papers on Accounting History.*
New York, 1984.

■ Previts, Gary John, and Alfred R. Roberts, eds. *Federal Securities Law and Accounting 1933-1970: Selected Addresses.*
New York, 1986.

■ *Reid, Jean Margo, ed. *Law and Accounting: Nineteenth-Century American Legal Cases.*
New York, 1988.

■ *Sheldahl, Terry K., ed. *Accounting Literature in the United States before Mitchell and Jones (1796): Contributions by Four English Writers, through American Editions, and Two Pioneer Local Authors.*
New York, 1988.

▪ Sheldahl, Terry K. *Beta Alpha Psi, from Alpha to Omega: Pursuing a Vision of Professional Education for Accountants, 1919-1945.*
New York, 1982.

▪ Sheldahl, Terry K. *Beta Alpha Psi, from Omega to Zeta Omega: The Making of a Comprehensive Accounting Fraternity, 1946-1984.*
New York, 1986.

▪ *Sheldahl, Terry K., ed. *Education for the Mercantile Countinghouse: Critical and Constructive Essays by Nine British Writers, 1716-1794.*
New York, 1988.

▪ Solomons, David. *Collected Papers on Accounting and Accounting Education (in two volumes).*
New York, 1984.

▪ Sprague, Charles F. *The General Principles of the Science of Accounts and the Accountancy of Investment.*
New York, 1984.

▪ Stamp, Edward. *Edward Stamp—Later Papers. See* Michael J. Mumford.

▪ Stamp, Edward. *Selected Papers on Accounting, Auditing, and Professional Problems.*
New York, 1984.

▪ *Staubus, George J. *Activity Costing for Decisions: Cost Accounting in the Decision Usefulness Framework.*
New York, 1988.

■ Storrar, Colin, ed. *The Accountant's Magazine—An Anthology.*
New York, 1986.

■ Tantral, Panadda. *Accounting Literature in Non-Accounting Journals: An Annotated Bibliography.*
New York, 1984.

■ *Vangermeersch, Richard G. *Alexander Hamilton Church: A Man of Ideas for All Seasons.*
New York, 1988.

■ Vangermeersch, Richard, ed. *The Contributions of Alexander Hamilton Church to Accounting and Management.*
New York, 1986.

■ Vangermeersch, Richard, ed. *Financial Accounting Milestones in the Annual Reports of the United States Steel Corporation—The First Seven Decades.*
New York, 1986.

■ *Walker, Stephen P. *The Society of Accountants in Edinburgh, 1854-1914: A Study of Recruitment to a New Profession.*
New York, 1988.

■ Whitmore, John. *Factory Accounts.*
New York, 1984.

■ *Whittred, Greg. *The Evolution of Consolidated Financial Reporting in Australia: An Evaluation of an Alternative Hypothesis.*
New York, 1988.

■ Yamey, Basil S. *Further Essays on the History of Accounting.*
New York, 1982.

■ Zeff, Stephen A., ed. *The Accounting Postulates and Principles Controversy of the 1960s.*
New York, 1982.

■ Zeff, Stephen A., ed. *Accounting Principles Through the Years: The Views of Professional and Academic Leaders 1938-1954.*
New York, 1982.

■ Zeff, Stephen A., and Maurice Moonitz, eds. *Sourcebook on Accounting Principles and Auditing Procedures: 1917-1953 (in two volumes).*
New York, 1984.

■ *Zeff, Stephen a., ed. *The U. S. Accounting Profession in the 1890s and Early 1900s.*
New York, 1988.

REPRINTED TITLES

- *American Institute of Accountants. *Accountants Index, 1920* (in two volumes).
  New York, 1921 (Garland reprint, 1988).

- American Institute of Accountants. *Fiftieth Anniversary Celebration.*
  Chicago, 1937 (Garland reprint, 1982).

- American Institute of Accountants. *Library Catalogue.*
  New York, 1919 (Garland reprint, 1982).

- Arthur Andersen Company. *The First Fifty Years 1913-1963.*
  Chicago, 1963 (Garland reprint, 1984).

- Bevis, Herman W. *Corporate Financial Reporting in a Competitive Economy.*
  New York, 1965 (Garland reprint, 1986).

- Bonini,. Charles P., Robert K. Jaedicke, and Harvey M. Wagner, eds. *Management Controls: New Directions in Basic Research.*
  New York, 1964 (Garland reprint, 1986).

- **The Book-Keeper and the American Counting Room.*
  New York, 1880-1884 (Garland reprint, 1988).

▪ Bray, F. Sewell. *Four Essays in Accounting Theory.* London, 1953. *Bound with* Institute of Chartered Accountants in England and Wales and the National Institute of Economic and Social Research. *Some Accounting Terms and Concepts.*
Cambridge, 1951 (Garland reprint, 1982).

▪ Brown, R. Gene, and Kenneth S. Johnston. *Paciolo on Accounting.*
New York, 1963 (Garland reprint, 1984).

▪ Carey, John L., and William O. Doherty, eds. *Ethical Standards of the Accounting Profession.*
New York, 1966 (Garland reprint, 1986).

▪ Chambers, R. J. *Accounting in Disarray.*
Melbourne, 1973 (Garland reprint, 1982).

▪ Cooper, Ernest. *Fifty-seven years in an Accountant's Office.* *See* Sir Russell Kettle.

▪ Couchman, Charles B. *The Balance-Sheet.*
New York, 1924 (Garland reprint, 1982).

▪ Couper, Charles Tennant. *Report of the Trial ... Against the Directors and Manager of the City of Glasgow Bank.*
Edinburgh, 1879 (Garland reprint, 1984).

▪ Cutforth, Arthur E. *Audits.*
London, 1906 (Garland reprint, 1982).

▪ Cutforth, Arthur E. *Methods of Amalgamation.*
London, 1926 (Garland reprint, 1982).

■ Deinzer, Harvey T. *Development of Accounting Thought.*
New York, 1965 (Garland reprint, 1984).

■ De Paula, F.R.M. *The Principles of Auditing.*
London, 1915 (Garland reprint, 1984).

■ Dickerson, R. W. *Accountants and the Law of Negligence.*
Toronto, 1966 (Garland reprint, 1982).

■ Dodson, James. *The Accountant, or, the Method of Bookkeeping Deduced from Clear Principles, and Illustrated by a Variety of Examples.*
London, 1750 (Garland reprint, 1984).

■ Dyer, S. *A Common Sense Method of Double Entry Bookkeeping, on First Principles, as Suggested by De Morgan. Part I, Theoretical.*
London, 1897 (Garland reprint, 1984).

■ *† Edwards, James Don. *History of Public Accounting in the United States.*
East Lansing, 1960 (Garland reprint, 1988).

■ *† Edwards, James Don, and Robert F. Salmonson. *Contributions of Four Accounting Pioneers: Kohler, Littleton, May, Paton.*
East Lancing, 1961 (Garland reprint, 1988).

■ *The Fifth International Congress on Accounting, 1938 [Kongress-Archiv 1938 des V. Internationalen Prüfungs- und Treuhand-Kongresses].*
Berlin, 1938 (Garland reprint, 1986).

■ Finney, A. H. *Consolidated Statements.*
New York, 1922 (Garland reprint, 1982).

■ Fisher, Irving. *The Rate of Interest.*
New York, 1907 (Garland reprint, 1982).

■ Florence, P. Sargant. *Economics of Fatigue and Unrest and the Efficiency of Labour in English and American Industry.*
London, 1923 (Garland reprint, 1984).

■ *Fourth International Congress on Accounting 1933.*
London, 1933 (Garland reprint, 1982).

■ Foye, Arthur B. *Haskins & Sells: Our First Seventy-Five Years.*
New York, 1970 (Garland reprint, 1984).

■ *† Garner, Paul S. *Evolution of Cost Accounting to 1925.*
University, Alabama, 1925 (Garland reprint, 1988).

■ Garnsey, Sir Gilbert. *Holding Companies and Their Published Accounts.* London, 1923. *Bound with* Sir Gilbert Garnsey. *Limitations of a Balance Sheet.*
London, 1928 (Garland reprint, 1982).

■ Garrett, A. A. *The History of the Society of Incorporated Accountants, 1885-1957.*
Oxford, 1961 (Garland reprint, 1984).

■ Gilman, Stephen. *Accounting Concepts of Profit.*
New York, 1939 (Garland reprint, 1982).

■ Gordon, William. *The Universal Accountant, and Complete Merchant* ... [Volume II].
Edinburgh, 1765 (Garland reprint, 1986).

■ Green, Wilmer. *History and Survey of Accountancy.*
Brooklyn, 1930 (Garland reprint, 1986).

■ Hamilton, Robert. *An Introduction to Merchandise, Parts IV and V (Italian Bookkeeping and Practical Bookkeeping).*
Edinburgh, 1788 (Garland reprint, 1982).

■ Hatton, Edward. *The Merchant's Magazine; or, Tradesman's Treasury.* London, 1695 (Garland reprint, 1982).
Hills, George S. *The Law of Accounting and Financial Statements.*
Boston, 1957 (Garland reprint, 1982).

■ *A History of Cooper Brothers & Co. 1854 to 1954.*
London, 1954 (Garland reprint, 1986).

■ Hofstede, Geert. *The Game of Budget Control.*
Assen, 1967 (Garland reprint, 1984).

■ Howitt, Sir Harold. *The History of the Institute of Chartered Accountants in England and Wales 1880-1965, and of Its Founder Accountancy Bodies 1870-1880.*
London, 1966 (Garland reprint, 1984).

■ Institute of Chartered Accountants in England and Wales and The National Institute of Social and Economic Research. *Some Accounting Terms and Concepts.* *See* F. Sewell Bray.

- Institute of Chartered Accountants of Scotland. *History of the Chartered Accountants of Scotland from the Earliest Times to 1954.*
  Edinburgh, 1954 (Garland reprint, 1984).

- *International Congress on Accounting 1929.*
  New York, 1930 (Garland reprint, 1982).

- Jaedicke, Robert K., Yuji Ijiri, and Oswald Nielsen, eds. *Research in Accounting Measurement.*
  American Accounting Association,
  1966 (Garland reprint, 1986).

- Keats, Charles. *Magnificent Masquerade.*
  New York, 1964 (Garland reprint, 1982).

- Kettle, Sir Russell. *Deloitte & Co. 1854-1956.* Oxford, 1958. *Bound with* Ernest Cooper. *Fifty-seven Years in an Accountant's Office.*
  London, 1921 (Garland reprint, 1982).

- Kitchen, J., and R. H. Parker. *Accounting Thought and Education: Six English Pioneers.*
  London, 1980 (Garland reprint, 1984).

- Lacey, Kenneth. *Profit Measurement and Price Changes.*
  London, 1952 (Garland reprint, 1982).

- Lee, Chauncey. *The American Accomptant.*
  Lansingburgh, 1797 (Garland reprint, 1982).

- Lee, T. A., and R. H. Parker. *The Evolution of Corporate Financial Reporting.*
  Middlesex, 1979 (Garland reprint, 1984).

■ *† Littleton, A. C.. *Accounting Evolution to 1900.*
New York, 1933 (Garland reprint, 1988).

■ Malcolm, Alexander. *The Treatise of Book-Keeping, or, Merchants Accounts; In the Italian Method of Debtor and Creditor; Wherein the Fundamental Principles of That Curious and Approved Method Are Clearly and Fully Explained and Demonstrated ... To Which Are Added, Instructions for Gentlemen of Land Estates, and Their Stewards or Factors: With Directions Also for Retailers, and Other More Private Persons.*
London, 1731 (Garland reprint, 1986).

■ Meij, J. L., ed. *Depreciation and Replacement Policy.*
Chicago, 1961 (Garland reprint, 1986).

■ Newlove, George Hills. *Consolidated Balance Sheets.*
New York, 1926 (Garland reprint, 1982).

■ North, Roger. *The Gentleman Accomptant; or, An Essay to Unfold the Mystery of Accompts; By Way of Debtor and Creditor, Commonly Called Merchants Accompts, and Applying the Same to the Concerns of the Nobility and Gentry of England.*
London 1714 (Garland reprint, 1986).

■ **Proceedings of the Seventh International Congress of Accountants.* Amsterdam, 1957 (Garland reprint, 1988).

■ Pryce-Jones, Janet E., and R. H. Parker. *Accounting in Scotland: A Historical Bibliography.*
Edinburgh, 1976 (Garland reprint, 1984).

- *Reynolds, W. B., and F. W. Thornton. *Duties of a Junior Accountant* [three editions].
  New York, 1917, 1933, 1953
  (Garland reprint, 1988).

- Robinson, H. W. *A History of Accountants in Ireland.*
  Dublin, 1964 (Garland edition, 1984).

- Robson, T. B. *Consolidated and Other Group Accounts.*
  London, 1950 (Garland reprint, 1982).

- Rorem, C. Rufus. *Accounting Method.*
  Chicago, 1928 (Garland reprint, 1982).

- Saliers, Earl A., ed. *Accountants' Handbook.*
  New York, 1923 (Garland reprint, 1986).

- Samuel, Horace B. *Shareholder's Money.*
  London, 1933 (Garland reprint, 1982).

- *The Securitites and Exchange Commission in the Matter of McKesson & Robbins, Inc. Report on Investigation.*
  Washington, D. C., 1940 (Garland reprint, 1982).

- *The Securities and Exchange Commission in the Matter of McKesson & Robbins, Inc. Testimony of Expert Witnesses.*
  Washington, D. C., 1939 (Garland reprint, 1982).

- Shaplen, Roger. *Kreuger: Genius and Swindler.*
  New York, 1960 (Garland reprint, 1986).

- Singer, H. W. *Standardized Accountancy in Germany. (With a new appendix.)*
  Cambridge, 1943 (Garland reprint, 1982).

■ *The Sixth International Congress on Accounting.*
London, 1952 (Garland reprint, 1984).

■ Stewart, Jas. C. (with a new introductory note by T. A. Lee). *Pioneers of a Profession: Chartered Accountants to 1879.*
Edinburgh, 1977 (Garland reprint, 1986).

■ Thompson, Wardbaugh. *The Accomptant's Oracle: or, a Key to Science, Being a Compleat Practical System of Book-keeping.*
York, 1777 (Garland reprint, 1984).

■ *Thornton, F. W. *Duties of the Senior Accountant.* New York, 1932. *Bound with.* John C. Martin. *Duties of Junior and Senior Accountants, Supplement of the CPA Handbook.*
New York, 1953 (Garland reprint, 1988).

■ Vatter, William J. *Managerial Accounting.*
New York, 1950 (Garland reprint, 1986).

■ Woolf, Arthur H. *A Short History of Accountants and Accountancy.*
London, 1912 (Garland reprint, 1986).

■ Yamey, B. S., H. C. Edey, and Hugh W. Thomson. *Accounting in England and Scotland: 1543-1800.*
London, 1963 (Garland reprint, 1982).